SOFTWARE QUALITY CONTROL, ERROR ANALYSIS, AND TESTING

SOFTWARE QUALITY CONTROL, ERROR ANALYSIS, AND TESTING

by

Judith A. Clapp   **Saul F. Stanten**
The MITRE Corporation

W.W. Peng   **D.R. Wallace**
National Institute of Standards and Technology

Deborah A. Cerino   **Roger J. Dziegiel, Jr.**
Rome Laboratory

Advanced Computing
and
Telecommunications Series

NOYES DATA CORPORATION
Park Ridge, New Jersey, U.S.A.

Copyright © 1995 by Noyes Data Corporation
Library of Congress Catalog Card Number: 94-35136
ISBN: 0-8155-1363-1

Transferred to Digital Printing, 2011

Printed and bound in Great Britain by
CPI Antony Rowe, Chippenham and Eastbourne

Library of Congress Cataloging-in-Publication Data

Software quality control, error analysis, and testing / by Judith A.
    Clapp et al.
            p.   cm. -- (Advanced computing and telecommunications series)
        Consists of 3 works: A guide to total software quality control by
    Judith A. Clapp, 1992; Software error and analysis by Wendy W. Peng,
    1993; and Increasing software confidence by Deborah A. Cerino, 1992.
        Includes index.
        ISBN 0-8155-1363-1
        1. Computer software--Quality control. 2. Computer software-
    -Testing. I. Clapp, Judith A. II. Clapp, Judith A. Guide to
    total software quality control. III. Peng, Wendy W. Software error
    analysis. IV. Cerino, Deborah A. Increasing software confidence.
    V. Series.
    QA76.76.Q35S65   1994
    005.1'068'5--dc20   94-35136
                                                              CIP

Preface

Part I is a guide that provides strategies and techniques for controlling the quality of software for mission–critical systems. Although designed for military applications, it also has important commercial aspects. It describes techniques to prevent, detect, and correct defects, and to make improvements in the processes and resources used to develop the software. It recommends use of a Total Software Quality Control Plan and shows how to create one prior to the start of system development. Volume 1 of Part I contains an overview of techniques and the planning process. Volume 2 of Part I is a compendium of descriptions of individual techniques. It was prepared by Judith A. Clapp, and Saul F. Stanten of MITRE Corporation, under contract to Rome Laboratory. The authors wish to thank Andrew Chroscicki of Rome Laboratory for his encouragement and guidance, as well as other individuals of MITRE who contributed their suggestions.

Part II provides guidance on software analysis. Software error analysis includes error detection, analysis, and resolution. Error detection techniques considered in the study are those used in software development, software quality assurance, and software verification, validation and testing activities. These techniques are those frequently cited in technical literature and software engineering standards or those representing new approaches to support error detection. The study includes statistical process control techniques and relates them to their use as a software quality assurance technique for both product and process improvement. Finally, several software reliability models are described. It was prepared by W.W. Peng, and D.R. Wallace, of the Systems and Software Technology Division, Computer System Laboratory, National Institute of Standards and Technology.

Part III describes the testing process and the results of a comparison of testing techniques via two test tools. In the past decade, many specialized software testing philosophies and testing techniques have evolved. Some of these testing philosophies are time–consuming and impractical while others are practical but only for small programs. Automating the testing process is a goal that needs to be attained for testing to be cost–effective and practical for any size or type of software program. Two testing techniques have been explored under Rome Laboratory (C3CB) R&D programs. These programs developed automated testing tools which support these techniques. One testing technique is mutation analysis and the other technique is decision–to–decision path analysis. It was prepared by Deborah A. Cerino and Roger J. Dziegiel, Jr. of Rome Laboratory, Griffiss AFB, NY.

Notice

The materials in this book were prepared as accounts of work sponsored by various government agencies. On this basis the Publisher assumes no responsibility nor liability for errors or any consequences arising from the use of the information contained herein.

The book is sold with the understanding that the Publisher is not engaged in rendering legal, technical, or other professional service. If advice or other expert assistance is required, the service of a competent professional should be sought.

Contents and Subject Index

PART I
A GUIDE TO TOTAL SOFTWARE QUALITY CONTROL

Volume 1
Overview of Techniques and the Planning Process

1. INTRODUCTION 3
  1.1   Purpose of the Guide 3
  1.2   Scope of the Guide 3
  1.3   Organization and Content of the Guide 4
  1.4   What is Software Quality 4
  1.5   What is Software Quality Control? 7
  1.6   Why is it Difficult to Control Software Quality? 7
  1.7   What Does Quality Control Cost? 8
  1.8   Why is it Important to Control Software Quality? 8
  1.9   Who Controls Software Quality? 9
  1.10 Who Has Been Responsible for Software Quality in the Past? 10
  1.11 When Should Software Quality Control be Applied? 10
       1.11.1 Basic Phases of a System Life Cycle 11

2. MODELS FOR SOFTWARE QUALITY CONTROL 13
  2.2   Introduction 13
  2.2   General Approaches to Software Quality Control 13
       2.2.1 Rome Laboratory's Software Quality Framework 13
       2.2.2 Goal Question Metric Paradigm 17
       2.2.3 Risk Management Model 18
       2.2.4 The Spiral Model of Software Development 19
       2.2.5 The Plan–Do–Check–Action Model of Quality Control 19
  2.3   The TSQC Model 20
       2.3.1 The Basic Elements of the TSQC Model 20
       2.3.2 What are the TSQC Parameters? 22
           2.3.2.1 Products 22

2.3.2.2 Processes 24
2.3.2.3 Resources 25
2.3.3 The TSQC Model in the System Life Cycle 26
2.3.3.1 Predevelopment 27
2.3.3.2 Development 28
2.3.3.3 Post Deployment Support 29
2.3.4 The TSQC Model in an Organization 29
2.4   How Does the TSQC Model Differ from the RSQF? 29

3. **SOFTWARE QUALITY CONTROL TECHNIQUES** 31
3.1   Introduction 31
3.2   Characteristics of Quality Control Techniques and Measures 31
3.2.1 Life Cycle Phase 31
3.2.2 Type of Control 31
3.2.3 Effect on Quality Control Parameters 32
3.3   Quality Control Issues and Techniques 32
3.3.1 What are the Quality Requirements for the Final Product? 33
3.3.1.1 Operations Concept Document 33
3.3.1.2 RFP Preparation and Review 33
3.3.1.3 Prototyping 33
3.3.2 Who Will be the Developer? 33
3.3.2.1 RFP Preparation and Review 34
3.3.2.2 The Software Engineering Institute Software Capability
Evaluation 35
3.3.2.3 Software Development Capability/Capacity Review 35
3.3.2.4 Software Engineering Exercise 35
3.3.3 What Can be Done to Prevent Quality Defects? 36
3.3.3.1 Standards 36
3.3.3.2 Software Engineering Prototype 37
3.3.3.3 Configuration Management 38
3.3.3.4 Performance Engineering 39
3.3.3.5 Software Engineering Environments 39
3.3.3.6 Reuse 40
3.3.4 How Can Quality be Checked 41
3.3.4.1 Reviews and Audits 41
3.3.4.2 Independent Verification and Validation 42
3.3.4.3 Requirements Verification Matrix 43
3.3.4.4 Software Quality Assurance 43
3.3.4.5 Testing 43
3.3.4.6 Reliability Modeling 44
3.3.5 What Kinds of Information Should be Available at Checkpoints 44
3.3.5.1 Requirements Traceability Matrix 45
3.3.5.2 Metrics 45
3.3.5.3 Software Problem Reports Analysis 46
3.3.5.4 Software Development Files 46
3.3.6 What Can the Contractor do to Improve the Process and Resources . . . 47
3.3.6.1 Cause and Effect Analysis 47
3.3.6.2 SEI Self–Assessment 47
3.4   Characterization of the Quality Control Techniques 47

3.4.1   Applicability of the Techniques 48
3.4.2   Type of Control 48
3.4.3   Relationship to the Quality Control Parameters 48

4. **APPLYING TOTAL SOFTWARE QUALITY CONTROL** 54
   4.1   **Introduction** 54
   4.2   **A Review of TSQC Planning Principles** 54
   4.3   **An Overview of the TSQC Planning Process** 55
   4.4   **The Total Software Quality Control Plan** 56
   4.5   **Planning Prior to Development** 57
         4.5.1   Defining the Software Quality Requirements 59
         4.5.2   Identifying Constraints 59
         4.5.3   Identifying Risks 60
                 4.5.3.1   Sources and Causes of Risk 60
                 4.5.3.2   Assessing Risks 62
         4.5.4   Selecting Software Quality Control Techniques and Activities 65
                 4.5.4.1   Using a Core Set of Techniques 66
                 4.5.4.2   Selecting Additional Techniques to Control Risk 66
         4.5.5   Applying the Techniques 70
         4.5.6   Refining the Selections 70
                 4.5.6.1   Reviewing Controls Over the Developer 71
                 4.5.6.2   Tailoring the Application of Techniques 72
                 4.5.6.3   Selecting the Level of Application of Techniques 72
                 4.5.6.4   Selecting Among Alternative Techniques 73
         4.5.7   Planning Checkpoints 73
                 4.5.7.1   Planning the Acquisition Strategy 74
                 4.5.7.2   Planning Information Requirements at Checkpoints 75
                 4.5.7.3   Reviewing and Refining Checkpoints 75
         4.5.8   Documenting an Overview of the TSQC Process 77
         4.5.9   Making Detailed Plans for TSQC Activities 78
   4.6   **Updating the TSQC Plan** 78
         4.6.1   After Developer Selection 78
         4.6.2   During Development 79

5. **SUMMARY AND CONCLUSIONS** 80
   5.1   **Summary** 80
   5.2   **Conclusions** 80
         5.2.1   What is the Current Status of Total Software Quality Control? 80
         5.2.2   What is Needed to Gain Greater Control Over Software Quality? 81
         5.2.3   What Can be Done Now? 81
   List of References 82

APPENDIX A: QUALITY GOALS, QUESTIONS, METRICS, REQUIREMENTS 85
   A.1   **Efficiency** 85
   A.2   **Integrity** 86
   A.3   **Reliability** 87

APPENDIX B: RISK ASSESSMENT QUESTIONNAIRE 90
   B.1   **Risk Areas** 90

B.2	**Use of Questionnaire**	91
B.3	**Requirements Risk Area**	91
B.4	**Development and Test**	93
B.5	**Maintenance Planning**	94
B.6	**Government**	94
B.7	**Developer**	95
B.8	**Schedule and Budget**	96

GLOSSARY 98

PART I

Volume 2
Descriptions of Individual Techniques

1. INTRODUCTION 101
   Purpose of the Guide 101
   Scope of the Guide 101
   Organization and Content of the Guide 102

2. CAUSE AND EFFECT ANALYSIS 104

3. CONFIGURATION MANAGEMENT 111

4. INDEPENDENT VERIFICATION AND VALIDATION 119

5. INSPECTIONS 126

6. PERFORMANCE ENGINEERING 131

7. PROTOTYPING 140

8. RELIABILITY MODELING 145

9. REQUIREMENTS TRACEABILITY 152

10. RFP PREPARATION AND REVIEW 158

11. SEI SOFTWARE CAPABILITY EVALUATION 164

12. SOFTWARE AUDIT 171

13. SOFTWARE DESIGN METRICS 177

14. SOFTWARE DEVELOPMENT CAPABILITY/CAPACITY REVIEW 182

15. SOFTWARE DEVELOPMENT FILES 186

16. SOFTWARE ENGINEERING EXERCISE 189

17. SOFTWARE ENGINEERING PROTOTYPE 195

18. SOFTWARE MANAGEMENT METRICS 200

19. SOFTWARE QUALITY ASSURANCE 210

20. SOFTWARE PROBLEM REPORT ANALYSIS 215

21. STANDARDS 223

22. TESTING 230

GLOSSARY 237

PART II
SOFTWARE ERROR ANALYSIS

EXECUTIVE SUMMARY 240

1. OVERVIEW 242
    1.1   Definitions 243

2. INTRODUCTION TO SOFTWARE ERROR ANALYSIS 245
    2.1   Cost Benefits of Early Detection 246
    2.2   Approach to Selecting Error Analysis Techniques 247

3. TECHNIQUES FOR DETECTING ERRORS 248
    3.1   Classes of Error Detection Techniques 248
    3.2   Techniques Used During the Lifecycle 249
           3.2.1   Requirements 251
           3.2.2   Design 252
           3.2.3   Implementation 252
           3.2.4   Test 254
           3.2.5   Installation and Checkout 255
           3.2.6   Operation and Maintenance 255
    3.3   Benefits of Classes of Error Detection Techniques 255

4. REMOVAL OF ERRORS 258
    4.1   Identification 258
    4.2   Investigation 260
    4.3   Resolution 261
           4.3.1   Resolution Plan 261
           4.3.2   Resolution Action 261
           4.3.3   Corrective Action 262
           4.3.4   Follow–Up 262
    4.4   Use of Individual Error Data 262

5. TECHNIQUES FOR THE COLLECTION AND ANALYSIS OF ERROR DATA   263
    5.1   Error History Profile / Database 263

	5.2	**Data Collection Process**	264
	5.3	**Metrics**	266
		5.3.1 Metrics Throughout the Lifecycle	268
		5.3.1.1 Metrics Used in All Phases	268
		5.3.1.2 Requirements Metrics	270
		5.3.1.3 Design Metrics	271
		5.3.1.4 Implementation Metrics	273
		5.3.1.5 Test Metrics	275
		5.3.1.6 Installation and Checkout Metrics	278
		5.3.1.7 Operation and Maintenance Metrics	278
	5.4	**Statistical Process Control Techniques**	279
		5.4.1 Control Chart	260
		5.4.2 Run Chart	
		5.4.3 Bar Graph	283
		5.4.4 Pareto Diagram	285
		5.4.4 Histogram	286
		5.4.5 Scatter Diagram	288
		5.4.6 Method of Least Squares (Regression Technique)	289
	5.5	**Software Reliability Estimation Models**	290

6. SUMMARY 295

7. REFERENCES 297

APPENDIX A: ERROR DETECTION TECHNIQUES 303

A.1	**Algorithm Analysis**	303
A.2	**Back–to–Back Testing**	303
A.3	**Boundary Value Analysis**	304
A.4	**Control Flow Analysis/Diagrams**	305
A.5	**Database Analysis**	305
A.6	**Data Flow Analysis**	306
A.7	**Data Flow Diagrams**	306
A.8	**Decision Tables (Truth Tables)**	307
A.9	**Desk Checking (Code Reading)**	308
A.10	**Error Seeding**	309
A.11	**Finite State Machines**	310
A.12	**Formal Methods (Formal Verification, Proof of Correctness, Formal Proof of Program)**	310
A.13	**Information Flow Analysis**	311
A.14	**(Fagan) Inspections**	311
A.15	**Interface Analysis**	312
A.16	**Interface Testing**	313
A.17	**Mutation Analysis**	314
A.18	**Performance Testing**	315
A.19	**Prototyping / Animation**	315
A.20	**Regression Analysis and Testing**	316
A.21	**Requirements Parsing**	316
A.22	**Reviews**	317
A.23	**Sensitivity Analysis**	317

A.24 Simulation 318
A.25 Sizing and Timing Analysis 319
A.26 Slicing 320
A.27 Software Sneak Circuit Analysis 320
A.28 Stress Testing 321
A.29 Symbolic Execution 322
A.30 Test Certification 322
A.31 Traceability Analysis (Tracing) 323
A.32 Walkthroughs 324

APPENDIX B: ERROR ANALYSIS TECHNIQUES CITED IN
SOFTWARE STANDARDS 325

PART III
INCREASING SOFTWARE CONFIDENCE: WHERE WE'RE HEADED
IN SOFTWARE TESTING TECHNOLOGY

1. INTRODUCTION 344

2. BACKGROUND 344

3. TESTING STRATEGIES 346
   3.1 Mutation Testing 346
   3.2 Decision to Decision PATH (DD–PATH) Testing—Branch Testing 347

4. AUTOMATED TESTING TOOLS 349
   4.1 MOTHRA 350
   4.2 RXVP80 353

5. THE TEST PROGRAM 354

6. CORRECT PROGRAM 356
   6.1 MOTHRA—Statement Analysis Mutants 356
   6.2 MOTHRA—Predicate and Domain Mutants 356
   6.3 RXVP80 363

7. DOMAIN ERROR 363
   7.1 MOTHRA—Statement Analysis Mutants 363
   7.2 MOTHRA—Predicate and Domain Mutants 368
   7.3 RXVP80 375

8. MISSING STATEMENT ERROR 377
   8.1 MOTHRA 377
   8.2 RXVP80 377

9. COMPUTATION ERROR 384
   9.1 MOTHRA 384
   9.2 RXVP80 389

10. CONCLUSION 389

PART I

A GUIDE TO TOTAL
SOFTWARE QUALITY CONTROL

Judith A. Clapp
Saul F. Stanten

The MITRE Corporation

1

PART I

Volume 1
Overview of Techniques
and the Planning Process

SECTION 1

INTRODUCTION

1.1 PURPOSE OF THE GUIDE

This guide is intended for Air Force personnel who are responsible for assuring that software in mission-critical systems attains and sustains a level of quality that is required for its effective use. Typical users of the guide will be in a program office, responsible for planning and overseeing the development of a system. Others concerned with the development of quality software may find it useful as well.

1.2 SCOPE OF THE GUIDE

The guide focuses primarily on the problems in quality control that are common to mission-critical systems with large amounts of software. These systems often have the following characteristics:

a. Requirements are difficult to define.

b. Meeting delivery schedules and budgets is as important as delivering quality.

c. The software plays a key role in achieving system requirements.

d. The software must meet rigid timing requirements.

e. The system must have very high reliability. Human lives may depend on its correct operation.

f. The system must be operational virtually all of the time.

g. The system may be embedded in another system that limits its size and accessibility for maintenance and repair, and increases the complexity of its external interfaces.

h. The system must be easy to repair and modify quickly, for a long time after it is fielded.

These requirements place a heavy responsibility, often with high risk, on those who must assure the quality of a mission-critical system and its software. The methods and techniques in this guide may be useful but less essential for small software developments or systems where requirements are less demanding.

3

The guide addresses these questions about software quality control:

a.   How do you define software quality requirements?

b.   How do you plan for achieving software quality?

c.   How do you build quality into software?

d.   How do you predict or measure software quality?

e.   What actions can you take to improve software quality?

1.3   ORGANIZATION AND CONTENT OF THE GUIDE

This report provides tutorial information for those learning about software quality control as well as practical guidance on controlling software quality. The sources of this guidance are software engineering theory and practices; DOD and especially Air Force regulations, standards, and guidance; published reports and books; and our own experiences and those of our colleagues who have participated in the development and maintenance of mission-critical systems.

The guide is divided into two volumes. The first volume presents a quality control model, basic concepts of software quality control, a brief summary of techniques that have been used to control the quality of software, and guidelines for the selection of appropriate software quality control techniques for a program.

The second volume of this guide presents a more detailed description of selected techniques for controlling software quality. Each is described in terms of what it is, when and how it can be used, and what is known about its benefits and costs.

The remainder of this section introduces terminology and concepts that are used throughout the document.

1.4   WHAT IS SOFTWARE QUALITY?

There is no single definition of software quality. It is different for each system. The definition we will use in this guide is:

Software quality is a set of measurable characteristics that satisfies the buyers, users, and maintainers of a software product.

From this brief definition, we can see the following:

a.   Software quality is an attribute of a software product.

b.   There can be many characteristics of a software product that define its quality.

- The customer should define what quality characteristics he or she requires and how to measure that the product satisfies those quality requirements.

- There can be more than one customer and each may have different requirements for quality, as shown in table 1-1.

Table 1-1. Examples of Software Quality Requirements

Customer	Quality Requirements
Buyer	Cost, efficiency in use of resources
User/Operator	Functionality, reliability, ease of use
Maintainer	Ease of change, expandable

The list of important characteristics may differ from one system to another. The criteria for satisfying the same characteristics may differ from one system to another.

Table 1-2 shows a set of customer-oriented quality characteristics for software products proposed by Bowen [BOW85]. Bowen calls these user/customer-oriented characteristics **quality factors.** This is just one view of software quality. Bowen then decomposes these quality factors into multiple software-oriented **quality criteria** whose presence contributes to achieving quality factors. Figure 2-2 in the next section illustrates the relationship between quality factors and quality criteria. The lowest level view of quality is **quality metrics** that correspond to the criteria and can be measured in software and its documentation to estimate the degree to which quality characteristics have been achieved.

Section 2.2.1, later in this guide, describes the Rome Laboratory's Software Quality Framework, which uses Bowen's hierarchical model to enable quantitative measurement of software characteristics, which can then be communicated in customer-oriented or customer-understood terms.

Table 1-2. Rome Laboratory Software Quality Factor Definitions

QUALITY FACTOR	DEFINITION
EFFICIENCY	Relative extent to which a resource is utilized (e.g., storage space processing time, communication time).
INTEGRITY	Extent to which the software will perform without failures due to unauthorized access to the code or data within a specified time period.
RELIABILITY	Extent to which the software will perform without any failures within a specified time period.
SURVIVABILITY	Extent to which the software will perform and support critical functions without failures within a specified time period when a portion of the system is inoperable.
USABILITY	Relative effort for using software (training and operation) (e.g., familiarization, input preparation, execution, output interpretation).
CORRECTNESS	Extent to which the software conforms to its specifications and standards.
MAINTAINABILITY	Ease of effort for locating and fixing a software failure within a specified time period.
VERIFIABILITY	Relative effort to verify the specified software operation and performance.
EXPANDABILITY	Relative effort to increase the software capability or performance by enhancing current functions or by adding new functions or data.
FLEXIBILITY	Ease of effort for changing the software missions, functions, or data to satisfy other requirements.
INTEROPERABILITY	Relative effort to couple the software of one system to the software of another system.
PORTABILITY	Relative effort to transport the software for use in another environment (hardware configuration and/or software system environment).
REUSABILITY	Relative effort to convert a software component for use in another application.

1.5   WHAT IS SOFTWARE QUALITY CONTROL?

Quality control is the set of methods used to achieve quality goals on a specific project and to continually improve the process so that higher and higher levels of quality can be achieved at lower and lower cost.

In this report, we define software quality control as follows:

> **Software quality control is the set of procedures used by organizations (1) to ensure that a software product will meet its quality goals at the best value to the customer, and (2) to continually improve the organization's ability to produce quality software products in the future.**

Based on this brief definition, we can observe the following:

a.   Software quality control is a process carried out by one or more organizations.

b.   The goal of software quality control is to deliver a satisfactory product to the customer at the best cost.

c.   The goal of software quality control for an organization also includes learning from each development so that software quality control will be better the next time.

In summary, software quality control is, first, a process of planning for, building in, measuring, assessing, and taking the appropriate actions to achieve the quality specified by the customer, and, second, the set of procedures, e.g., causal analysis, for continually improving the process by which one develops software. It follows that measurement is the basis for quality control and improvement.

1.6   WHY IS IT DIFFICULT TO CONTROL SOFTWARE QUALITY?

It is not easy to control software quality. There are many reasons why it may not be done, or not done well.

a.   Many of the factors that make it difficult to achieve software quality goals, such as system requirements, funds, and schedule, are beyond the control of the program office.

b.   Most acquisition and development managers focus on cost and schedule more than quality during software development. Cost and schedule status are easier to measure and more visible than the status of quality. They also affect the developer's profit and the program manager's reputation and career.

c.   Delivering within budget and on time can be at least as important to the customer as software quality because there are high expenses associated with not having the system available when it is needed.

    d.   If the program manager and/or the development manager are not responsible for defects that are uncovered after the system is delivered, then they may not be strongly motivated to control software quality during development if it means additional cost.

    e.   A large factor in achieving software quality is the development team. Variability in human performance during a labor-intensive software development makes it difficult to control software quality.

1.7   WHAT DOES QUALITY CONTROL COST?

Quality control costs time and effort. There are four sources of quality control costs.

    a.   Prevention costs, which include quality planning and other costs associated with preventing defects.

    b.   Appraisal costs incurred in evaluating product quality against established levels.

    c.   Internal failure costs caused by defective products or processes which result in rework.

    d.   External failure costs caused by defects reaching the customer.

1.8   WHY IS IT IMPORTANT TO CONTROL SOFTWARE QUALITY?

Deming [DEM86] and other leaders in quality control say that the real reason for controlling quality is to gain higher profits and increased competitiveness in the marketplace. The following are other reasons often cited for controlling software quality:

    a.   Some software quality requirements are critical to the use of the system, e.g., if defects would cause loss of large amounts of money or loss of life.

    b.   All mission-critical systems have some quality criteria for acceptance by the customer. Usually these criteria are evaluated at the end of the development by testing. It may be very costly in time and effort to remove defects that were introduced early in the development and not discovered sooner because of poor quality control.

    c.   Producing a quality product by "doing it right" can save money and time by avoiding rework.

d. Controlling quality can also control cost and effort. The same parameters that affect software productivity in cost estimation models also affect quality. In the Cost Constructive Model (COCOMO) model [BOE81], these include

- The team capability and experience
- The product requirements
- The development methods and tools
- The target hardware constraints
- The schedule constraint.

e. COCOMO data showed that reducing development costs at the expense of quality can lead to considerably higher maintenance costs.

1.9   WHO CONTROLS SOFTWARE QUALITY?

In the context of this guide, the Government is the buyer of the software system, and contractors develop the software. The respective roles for Government and industry in a system acquisition can vary from program to program, but both must be responsible for controlling software quality. The development contractors have direct control over the quality of the software since they possess the process. The Government has indirect control through the ability to approve or disapprove products based on the use of metrics or measurable characteristics.

The Government as the buyer probably performs these kinds of quality control functions:

a. Determines the quality requirements for the system

b. Determines the allocation of funds

c. Determines the schedule and milestones

d. Selects the development organization

e. Reviews, approves or disapproves, baselines, and accepts products.

There are many other tasks that must be done to control software quality. These will be described later in this guide. They may be done by government, industry, the developer, the buyer, or the user.

1.10   WHO HAS BEEN RESPONSIBLE FOR SOFTWARE QUALITY IN THE PAST?

A 1984 MITRE survey of managers of command and control systems under development revealed the software problems in table 1-3, listed from most to least frequently cited. The table also shows who is responsible for a problem. Although the bottom line is poor software quality control, all of the other factors contributed to poor quality.

Table 1-3. Most Frequent Software Problems and Responsibility

Problem	Responsibility
Too little time	Government
Complex set of requirements	Government
Large number of requirements	Government
High performance requirements	Government
Incorrect requirements specification	Government
Unstable changing requirements	Government
Poor design documentation	Developer
Difficult to determine requirements	Government
Inadequate personnel skills	Developer
Weak management by developer	Developer
Too little user involvement	Government
Inadequate tools, support software	Developer
Too little money	Government
Poor software quality control	Government & developer

1.11   WHEN SHOULD SOFTWARE QUALITY CONTROL BE APPLIED?

Software quality control must be applied throughout the life cycle of a system, i.e., pre-development, development, and maintenance. While every system may use a different sequence of activities to specify, develop, and maintain its software, there is a set of activities that is performed at some time in the life of most systems. We have grouped these activities into three basic phases which will be used to describe when specific software quality control techniques are applicable.

1.11.1 Basic Phases of a System Life Cycle

In this guide, we will use the following basic phases, which can be combined to represent a variety of life cycles: Predevelopment, Development, and Maintenance or Post Deployment Software Support (PDSS). Table 1-4 shows examples of activities associated with each phase.

Table 1-4. Examples of Life Cycle Phases and Activities

Predevelopment	Development	PDSS
Concept Definition	Requirements Analysis	Repair
Prototyping	Design	Enhance
Requirements Specification	Code Unit Test	Adapt (new hardware, operating system)
RFP Preparation	Integration Test	
Source Selection		
Contract Award		

These phases may occur many times during a system's life, sequentially or overlapping in time. For example, phases of an evolutionary acquisition are represented in figure 1-1.

After a system is fielded, parts of the predevelopment phase are repeated to define new requirements based on feedback from operational experience. Then a new development is initiated, integrated with the prior system, fielded, and maintained.

The phases of an incremental development are represented in figure 1-2.

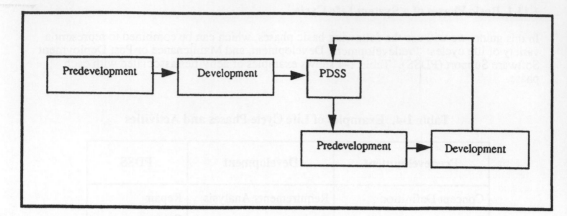

Figure 1-1. Phases of an Evolutionary Acquisition

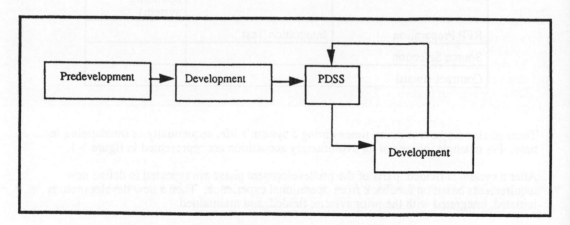

Figure 1-2. Phases of an Incremental Development

In this case, following initial delivery, additional software is developed for the fielded system, in accordance with the specifications provided during predevelopment, and then it is maintained as part of the next release. Other life cycles can also be represented.

SECTION 2

MODELS FOR SOFTWARE QUALITY CONTROL

2.1 INTRODUCTION

In the previous section, we defined software quality control. In this section, we describe and compare some general approaches that have been used for software quality control. Then we present a model, called the Total Software Quality Control (TSQC) model, that builds on and extends the Rome Laboratory Software Quality Framework (RSQF) to make a more complete framework for planning, monitoring, and improving software quality control.

2.2 GENERAL APPROACHES TO SOFTWARE QUALITY CONTROL

2.2.1 Rome Laboratory's Software Quality Framework

The Rome Laboratory Software Quality Framework [BOW85] is one of the earliest systematic methods for specifying, predicting, and evaluating software quality. It has become a de facto standard for software quality evaluation. It uses a hierarchical model for defining and measuring quality in software products (see figure 2-1). User/customer-oriented views of quality in a product, called **quality factors**, are at the top level of the hierarchy. These were listed in table 1-2. At the next level are software-oriented characteristics, called **quality criteria**, that act to define and link user/customer-understood characteristics of quality into software characteristics (see figure 2-2). These software characteristics are defined at the third level into metrics that are measurable characteristics of those software characteristics defined at level two. The metrics are sets of questions about the software specifications and the design that are answered at major milestones during the development. The following example is taken from Bowen:

Quality Factor:	Reliability
Quality Criteria:	Accuracy, anomaly management, simplicity
Questions:	Accuracy
SRR:	Are there accuracy requirements for all applicable inputs associated with each applicable function (e.g., mission-critical function)?
PDR:	Do the numerical techniques used in implementing applicable functions (e.g., mission-critical functions) provide enough precision to support accuracy objectives?

13

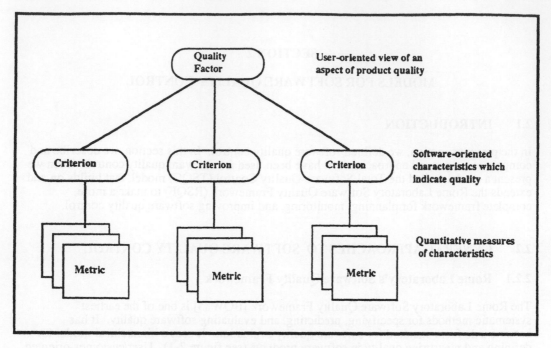

Figure 2-1. Software Quality Model

As an approach to quality control, the model's main features are

a. Numeric quality goals are defined for the product under development by identifying the quality factors required. Typically, no more than three factors are specified on a project. A method for determining what factors to apply is described in volume II of [BOW85]. The metrics can also be used as requirements, so that these features can be assured to be present in the software.

b. Quality is evaluated or predicted for the final product at a series of decision points during development by responding to questions in worksheets applied to products available at that time. These are the review criteria. See volume III of [BOW85] for details of the quality evaluation method.

c. The responses are used to calculate quality criteria and factor scores. The achieved scores are then compared with the goals.

d. If quality achieved meets or exceeds goals, no action is taken. If quality achieved is less than the goal, questions with negative responses are examined to determine where deficiencies in quality exist. Action is then taken to improve quality. Requirements can be changed or products reworked until goals are met.

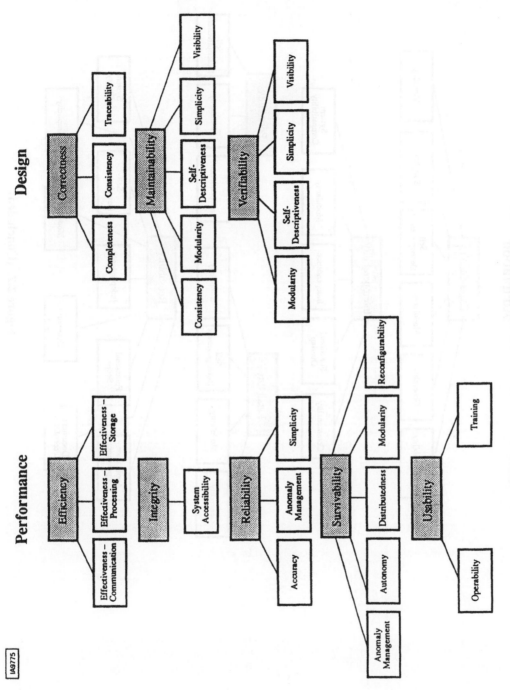

Figure 2-2. Quality Factor and Quality Criteria Relationships

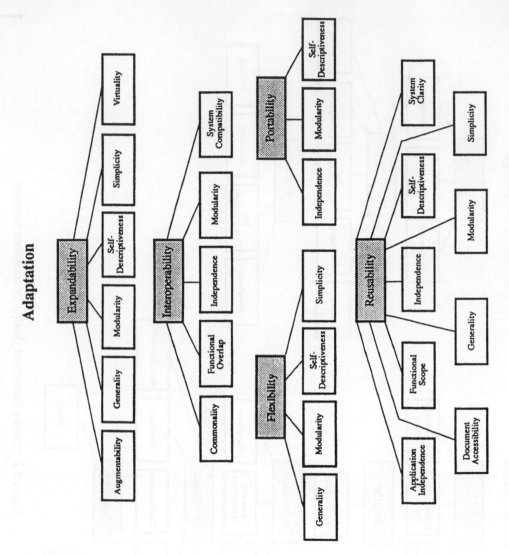

Figure 2.2. (Concluded)

2.2.2   Goal Question Metric Paradigm

The Goal Question Metric (GQM) approach [BAS89] is another method that can be used for defining quality goals and monitoring how well they are being met. GQM consists of the following steps:

a.   Goals are specified for any aspect of a project including products, processes, and resources. Goals can be formulated to provide a better understanding of what happens during development, to evaluate what is done, or to improve over past performance.

b.   For each goal, a series of questions is derived whose answers will reveal whether the goal is being achieved.

c.   The questions are then mapped into metrics that can be used to answer the questions, and plans are made for data collection and analysis.

d.   Data are collected for the specific project and used over the long term to set new goals for continuous improvement.

Grady [GRA87] provides an excellent example of the application of GQM to software maintainability. The following is an adaptation of an example from that article:

Goal: Improve post-release quality (maintainability)

Questions: How effective is the development process in preventing defects?
                    What defects are getting through? Why?

Metrics: Post-release defect density
                    Post-release defect frequency by category
                    Frequency distribution of causes of defects
                    Frequency distribution of phase when defects occurred

Appendix A gives further examples of the use of the GQM model for measuring achievement of quality factor goals.

The GQM approach is similar to the RSQF, but differs in the following ways:

a.   It is broader in its application of metrics that can focus on the quality of processes as well as products.

b.   It has no predefined set of questions although reuse of questions is encouraged.

c.   It emphasizes collecting data to understand what happens during a process and how it can be improved as part of long-term improvement in the performance of an organization, as well as for specific project quality control.

2.2.3   Risk Management Model

Risk management is a systematic approach to identifying and controlling those factors in a software development that are most likely to jeopardize the successful achievement of goals, including software quality goals. Boehm [BOE89] gives an excellent description of a risk management process for software. He describes two parts to risk management, risk assessment and risk control, and the techniques that can be used to accomplish them. Other discussions of risk management for software can be found in [CHA90] and in the articles in the Boehm book. For the program manager, a pamphlet has been written [AFS88a] that describes methods for software risk management.

The risk management approach generally involves the following steps:

a.   Identify the risks associated with the current status of the product requirements, processes, and resources based on general experiences with problems in software development and specific difficulties presented by this project.

b.   Evaluate the probability of the risks occurring, and the cost impact they would have on the project.

c.   Prioritize the risk items based on those that have the highest probability of occurring and can cause the most serious defects in the product.

d.   Select risk control techniques based on risk priorities and project constraints, and formulate a plan for using them.

e.   Carry out the plans and monitor the progress in reducing and resolving risks using techniques such as milestone reviews.

f.   After each assessment, take corrective action if necessary and repeat the process to reevaluate and reprioritize risks.

The risk management approach to quality control differs from the RSQF and the GQM approaches in two ways:

a.   The investment in quality control techniques is directed at areas where there is the greatest potential for failures that would critically affect the successful delivery of the system.

b.   The choice of appropriate quality control techniques is an integral part of the risk management approach, whereas the two previous approaches are more directed toward selecting quality goals and monitoring progress toward meeting those goals.

2.2.4   The Spiral Model of Software Development

The spiral model of software development [BOE88] is an example of a risk-driven model of software development. The spiral model is largely based on a series of prototype developments, each of which is directed toward obtaining information that will reduce the significant software risks and lead to specification of the system and its design. The spiral model provides for the adaptation of the product and the development process.

2.2.5   The Plan-Do-Check-Action Model of Quality Control

The basic Plan, Do, Check, Action (PDCA) model was first proposed in 1939 by Shewart as a quality improvement approach to manufacturing. It was widely advocated by Deming [DEM86] to help in the recovery of Japanese industry after World War II, and adopted by the Japanese with great success. It is shown in figure 2-3 and briefly described below. In a later section of this guide, we show its applicability to software quality control.

    a.   **Planning** involves setting goals or standards for the quality of the products that will be generated, for the process that will be used to generate them, and for resources. Goals are based on past performance and desired improvements in product, process, and resource quality.

        •   Goals can be quantitative, such as the maximum number of defects that will be found in the software per thousand lines of code (defect density) during testing or within the first six months after delivery to customers.

    b.   **Doing** involves developing the products using the process that was defined during the Planning phase.

        •   The quality is either engineered into the products or defects will occur. Defects could be caused by the process, or by the resources used (e.g., people, tools, material).

    c.   **Checking** involves evaluating or testing a product to determine if the goals have been met and to identify causes of deviations.

    d.   **Acting** involves correcting the problems that were found, and identifying areas where improvements can be made. This becomes the basis for the next planning cycle.

A similar model of quality control has been succinctly described in [FEI83] as a management tool with the following four steps:

    a.   Setting quality standards

    b.   Appraising conformance to these standards

    c.   Acting when the standards are exceeded

    d.   Planning for improvement in the standards.

The PDCA cycle is general enough to be compatible with the prior models. Its features of interest to software quality control are the following:

    a.   It is an iterative improvement process for an organization to use over the long term to set new goals and to increase its performance.

    b.   It depends on data collection and checking as a basis for setting new goals.

    c.   It focuses on measurement of processes and resources as well as products to find causes of deficiencies and opportunities for improvement.

2.3   THE TSQC MODEL

The TSQC model is a framework for organizing and presenting guidance on how to plan for and control the quality of software within an organization in a particular development (intra-process model). It can also serve as a framework for accumulating information across many programs that can be used over the long term to formulate quantitative relationships between quality control options and the resulting quality of software, which can lead to process improvement (inter-process model). It is based on the RSQF model with the incorporation of extensions derived from the other models previously described.

2.3.1   The Basic Elements of the TSQC Model

Figure 2-3 shows the basic elements of the TSQC model and the relationships among them.

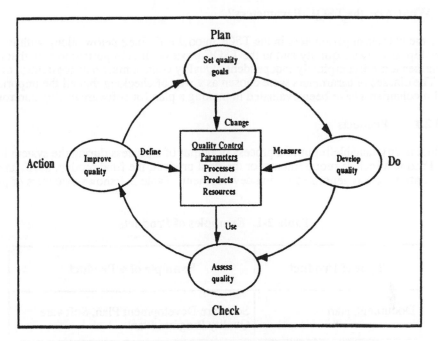

Figure 2-3. The Total Software Quality Control Model

The model can be described as follows:

a.   The total software quality control process consists of regulating all of the parameters that can affect the quality of the final software product.

b.   The three classes of parameters that control software quality are

•   Products—what is generated
•   Processes—how it is done
•   Resources—what is used to do it.

The total quality control process consists of the following activity cycle:

a.   Plan: define the requirements for the parameters.

b.   Do: use the defined parameters.

c.   Check: determine if requirements are being met through review, measurement, and test.

d.   Action: correct the parameter requirements and/or repeat the work.

2.3.2   What Are the TSQC Parameters?

Each of the classes of parameters in the TSQC model is defined below, along with its relationship to software quality and to the TSQC process. It is important to note that the three classes are not completely independent. Quality control must balance control of each class. The classes of parameters were chosen as a way of checking that all the important control mechanisms have been evaluated in making a plan for software quality control.

2.3.2.1   Products

A product is any tangible input to a process or output of a process during the system life cycle. Products include requirements for the final product, the final product itself, and intermediate products generated during development. Table 2-1 shows examples of products.

Table 2-1. Examples of Products

Type of Product	Example of a Product
Document, plan	Software Development Plan, Software Quality Program Plan
Document, specification	System/Subsystem Specification
Document, intermediate product	Software Design Document
Software, code	Prototype, final system
Data	Error reports, test case results, cost data

The Impact of the Final Product Requirements on Software Quality

The quality requirements for the product that is being developed, referred to here as the "final product," vary in the difficulty or risk in achieving them, e.g., 24-hour-a-day system availability despite equipment downtime is harder to achieve than batch processing that can tolerate four hour interrupts in operation. System requirements have been a major source of problems in implementing C^3 systems. Section 4 lists some of the areas of risk in specifying requirements.

The Impact of Intermediate Products on Software Quality

Intermediate products are the outputs of steps in the development process that may also be inputs to subsequent steps. Figure 2-4 illustrates the dual role of intermediate products as inputs and as outputs.

The quality of the outputs of a process can be no better than the quality of its inputs. If an input has defects, new work will be based on that defect, and the impact will continue to multiply downstream until the defect and all subsequent defects derived from it are removed. The feedback of defects to earlier processes and rework of earlier products delay the delivery of a product and increase the risk that some defects will not be found or removed in time for product delivery.

The roles of intermediate products in controlling software quality are

a. An indicator of the quality of work that has been done up to that point; e.g., the software architecture shows the skills of people to use their design process, and their understanding of the application and the technology needed.

b. A predictor of the quality of the final product; e.g., the design can be evaluated to determine if the final system will be reliable and maintainable.

c. The specification for the next set of steps; e.g., the software design is the specification for the coders to implement.

d. A means of eliminating errors and their causes before they reach the final product; e.g., errors in the software design will become errors in the code unless they are removed before coding begins. Causal analysis is a method for determining the cause so that it can be removed and so that similar defects will not occur in the future.

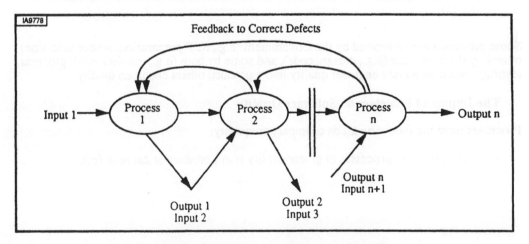

Figure 2-4. Products as Inputs and Outputs

2.3.2.2   Processes

Processes are the management and technical activities performed to develop, maintain, and assure the quality of the software. Management processes include planning and monitoring work, and allocating resources and work among organizations. Technical processes are characterized by the software engineering methods and tools used to develop and maintain the software. Inputs to these processes include products generated in previous phases and available resources. Table 2-2 shows examples of processes.

Table 2-2. Examples of Processes

Type of Process	Example of a Process
Management/technical	RFP preparation
Management/technical	Source selection
Management	Monitor work progress, resource use
Management	Select, approve development standards
Management	Assign responsibilities to subcontractors
Management/technical	Configuration management
Technical	Design, code, test software
Technical	Develop a prototype
Technical	Review design

Some processes are performed by the Government (e.g., RFP preparation, source selection), others by the contractor (e.g., design, code), and some by both (e.g., monitor work progress, testing). Some processes engineer quality into a product, others check on quality.

The Impact of Processes on Software Quality

Processes have the following kinds of impact on quality:

a.   Development processes engineer quality into a product or cause defects.

b. Processes are used to check that quality has been achieved in the products, development processes, and resources used in software development.

c. The number of organizations involved in a process and their relationships affect the probability that faults will be introduced, and the probability that faults will be found and fixed.

   • Complex technical, management, and physical interfaces between a contractor and subcontractors can lead to errors and inconsistencies among the parts of the system they each develop.

   • The amount of independence and authority a quality assurance organization has can determine how well it can enforce standards.

d. Studies of the psychological, social, and organizational factors in software development processes show these factors have strong effects on software productivity and quality [CUR88].

2.3.2.3   Resources

Resources are the time, dollars, people, and equipment used by the processes that are applied to delivering quality software products. Table 2-3 shows examples of the kinds of resources that are important in controlling software quality.

Table 2-3. Examples of Resources

People
Software development environment
Software test facility
System hardware, computers
Schedule for development
Funding

Impact of Resources on Software Quality

The quality and quantity of resources affect software quality in the following ways:

a. The personnel/team capability is considered the most influential factor in software productivity, according to the COCOMO cost model.

   • Differences among programmers are often of sufficient magnitude to disguise performance effects due to software "characteristics or practices." [CUR81]

- One of the most salient problems in software development and maintenance of large, complex systems is the "thin spread of application domain knowledge." [CUR88]

b.   Insufficient time and money cause a decrease in software quality control activities (see section 1).

c.   Insufficient, inadequate, or unreliable software development environments or software test facilities can cause increases in the rate at which defects are introduced and the time it takes for them to be discovered and removed.

- When the compiler is unreliable or poorly documented, people have difficulty generating and testing software. This can lead to increased development time and cost as well as decreased quality.

- If the software development facility cannot be used for integrating software, then the test facility may have to stop testing to support development and repair of detected defects.

- As software approaches the limits of the speed and storage capacity of processors, more work is needed to optimize the size and run time to meet performance requirements. Such optimization usually compromises design clarity, maintainability, and adaptability.

2.3.3   The TSQC Model in the System Life Cycle

The TSQC model applies the basic elements described above to all of the phases of the system life cycle as shown in figure 2-5.

The discussion below assumes that each phase happens only once, but it could occur more than once as shown in section 1. For every occurrence of a phase, the activities described below could be applied, with tailoring if necessary.

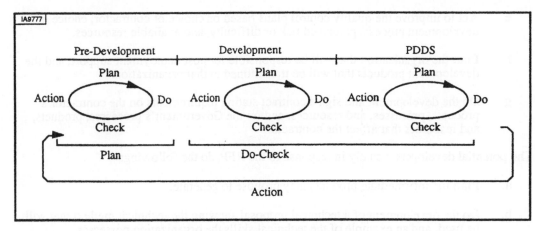

Figure 2-5. The TSQC Model

2.3.3.1   Predevelopment

The predevelopment phase covers activities related to the acquisition of a system that occur prior to the commencement of the system's development. During predevelopment, the Government usually performs studies to establish requirements, issues an RFP, conducts a source selection, and awards a contract to a system developer. The following kinds of activities in the PDCA cycle are performed (usually by the Government as buyer and user) to define the requirements and standards for the three classes of software quality control parameters. Other activities may be performed in this phase or in a subsequent phase.

a. **Plan** the software quality control process to be used, and the criteria for selection of a developer based on available resources, perceived risk or difficulty, past experience and assets, and proven software engineering technology such as tools and methods.

b. **Do** the development of the RFP package, which contains

- The specification for functional and quality requirements
- The statement of work
- Criteria for source selection
- Instructions for proposal evaluation
- Schedule information
- Deliverable product requirements.

c. **Check** the quality of the RFP package, and **act** to improve it if necessary.

d. **Check** offerors' responses to the RFP against criteria and select one.

e.   **Act** to improve the quality control plans based on choice of contractor, choice of development process, perceived risk or difficulty, and available resources.

f.   **Plan** the organization that will be responsible for post deployment support, and the development products that will be transitioned to that organization.

g.   **Do** the development and sign a contract stating requirements on the contractor's products, processes, and resources, and on the Government's processes, products, and resources that affect the contractor.

The potential developers, usually in response to the RFP, do the following:

a.   **Plan** the intermediate products they propose to generate.

b.   **Do** the development of a technical proposal showing the technical method that will be used, and an example of the technical skills the organization possesses.

c   **Plan** the funds, schedule, staffing resources, development facilities, and system computer resources they propose to use.

d.   **Plan** the methods they will use for checking software quality and making adjustments to correct deficiencies in their products.

In some cases (described in the next section), the developer may be asked to demonstrate his software engineering capabilities during source selection.

2.3.3.2   Development

This phase covers activities from commencement of development to the delivery and acceptance of an operational capability by a user. The following are representative activities in this phase:

a.   **Plan** the detailed development process to be followed, resources to be used, and products to be generated, based on requirements and on risks. This is usually done by the developer and approved by the Government.

b.   **Do** the execution of the plans for development using the resources planned. This is done by the developer.

c.   **Check** for conformance to plans and for achievement of expected results. This is done by the developer and the Government.

d.   **Act** to improve plans, processes, allocation of resources, and products. Review and revise risks based on results of the checking process. This should be done by the developer with Government approval if prior plans are on contract. It may also be done by the Government when contractual issues are involved.

2.3.3.3   Post Deployment Support

In this phase, the system will undergo maintenance activities to repair defects, to make changes due to requirements changes, and to improve the system performance. The following kinds of quality control activities may occur:

a.   **Plan** the PDSS process for handling defects if not already planned.

b.   **Check** that defects are corrected.

c.   **Check** and record data on defect density and rate of repair to determine when changes are needed to increase efficiency, improve quality, and reduce cost.

d.   **Act** to provide data for inter-project studies of factors that affect the quality of delivered software with respect to its operational performance and supportability.

2.3.4   The TSQC Model in an Organization

For an organization that participates in many programs, a PDCA cycle can help to improve the overall performance of the organization by influencing and improving the way quality control is performed in all programs. The organization issues standards and policies, and establishes the goals or norms for all of its programs. The basis for these decisions should come from an analysis of what has happened on individual programs. The factors that contributed to achieving or not achieving quality goals need to be determined. As figure 2-5 shows, each system should contribute to that knowledge, and use that knowledge in formulating its plans.

2.4   HOW DOES THE TSQC MODEL DIFFER FROM THE RSQF?

The TSQC model incorporates and extends the RSQF in the following ways as shown in figure 2-6.

a.   Meeting software quality factor requirements is the goal of both the RSQF and the TSQC model.

b.   The RSQF criteria apply to products only, while the TSQC criteria apply to products and resources as well, because of their influence on quality.

c.   The RSQF uses only one quality control technique, namely a questionnaire, for evaluating products at milestones. The TSQC model includes multiple techniques for achieving those product criteria; e.g., to achieve "completeness," processes might be used such as developing a Requirements Traceability Matrix, using an IV&V contractor, and hiring people who understand the application domain. These techniques employ processes and resources.

d.   The RSQF covers Government evaluation of products generated by the developer. The TSQC model includes activities and evaluations by the Government prior to the commencement of development.

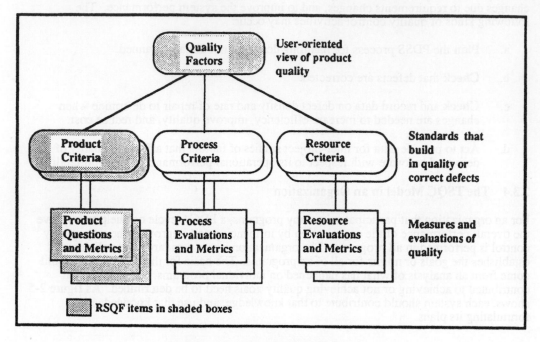

Figure 2-6. Extending the RSQF

SECTION 3

SOFTWARE QUALITY CONTROL TECHNIQUES

3.1 INTRODUCTION

In the prior section, a TSQC model was presented for performing software quality control within three phases that occur during a system life cycle. The model uses the PDCA cycle to control three kinds of software quality control parameters.

In this section, we present brief descriptions of some of the kinds of quality control techniques that are available and how they can be used to support activities of the Government and the contractor. Some of these techniques, marked with an asterisk, are described in much fuller detail in volume 2 of this report, which can serve as a reference document for applying them.

In section 4, we describe a method for determining which quality techniques may be appropriate for a specific program.

3.2 CHARACTERISTICS OF QUALITY CONTROL TECHNIQUES AND MEASURES

Quality control techniques can be characterized in ways that help to identify when they might be useful. Tables 3-1, 3-2, and 3-3, at the end of this section, summarize these characteristics for a set of quality control techniques.

3.2.1 Life Cycle Phase

Each of the quality control techniques is applicable to one or more of the life cycle phases described in section 1. Planning, prior to development, must ensure that provisions have been made for using the selected techniques in the appropriate phases to follow. Table 3-1 shows techniques categorized by life cycle phase.

3.2.2 Type of Control

Quality control techniques can be classified by their purpose. Some are intended to avoid making errors; others detect when errors have been made. Today, we need both kinds of techniques, since there are no techniques that reliably prevent defects from occurring. The "planning" and "doing" stages of the TSQC model are preventive; the "checking" and "action" stages of the TSQC model are detective. Table 3-3 shows techniques categorized by the type of quality control.

31

a. Preventive Quality Control — Do it right.

Preventive methods avoid defects by setting standards for processes, products, and resources. The choices are derived from sound software engineering principles and from past experiences with similar systems, within the same organization or similar organizations, that have demonstrated which techniques lead to higher quality products and which factors cause defects.

Standards may be processes to follow, quantities of and qualifications for resources, and normal values for what results to expect, such as density of errors found in testing and productivity during coding.

b. Detective Quality Control Techniques — Find deficiencies and fix them.

Detective techniques look for deficiencies in products, processes, and resources. These techniques assess the quality of the intermediate products and look for defects that must be corrected. Some detective techniques analyze the causes of defects in the processes and resources used to produce products. These analyses can lead to corrective actions that are preventive for the remainder of that development or for future developments.

Detective techniques also compare standards against actual products, processes, and resources, on the assumption that digression from standards will lead to lower quality.

3.2.3   Effect on Quality Control Parameters

The TSQC model states that quality is achieved by regulating the quality control parameters. Therefore, the relationship between the quality control techniques and the products, processes, and resources they can affect helps determine the relevance of a technique, especially when the parameter type causing defects has been identified and corrections are needed. Table 3-3 shows examples of how the quality control parameters are affected by the quality control techniques.

3.3   QUALITY CONTROL ISSUES AND TECHNIQUES

The following is a list of decisions to be made concerning software quality control by a program office or a developer, with brief descriptions of techniques that are relevant to each decision. The techniques whose titles are followed by an asterisk (*) are described more fully in volume 2 of this report. If a technique is applicable to more than one decision, it is cited in each place but is described only once unless it is applied differently.

3.3.1   What Are the Quality Requirements for the Final Product?

Quality requirements include operational requirements such as usability and survivability, as well as implementation qualities such as maintainability. Not only must the quality requirements be stated, but they must be stated well.

3.3.1.1   Operations Concept Document

One of the most important ways to define requirements is through an operations concept document that describes how the system will be used. It is a description of the dynamics of its use and how use changes over time. This view is necessary when establishing quality requirements and prioritizing them. Sometimes an operations concept document does not exist at the time a system development begins, and its lack adversely affects the quality of the system.

3.3.1.2   RFP Preparation and Review*

The system level requirements are usually contained in the System/Subsystem Specification (SSS) which is part of the RFP package. This is the place where the quality requirements should be defined. A comprehensive review should be done prior to its release to assure that the requirements are clearly and completely defined, and are verifiable.

The RSQF software quality factors (in table 1-1) are a list that should be used in identifying what qualities are important in the final product and how important they are. This list should be tailored to those factors important for the system to be developed, and augmented by any important qualities not in the list.

3.3.1.3   Prototyping*

If there is uncertainty about requirements, the Government or the developer can use prototyping to determine the correct requirements. Prototypes are limited implementations to learn something. Prototypes of the user interface can clarify the functional requirements and the operations concept. The user interface includes the displays and actions available to an operator, the sequence and set of actions needed to perform a task, and the expected system response. Users should be involved in reviews of prototypes when operator interfaces are an important requirement to be resolved. Other prototypes may show the effects of alternative technical requirements such as communications protocols, or the technical feasibility of requirements such as accuracy. To learn what algorithms should be specified, prototype software might be developed and evaluated.

3.3.2   Who Will Be the Developer?

Since the development team is probably the most significant contributor to software quality, this decision is one of the most significant that a program office can make. There are many techniques that support this decision. Those listed here are appropriate to the award of a contract. An Air Force Systems Command pamphlet [AFS90] recommends a planned approach to evaluating a developer during source selection, called the Software Development Capability Assessment. The areas of evaluation it suggests are

    a.   Program Management

    b.   Planning and Execution

    c.   Configuration Management

    d.   Quality Assurance

    e.   Review and Testing

    f.   Training

    g.   Process Focus.

A set of techniques for determining who will be the developer is described below.

3.3.2.1   RFP Preparation and Review*

The RFP package contains the criteria that will be used to select among competing offerors. It also specifies in the section on Instructions for Proposal Preparation (IFPP) the information the offerors must provide to help in that selection.

Important criteria are

    a.   The developer's software engineering methods, standards and practices, and development environment (tools and facilities)

    b.   The developer's ability to staff the program with people who have knowledge of the application area or mission

    c.   The developer's ability to staff the program with people who have competence and experience in software engineering and are trained and experienced in using the process proposed by the developer

    d.   The maturity of the software engineering and management processes proposed (see [HUM87] for definition of maturity)

    e.   The quality assurance and configuration management activities proposed by the developer

    f.   The developer's management commitment to the program, and understanding of software development management techniques

g.   The organizational structure within the developer's company and among associate contractors, and the distribution of work among components of the organizations

h.   The soundness of the offeror's technical proposal

i.   The credibility of the cost and schedule proposals.

The RFP preparation and review techniques, described in volume 2, should check that these criteria have been reflected in the RFP package.

3.3.2.2   The Software Engineering Institute Software Capability Evaluation*

The Software Engineering Institute (SEI) Software Capability Evaluation (SCE) is a procedure for assessing the ability of an organization to control and improve its software development process and its capability to use modern software engineering technology [HUM87]. It was developed by the SEI to provide objective and consistent assessments that can be compared across organizations and within the same organization at different points in time. It can be used by an organization to assess its own strengths and weaknesses, and by the Government to assess contractors as part of source selection or while they are under contract. It uses evidence from past performance as a predictor of future performance. A questionnaire with yes-no answers and an on-site visit are used to collect information for the evaluation.

3.3.2.3   Software Development Capability/Capacity Review*

The Software Development Capability/Capacity Review (SDCCR) is a technique for evaluating an organization's capability to develop software for a particular system [ASD87]; it is an integral part of the source selection process. The offerors are required to respond with information on the software development tools and methods they propose to use on the specific development, with examples of their use and data on tool performance. The evaluation includes an in-plant review at an offeror's facilities using a predefined set of open-ended questions. An Air Force Systems Command (AFSC) pamphlet [AFS90] shows how the SDCCR and the SCE can be used during source selection. The primary difference between the two is the emphasis of the SDCCR on evaluation of an organization relative to a specific software development project. Its output is an assessment for source selection rather than a score. Its scope includes systems engineering as well as software engineering.

3.3.2.4   Software Engineering Exercise*

The Software Engineering Exercise (SEE) [SCH89] can be used by the Government during the source selection process as part of the technical evaluation of the offerors. It is an exercise in software engineering that each offeror is given after the proposals have been submitted. It requires an offeror to carry out part of the development of a mini-system with a small team. The SEE enables the Government to evaluate each offeror's ability to apply its proposed software development process, tools, and techniques, and to illustrate its knowledge and expertise in pertinent technology areas. The products of the SEE are evaluated and the team is interviewed. The results are considered in the source selection.

3.3.3   What Can Be Done to Prevent Quality Defects?

Preventing quality defects requires action by both the Government and the development organizations. The Government can perform activities that prevent or anticipate problems. The Government can also require the developer to use quality control techniques intended to prevent defects from occurring. These must be planned before the development begins and be written into the contract. The contractor or developer can also elect to use techniques that prevent defects. Some techniques prevent defects by finding problems early and correcting them. In that sense, many detective techniques are also preventive.

The following list includes techniques performed by either the Government, the developer, or both. In the latter case, they may be performed somewhat differently or with different emphasis. The descriptions will indicate this.

3.3.3.1   Standards*

Standards define the practices to be followed by organizations. There are both Government and developer standards that affect software quality by constraining the processes and resources that are used, and the products that are generated.

Government Standards

Government regulations and standards provide consistency across programs in organizations that manage the development and maintenance of Government systems by the use of certain practices. They are usually based on past experience in the technology and practices that have contributed to a successful program. Use of Ada is an example of a requirement that affects the process and tools used for development. The requirement to document a Software Development Plan and Software Standards and Procedures are other examples intended to prevent quality problems from arising.

Some of the regulations and standards specify activities of the Government and of the contractor to control the quality of software, such as the following:

a.   DOD-STD-2167A specifies the activities in the software development process that a developer is expected to perform. It also specifies the reviews the Government should conduct and evaluation criteria at those reviews.

b.   MIL-HDBK-287 gives tailoring instructions for DOD-STD-2167A.

c.   DOD-STD-2168 specifies requirements for the development, documentation, and implementation of a software quality program by the developer [DOD88a].

Developer Standards

The SEI SCE establishes the importance of documented software development standards to a development organization. Developer standards accomplish the following:

a.   Make their process repeatable

b.   Allow investment in tools adapted to their process

c.   Allow training of staff to the process

d.   Allow measurement and improvement of their process.

The developer can be required to deliver to the Government documentation of their standards and practices for software development. This can be done in a Software Development Plan [DI-MCCR-80030A] and in a Software Standards and Procedures Manual.

Technical Standards

There are a growing number of Government and industry technical standards for commonly used functional components and their interfaces. Examples are the Portable Operating System Interface (POSIX), X Windows for management of user interfaces, and Government Open Systems Interconnection Profile (GOSIP) for communications. The use of these standards can contribute to the quality of the software in a number of ways.

a.   Provide well-defined specifications

b.   Enhance interoperability with other systems

c.   Enhance maintainability by using proven or popular designs

d.   Enhance portability, flexibility, and adaptability by using interfaces for which there may be more than one software product available.

The quality of the standards themselves must be considered before they are adopted.

3.3.3.2   Software Engineering Prototype*

The Software Engineering Prototype (SEP) is similar to the Software Engineering Exercise, but it occurs after the developer is on contract. The SEP is an exercise in which the Government requires the developer to demonstrate how its organization uses its software development process to carry out the development of a small portion of the system requirements described in a mini-system specification. That specification, accompanied by a set of instructions, is delivered to the contractor approximately at the time of the System Design Review (SDR). It can serve the following purposes:

a.   It can show the Government, prior to major software development, how well the contractor team can adhere to its development process and satisfy the quality requirements of its products.

b.   It can show the use of the software development environment and how well the team understands it.

c.   It can show how well the team understands the application and relevant software engineering principles.

d.   It allows the contractor and the Government to make improvements in the process.

e.   The products may be used as part of the actual system.

3.3.3.3   Configuration Management*

Configuration management [BER84] [SCH87] is the discipline of identifying the configuration of a system for the purpose of systematically controlling changes and maintaining the integrity and traceability of the configuration throughout the system life cycle. According to MIL-STD-483A [MIL85a], configuration management consists of

a.   Identification and documentation of the functional and physical characteristics of the configuration item

b.   Control of changes to those characteristics

c.   Record keeping and status reporting.

Configuration management by the Government during development includes controlling changes to the system functional and performance requirements. This can be done by chairing and being members of a Configuration Control Board that approves requirements changes. Similarly, a developer may have a Configuration Control Board that controls changes to software that do not affect requirements. When software is released to the Government and accepted, the Government must assure that configuration management is conducted for the software requirements, implementation, and related deliverables.

Configuration management by the contractor is an important way to identify and control evolving versions of software and documentation. It is essential in coordinating activities such as integration of components, testing, repair or other modification of software, and documentation, especially when multiple users and organizations participate.

3.3.3.4   Performance Engineering*

Performance engineering refers to activities that estimate, measure, and control the timing of systems. It can be used by the Government, the developer, or both. It provides assurance that a system design meets these kinds of system requirements.

a. **Execution time**—the time to execute a specific function.

b. **Response time**—the time a system takes to respond to an input by changing its state or generating an output.

c. **Throughput**—the rate at which the system can perform a function or handle a particular processing load.

d. **Reserve**—unused but usable processing time, input/output (I/O) capacity, and memory for future changes in requirements.

Performance engineering is an essential activity for real-time systems, where requirements for system response may be in the range of milliseconds, with little tolerance for deviations. It is also important for systems that have larger ranges of response times and throughput requirements, if there is any uncertainty about timing that results from the system and software design. With distributed system architectures and concurrent processing, understanding and predicting performance have become very difficult. Techniques for performance engineering include analytical modeling, simulation, and selective benchmarking of hardware and software. These techniques can be used to detect design defects that might not be discovered until major portions of the system have been integrated and executed, and timing measurements taken. At that time, making software design or hardware changes can be very expensive.

The Government can use performance engineering to determine the technical and economic feasibility of performance requirements prior to issuing the RFP, and during development to independently anticipate or validate design decisions that the contractor makes. Performance engineering techniques have also been used by the Government to prepare for evaluation of offerors' technical proposals. When the developer uses performance engineering, a timing and sizing report can be generated for Government review.

3.3.3.5   Software Engineering Environments

A software engineering environment consists of an integrated set of automated tools that are used by developers to support the activities in their development process. Included in a software engineering environment are Computer-Aided Software Engineering (CASE) tools, which are commercially available, as well as tools developed by the contractor to aid in development. These tools have the following kinds of impact on software quality:

a. Assist in generation, modification, and management of software and associated documentation, such as designs and specifications.

b.   Evaluate design and software by measuring characteristics (see Software Design Metrics).

c.   Perform checking for consistency in parts of the documentation and in the associated design, including interfaces.

d.   Automate configuration management.

e.   Detect deviations from coding standards.

f.   Measure the extent of test coverage.

g.   Generate code from other forms of documentation, such as graphs, tables, and dictionaries.

3.3.3.6   Reuse

"Reuse" means using something that has been previously developed. System and software designs as well as complete components of software may be reused. Reused software components are sometimes referred to as Nondevelopmental Items (NDI). Reuse can reduce the amount of new software that must be developed, with the goal of increasing productivity and quality.

There are several kinds of reusable software.

a.   Software that is developed once for a system and used more than once in that system, e.g., Ada generics

b.   Commercial off-the-shelf (COTS) software that is presumed to be widely used, self-contained, well-documented for users, reliable, and supported

c.   Other off-the-shelf software which may be Government furnished, probably developed for a system with similar requirements or developed by a contractor as part of a research program

d.   Modified software, which is one of the above categories of reusable software that is modified.

There is a growing trend in the Department of Defense to establish collections of reusable software components for a particular application domain, such as command and control, and standard designs for the software architecture. The goal is to quickly assemble prototypes or operational systems from these components.

The effect of reuse on the quality of the software in the new system depends on the quality of the software that is reused, and how well it can be integrated with other existing software. Maintainability is an issue for COTS software, since only the vendors may be able to modify or repair their software components.

3.3.4   How Can Quality Be Checked?

In the TSQC model, checking quality means checking the developer's processes and resources as well as products. It also means predicting quality as well as evaluating it. Quality can be checked at major checkpoints or on a continuous basis. Examples of both kinds of techniques are described here. Some techniques are used by the Government or any organization independent of the developer. Others are primarily used by the developer and should be integral to the development process.

3.3.4.1   Reviews and Audits

Government Reviews

Government reviews provide points during a development when the Government has visibility into what the contractor is doing by receiving information that can be used for checking and evaluation. Some examples of reviews are given below.

Formal Government reviews are usually scheduled to coincide with the completion of each major development activity. The purpose of these reviews is to measure the progress of the program against the planned schedule, to provide a check on the quality of the work to date, and to prevent defects or misunderstandings from propagating to future work. Both the products produced and the plans for the processes and resources to be applied during the subsequent development activities are reviewed.

For DOD-STD-2167A [DOD88b] these reviews include SDR, the Software Specification Review (SSR), the Preliminary Design Review (PDR), the Critical Design Review (CDR), and the Test Readiness Review (TRR). The content of these reviews usually is a tailored version of the definitions found in MIL-STD-1521B [MIL85b]. The same review may occur several times for different parts of the system. If the review is formal, the Government can decide to either pass the contractor or have the review repeated, and can require completion of action items from the review.

It is sometimes advantageous to use informal Government reviews, such as technical interchange meetings. These have a less elaborate structure, and hence less preparation time for the contractor. These reviews provide visibility without allowing the Government to officially redirect the contractor, unless there are provisions in the contract. Continuous on-site oversight is another alternative. These techniques can prevent surprises at formal reviews.

The Software Audit*

The Software Audit (SWA) [ATT90] is a specific example of a Government review that is not found in a regulation, specification, or standard. It was devised by The MITRE Corporation for the Electronic Systems Division (ESD) of the Air Force. It is normally held at the time of the SSR. The SWA evaluates the products and resources available at that time including: the SRSs, interface requirements specification (IRS), Software Development Plan (SDP), Interface Control Documents (ICDs), and the software engineering environment.

This is a critical point for software development, because the software engineering must have been done well or the software development will have problems. The SWA serves the following purposes:

a.   To assess whether the contractor has performed the requisite requirements analysis and systems engineering and is well-prepared to continue into the software preliminary design phase

b.   To determine that the developer has a suitable SDP

c.   To assess the completeness of the SRSs and the requirements decomposition

d.   To review timing and sizing analyses, user interface design, test concepts, and plans or preparation for the design.

The SWA gives the program an overall pass or fail evaluation as well as individual ratings for criteria. This audit's results can be used to determine if the development may proceed.

Inspections*

Inspections are reviews used by developers prior to software testing to detect and remove defects as early as possible within the development process. Inspections can be informal or formal, but they are usually carried out by a small group of peers. The inspection usually reviews designs and code, but specifications, plans, and test procedures can also be inspected. The formal inspection process described by Fagan [FAG79] is very structured both in the steps to prepare, conduct, and follow up on an inspection, and in the roles of people in the group who do the inspection.

Inspections can improve quality by removing defects, and increase productivity by removing them early before they propagate into later development stages. Informal inspections, called "peer reviews" or "walk-throughs" have been used successfully for some time to find defects and to inform people working on related parts of a system about the interfaces and assumptions that have been made about their parts. NASA experiments showed that this is a very cost-effective technique because of the savings from early detection and correction of defects.

3.3.4.2   Independent Verification and Validation*

The Government can use an organization that is independent of the developer's organization to evaluate software products against technical specifications during a system development. The Independent Verification and Validation (IV&V) organization can provide continuous objective visibility into the quality and status of the development, rather than intermittent visibility at reviews. The IV&V process includes requirements verification, design verification, code verification, program validation, and document verification. These activities must be performed in parallel with, and complement, the software development process to achieve the early exposure of product defects. Specific activities performed during

IV&V can be found in AFSC/AFLC Pamphlet 800-5 [AFS88b], and techniques for use in IV&V are listed in [WAL89].

The contractor could also use an internal organization independent of the developers to perform verification and validation functions.

3.3.4.3   Requirements Verification Matrix

The Requirements Verification Matrix (RVM) is one of the principal vehicles for establishing the verification method for each requirement and capability of the system. The verification methods include inspection, demonstration, test, and analysis. The RVM is initially generated by the Government in the SSS to specify how the system level requirements are to be verified. The contractor uses this information to help establish a software level RVM, which indicates how the software requirements are to be verified. A software RVM is generated for each Computer Software Configuration Item (CSCI) and is documented within each SRS.

3.3.4.4   Software Quality Assurance *

Software Quality Assurance (SQA) refers to a set of quality control activities performed by the developer, and is also used to designate a group within the developer's organization, independent of the developers, that performs those activities. Traditional SQA organizations check conformance to the standards for processes and procedures defined for a project, and to the standards established for documentation. The assumption is that adherence to these standards will assure quality. SQA functions do not usually include a review of the technical content of the products. In some organizations, the role of SQA groups is becoming larger, encompassing more of the activities associated with software quality control, such as testing.

3.3.4.5   Testing*

Testing, unlike many other methods of checking quality by reviewing documents, evaluates the software product by running part or all of the system. Testing is performed by the contractor during development, and by the Government and the contractor as part of the acceptance process.

Usually Government testing is performed at the end of a development, or prior to release of a version of the system to the Government. However, the Government can be involved in the contractor's testing in the following kinds of ways:

a.   Reviewing and approving the contractor's test plans and procedures

b.   Reviewing and approving the Requirements Verification Matrix that determines how each requirement or set of requirements will be verified—verification may be performed by inspection, test, analysis, or demonstration

c.   Providing test equipment, facilities, and operators

      d.   Providing operational scenarios or other requirements for the contractor's tests.

Tests range from informal testing by the contractor through formal qualification and acceptance testing, to formal operational testing. Not every program uses every level of testing for every part of the system. The decision depends on how important that level of testing is in assuring the quality of the system. Each level of testing has its own objectives.

      a.   Low level unit testing and Computer Software Component (CSC) integration testing are performed by the contractor to detect and correct software defects.

      b.   Preliminary Qualification Tests (PQT) are performed by the contractor to verify that each CSCI satisfies the software requirements as specified in its SRS. PQTs employ Government-approved test procedures; these tests do not necessarily require Government witnessing. They do not require Government approval.

      c.   Formal Qualification Tests (FQT) are the official mechanism for approval of CSCI tests. Approved test procedures, Government witnessing, and approval of the test results are usually required.

      d.   Development Test and Evaluation (DT&E) involves testing the system with all its hardware and software elements integrated. These tests are usually carried out at the contractor's facilities, and require Government-approved test procedures, Government witnessing, and approval.

      e.   Initial Operational Test and Evaluation (IOT&E) expands the DT&E test to operational testing in the field. These tests also require Government-accepted test procedures, Government witnessing, and approval. After the approval of IOT&E and the resolution of any outstanding software, documentation, and test issues, the DD250 form is signed. This represents the official turnover of the accepted software to the Government.

3.3.4.6   Reliability Modeling*

Software reliability modeling represents a statistical means of analyzing software failure data. Data on the times when software failures occur, determined during operational test or PDSS, are applied to one or more models of software reliability to predict the reliability growth of the software. This technique is appropriate when the software reliability requirement is specified in terms of software failures per 1000 CPU hours or the probability that the software will not fail in a given time period. It is also appropriate for predicting when operational testing of the software will be complete.

3.3.5   What Kinds of Information Should Be Available at Checkpoints?

At checkpoints, information must be available on products, processes, and resources. Government checkpoints are used to evaluate the quality of end products, or to predict their quality. Defects can also be uncovered at these reviews.

The following kinds of information are specified as deliverables in DOD-STD-2167A:

a.   Plans—how the developer will perform its activities

b.   Status—how much work has been done, how much of resources has been used

c.   Product documentation—external and internal descriptions

d.   User documentation—operator, maintainer

e.   Analyses of the product that demonstrate quality.

Descriptions of these kinds of products can be found in the Data Item Descriptions (DIDs) associated with DOD-STD-2167A. Some of them directly affect the quality of the final system, e.g., user documentation can affect usability. Others check on the status to predict quality. Others check for conformance to established requirements. We have chosen to describe several other deliverables that are important to software quality control.

3.3.5.1   Requirements Traceability Matrix*

The Requirements Traceability Matrix (RTM) is an example of a product that is specified within DOD-STD-2167A as part of the SRS and plays an important role in controlling software quality. It provides a mapping from the requirements in the System/Subsystem Specification to the CSCIs where those requirements have been allocated, and a mapping from each CSCI to the requirements in the SSS, Prime Item Development Specification, or Critical Item Development Specification that the CSCI implements. The RTM is generated by the developer, often with the aid of automated tools, as a required part of the Software Requirements Specification. It is helpful to the developer and to the Government in assuring the completeness of the system requirements allocation to software, and in planning tests of system and software requirements.

3.3.5.2   Metrics

Metrics are collected and analyzed during software development to estimate or evaluate progress and the quality of the final product. The Government can impose metrics on a contractor as a form of reporting. Some kinds of metrics are listed below.

Management Metrics*

The purpose of management metrics is to provide management with a simple set of high level views of the status of a development program to indicate potential software development problems that should be investigated and explained [SCH88] [AFS86]. These are mostly quantitative measures that are taken at regular intervals during a development, and are presented graphically on a time line that shows planned versus actual status for products, processes, and resources. This format allows recognition of trends that may indicate plans cannot be met. Product characteristics include software size and design complexity. Process characteristics include requirements stability (changes in requirements over time) and work accomplished against plans. Resource characteristics include software personnel available, and percent of processing, memory, and communications bandwidth used versus required reserve.

Software Design Metrics*

Software design metrics evaluate characteristics of the design and code that are hypothesized to correlate with software quality factors, such as reliability, maintainability, expandability, flexibility, reusability, and portability. A great deal of research has been performed to establish these correlations, but the results are not conclusive or consistent for many of the measures [CAR90]. These metrics measure the structure within and among system modules [MCC76], [HEN81]. These metrics involve computations based on a representation of the design features, as in a Program Design Language or programming language. If the system is large, it may be necessary to use automated tools to scan the design language and compute the metrics. Design metrics have been used as criteria for evaluating, simplifying, and approving or accepting software for delivery. They allow test planning to focus on the more complex parts of a system.

3.3.5.3   Software Problem Reports* Analysis

Software Problem Reports (SPRs) can be used throughout a development to record defects that are found, when and where they occurred, their causes, how they can be fixed, and when the fix has been verified. The same kinds of reports (also called Software Change Reports) can also be used to record changes that are needed in requirements specifications or documents. The DID for an SDP suggests data items that can be included in an SPR. Traditionally, SPR data have been collected after the software has been placed under configuration control during software integration, system test, and PDSS activities.

The data can be used by the Government to monitor the quality of the development activities, to measure the efficiency of the testing and error correction processes, to estimate the reliability of the final product, and to predict when testing will be completed. To do so requires curves of "normal" or expected defect densities and rates of defect detection and correction.

SPRs should be used by the developer for the same reasons the Government uses them, as well as to identify parts of the process or parts of the software that are prime contributors to problems so improvements can be made. The data supports other quality control techniques such as reliability modeling and causal analysis. Such data, collected during PDSS, allows correlation of the quality of the delivered product with the development process that was used to identify improvements in an organization's development process.

3.3.5.4   Software Development Files*

Software Development Files (SDFs), also called Software Development Folders, are repositories for information about each software unit under development. Each file contains information related to a unit that will help someone else understand it and check its status.

For example, the latest listing of the design and code, test cases, and test results will be in the files. The advantages are

a. They facilitate audits, inspections, reviews of progress, and analysis of problems related to a unit.

b. They help SQA organizations to determine whether standard development procedures are being followed, with sign-off required for completion of each step in the process.

c. They support Configuration Management by keeping current versions of software and documentation.

The SDP should describe the developer's use of SDFs and the file contents. They can be required by the Government as part of the contract, but most contractors use them anyway.

3.3.6   What Can the Contractor Do to Improve the Process and Resources?

There are a number of techniques that a contractor can perform to improve the process and resources, without the Government having to impose project-specific requirements. These tend to focus on long term quality improvement, and span all or most of the software development and test projects within the contractor's organization.

3.3.6.1   Cause and Effect Analysis*

Cause and effect analysis attempts to identify the specific causes of a series of defects. Defects are then prevented either by changing the processes or resources on the current project or by modifying the institutionalized processes or resource selection criteria for future projects. Mays [MAY90] describes a formal process which consists of identifying the root cause of a defect, providing suggestions for preventive actions, creating action teams to implement the preventive action, holding meetings to increase awareness of the quality issues specific to each development phase, and providing for data collection and analysis activities.

3.3.6.2   SEI Self-Assessment

The contractor can use self-assessment to determine where the software development process is weakest, and where it has improved. There are published procedures for conducting a self-assessment, which is similar to an SCE; the major difference is that it is conducted within the organization, although there is an option to call in another organization such as the SEI to assist. The results do not have to be shared with the Government. Its use within a development is to take corrective action.

3.4   CHARACTERIZATION OF THE QUALITY CONTROL TECHNIQUES

This section contains the tables that categorize the quality control techniques discussed above, which are elaborated in volume 2.

3.4.1 Applicability of the Techniques

The applicability of each of the quality control techniques to the life cycle phases is shown in table 3-1.

3.4.2   Type of Control

Table 3-2 shows the relationship of the various quality control techniques to the PDCA paradigm of the TSQC model, which is shown in terms of the preventive (plan-do) and detective (check-action) nature of the techniques. Some of the techniques possess both preventive and detective characteristics.

3.4.3   Relationship to the Quality Control Parameters

The TSQC model states that quality is controlled by measuring and controlling the quality control parameters. The product, resource, and process characteristics that are affected by each of the quality control techniques are shown in table 3-3.

Table 3-1. Applicability of the Quality Control Techniques

QC Technique	Applicable Life Cycle Phase		
	Predevelopment	Development	PDSS
Cause and Effect Analysis		x	x
Configuration Management		x	x
Government Reviews		x	
IV&V	x	x	
Inspections		x	
Management Metrics		x	
Performance Engineering	x	x	
Prototyping	x	x	
Reliability Modeling		x	x
Requirements Traceability Matrix		x	x
Requirements Verification Matrix	x	x	
RFP Preparation and Review	x		
Software Audit		x	
SEI Software Capability Evaluation	x	x	
Software Design Metrics		x	x
Software Development Capability/Capacity Review	x		
Software Development Files		x	
Software Engineering Environment		x	x
Software Engineering Exercise	x		
Software Engineering Prototype		x	
Software Quality Assurance		x	x
SPR Analysis		x	x
Standards	x	x	x
Testing		x	x

Table 3-2. Preventive and Detective Quality Control Techniques

QC Technique	Preventive—Plan and Do	Detective—Check and Action
Cause and Effect Analysis	Suggests changes to product, process, and resources to prevent problems in the current project or in future projects	
Configuration Management	Controls the official software configuration and thus prevents the introduction of new defects	
Government Reviews	Reviews and suggests improvements to software development plans, standards and practices, configuration management plans, quality assurance plans, test plans	Reviews specific products and analyses to find defects and inconsistencies
Independent Verification and Validation		Provides early detection and correction of requirement, design, and coding errors; involves independent testing of software end product
Inspections	Detects and corrects design and code defects prior to test; test and integration problems are thus prevented	Detects and corrects design and code defects
Management Metrics	Detects program problems early and modifies quality control parameters to correct the negative trends	
Performance Engineering	Provides a means early in the program to detect potential performance problems by modeling	Measures actual performance of the system and its components to determine if allocated timing budgets are being satisfied
Prototyping	Provides early identification of potential requirements and some problems; obtains early concurrence from the user on the user interface design	
Reliability Modeling		Provides a measure of attainment of software reliability requirements; predicts the amount of additional testing or system use necessary to attain the required level of reliability
Requirements Traceability Matrix		Provides a means to determine that the software requirements are complete
Requirements Verification Matrix		Establishes the method of verification for each requirement; establishes one of the criteria for checking that the test plan and procedures are complete

Table 3-2. (Concluded)

RFP Preparation and Review	Eliminates system specification problems; establishes formal checking activities; defines acceptance criteria	Detects and corrects defects in the RFP
Software Audit	Identifies key risk areas in the development process and suggests ways in which the risks may be avoided	Detects if the work to date indicates that the contract is in serious schedule, cost, or quality trouble
SEI Software Capability Evaluation	Evaluates contractor's software development process; determines the level of maturity to prevent problems during development	
Software Design Metrics	Detects design problems early and modifies the design to prevent introduction of defects	Detects and corrects design and code problems
Software Development Capability/Capacity Review	Evaluates contractor with a sufficiently mature development process to prevent problems during development	
Software Development Folders	Used to prevent repetitive development mistakes and prevent maintenance problems; content of folders could be used as input to cause and effect analysis	Repository of software development information; input for checking conformance to standards
Software Engineering Environment	Provides integrated set of development tools and procedures; prevents defects by automating internal consistency checking	
Software Engineering Exercise	Enables the Government to evaluate a potential contractor's software development process and assists in the selection of a contractor.	
Software Engineering Prototype	Similar to SEE but more intensive; enables early detection of development process flaws and prevents misunderstandings in the requirements specification and the content and form of other required documentation	
Software Quality Assurance		Detects defects in specific products through a systematic analysis of each product by means of check lists based on established standards
SPR Analysis		Process is geared towards tracking the resolution of specific software problems
Standards	Prevents defects by establishing consistency in the development of the software products and in the use of the processes	
Testing		Verifies that the software, as implemented, satisfies the requirements as specified in the SRSs and IRS

Table 3-3. Quality Control Techniques and Quality Control Parameters

QC Technique	Quality Control Parameters		
	Products Affected	Processes Affected	Resources Affected
Cause and Effect Analysis		Requirements analysis SW development & test	Personnel Facilities Schedule
Configuration Management	Requirements Interfaces Code and associated documentation	CM SQA	
Government Reviews	Requirements, design, code, and test documentation Interfaces	Requirements analysis SW development and test Test plans	Personnel Facilities Schedule
Independent Verification and Validation	Requirements, design, code, and test documentation Timing and sizing	Requirements analysis SW development & test	Facilities
Inspections	Design and Code documentation		
Management Metrics	Requirements Design Code	Requirements analysis SW development & test Software development tools SW status	Computer resources Personnel Budget and schedule
Performance Engineering	Design Code Timing and sizing	Test	
Prototyping	Requirements User interface	SW development & test	Facilities
Reliability Modeling	Design Code		Schedule remaining for test and evaluation.
Requirements Traceability Matrix	Requirements, design, and test plans and procedures	Requirements analysis	
Requirements Verification Matrix	Requirements, test plans and procedures	Test	
RFP Preparation and Review	Requirements Interfaces	Proposal process Acquisition process SW development & test Review process	Schedule Facilities Developer selection
Software Audit	Requirements Interfaces Timing and sizing	Requirements analysis SW development & test Prototyping process CM SQA	Personnel Management Development and test facilities
SEI Software Capability Evaluation		SW development & test	
Software Design Metrics	Design Code		

Table 3-3. (Concluded)

Software Development Capability/Capacity Review		SW development & test	
Software Development Files	Design, code, test, SPR documentation	SW development & test SQA CM	
Software Engineering Environment		SW development & test	Tool set Facilities
Software Engineering Exercise		SW development & test Software development tools	Tool set Facilities
Software Engineering Prototype		SW development & test Software development tools	Personnel Tool set Facilities
Software Quality Assurance	Requirement, design, code, and test documentation	Requirements analysis SW development & test SQA	
SPR Analysis	Software problem documentation	SW development & test SQA CM	
Standards	Interface standards	Acquisition process SW development & test	Personnel Tool set Facilities
Testing	Code Test documentation	Test procedures	

SECTION 4

APPLYING TOTAL SOFTWARE QUALITY CONTROL

4.1   INTRODUCTION

The previous sections described general approaches and some techniques for controlling software quality. In this section, we provide guidelines for selecting and applying a set of techniques and measures for a specific program.

An overview of the Total Software Quality Control Process within a system acquisition is shown in figure 4-1. As described in prior sections, the TSQC process uses the PDCA cycle. In this section, most of the emphasis is on planning prior to system development. For many programs, the die is cast before the major development effort has begun. The Do, Check, Action parts of the process will have been determined by the planning. If planning is not done well, changes will occur because problems have forced change, not because there were checkpoints planned where constructive changes could be made.

4.2   A REVIEW OF TSQC PLANNING PRINCIPLES

Although most of these principles have already been stated, we summarize again the principles that will be used to apply the TSQC model.

a.   Software quality control is achieved by controlling three types of parameters (products, processes, resources).

b.   The choice of quality control techniques should depend on the level of risk associated with the most critical requirements for the system.

c.   Risk may often be reduced by buying information. That is, resources may be expended early in the program on special studies, evaluations, prototypes, simulations, etc., to develop a better understanding of requirements, technical solutions, or the quality of the processes and resources that are being used.

d.   The investment in software quality control must be affordable.

e.   If the schedule and budget provided for the program are too small, acceptable quality may not be achievable with any affordable quality control approach.

f.   Preventive quality control techniques are preferable to detective techniques, but there are few guaranteed preventive techniques, so detective techniques that perform checking and checkpoints for corrective action will also be necessary.

g. Every development organization has a software development process, good or bad. Changes to it usually take time and are gradual. The Government cannot impose a totally new process on a developer and expect to reap benefits immediately.

4.3 AN OVERVIEW OF THE TSQC PLANNING PROCESS

The basic TSQC planning process is shown in figure 4-1. Decisions about which TSQC activities to use are based on prior experience with what works, constraints that limit choices, the specific requirements of the program, and the risks that must be overcome to meet the requirements.

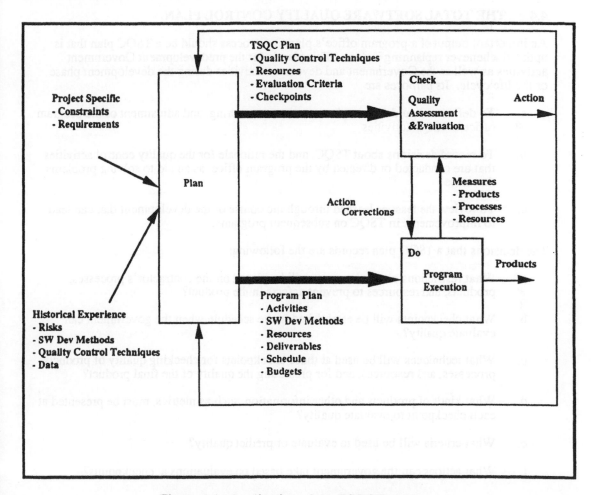

Figure 4-1. Application of the TSQC Process

The outputs of the planning process are two kinds of plans: a program plan and a TSQC plan. The latter is proposed here as part of the TSQC approach to achieving software quality. These two plans drive the **Doing** and **Checking** parts of the PDCA cycle for the system development by specifying what will be done and how it will be done, as well as when and what will be checked. Checking can result in **Actions** that correct and improve the current development and close the loop back to replanning.

Because a TSQC plan is the key to controlling software quality, the remainder of this section discusses the activities that lead to the development of a TSQC plan and its modification during system and software development.

4.4   THE TOTAL SOFTWARE QUALITY CONTROL PLAN

An important output of a program office's planning process should be a TSQC plan that is updated whenever replanning is done. This plan is for the predevelopment Government activities as well as the Government and developer activities during the development phase of the life cycle. Its purposes are

a.   To define and guide the implementation, monitoring, and adjustment of the program office's TSQC activities

b.   To record decisions about TSQC, and the rationale for the quality control activities that are conducted or directed by the program office, as an aid to solving problems that arise

c.   To review the lessons learned through the course of the development that can lead to improvements in TSQC on subsequent programs.

The decisions that a TSQC plan records are the following:

a.   What restrictions or requirements will be placed on the contractor's processes, products, and resources to prevent defects in the product?

b.   What checkpoints will be established in the schedule when the government can evaluate quality?

c.   What techniques will be used at those checkpoints for checking quality of products, processes, and resources, and for predicting the quality of the final product?

d.   What kinds of products and other information, such as metrics, must be presented at each checkpoint to evaluate quality?

e.   What criteria will be used to evaluate or predict quality?

f.   What actions can the government take based on evaluations at checkpoints?

g.   What resources does the government need?

Table 4-1 shows the table of contents of a TSQC plan. The following paragraphs describe ways to generate and update the information in the TSQC plan.

4.5   PLANNING PRIOR TO DEVELOPMENT

Planning prior to development by the Government can be reduced to answering these few questions:

a.   What do you want to have delivered?

b.   What might prevent you from getting it?

c.   What can you do about it?

Assuming there will be an RFP leading to the selection of a contractor, the planning activities should affect the RFP package in the following ways:

a.   Specification of quality requirements for the system

b.   Specification of criteria and methods for verifying that the requirements have been met

c.   Specification of source selection criteria and their priorities with respect to software

d.   Specification of information to be furnished with proposals

e.   Specification of quality control tasks for the developer and deliverables

f.   The type of contract and terms and conditions, if not already previously decided.

In preparation for issuing the RFP, the Government might conduct a Concept Definition or Demonstration/Validation phase to better define requirements, to conduct special studies to examine the technical feasibility of requirements, and to identify technical alternatives.

The following activities illustrate how to generate the information in the TSQC plan prior to issuing an RFP. Many of them are relevant for any organization planning a major software development. These activities are not the only ways to develop a TSQC plan, nor is there only one order for doing it. What matters is making the decisions represented in the plan, and documenting them. The TSQC plan should be carefully reviewed before it is implemented, and periodically checked during development to see that its assumptions are still valid, and to update it and replan when changes have occurred.

Table 4-1. Table of Contents of the TSQC Plan

A Total Software Quality Control Plan

1.0 Background

A brief description of the mission of the system, the estimated or actual size of the software, and representations of the system and software architecture.

2.0 Software Quality Requirements

Prioritized list of quality factors and quality requirements for the system and its software.

3.0 Constraints

List of predetermined requirements or limitations on products, processes, and resources of the government and the developer.

4.0 Software Risks

Prioritized list of specific risks, or areas of risk at the current time

5.0 Overview of the TSQC Process

Schedule of TSQC activities selected for the government and
    for the contractor
Risks that have been addressed by this version of the plan
When checkpoints will occur
Purpose of the checkpoint
Schedule of Government staffing requirements

6.0 TSQC Activities

For each activity the following will be recorded:

Description, including purpose
Who will do it and when will it occur
Checkpoints
    When they occur
    Information available at the checkpoint
    Thresholds for action and actions planned

4.5.1 Defining the Software Quality Requirements

Quality control begins with the definition of quality requirements.

"You can't achieve quality unless you can specify it." [DEU88]

The specification of quality requirements must be done well.

"...high-quality products are rarely developed from low-quality requirements." [HUM89]

Initially, quality requirements are specified for the whole system and are not limited to the software. The requirements should be prioritized to distinguish those most critical to the success of the system. They should be clearly stated in the SSS, and they should be included or referenced in section 2 of the TSQC plan. The simplest description is an ordered list of qualities, as shown in table 1-1, with weights to indicate their relative importance. A more detailed representation could be those individual requirements in the SSS that are considered most critical, and the quality factors that are involved.

The system and software quality requirements, as stated in the SSS, should be carefully reviewed. Volume 2 of this guide contains criteria for preparing and reviewing the SSS as part of the RFP Package Preparation and Review technique.

4.5.2 Identifying Constraints

Every program begins with constraints levied on the program office that are often outside its control. Some constraints, such as too little time, become sources of risk. In any case, constraints limit the choices open to a program office for carrying out TSQC activities. In section 3 of the Plan, the constraints and the reasons for them should be specified.

The following is a list of the kinds of initial program constraints that should be enumerated:

a. **Schedule**: dates for delivery of products, and when intermediate milestones or decisions must occur.

b. **Funding**: amount and source of money available for the work and facilities, when it is available, and uncertainty about its availability.

c. **Government organizations** involved: roles and interactions of users, buyer, testing organizations, maintenance organization, and any others.

d. **Other Government resources** (in addition to funding and schedule): need for and availability and quality of Government-furnished equipment, programs, and information.

e.   **Type of contract:** conditions of the contract that determine how much interaction is allowed between the Government and the contractor, and what incentives or disincentives are offered for achieving quality.

f.   **Requirements on the developer:** what limits must be placed on the process, products, and resources due to regulations and standards, or due to other constraints on this program.

4.5.3   Identifying Risks

Use of risk management as an approach to controlling software quality was described in section 2 of this report. This approach takes two steps: identification of risks, and then control of risks through use of TSQC activities to prevent or diminish the effect of risks that are most likely to prevent quality goals from being met. An important TSQC planning step is to perform risk identification or assessment, which involves identifying risks and estimating their probability of occurring, or prioritizing them. The result of risk identification should be a list of risks that is documented in section 4 of the TSQC plan; if possible, these risks should be prioritized.

4.5.3.1   Sources and Causes of Risk

One approach to identifying risk is to understand the potential sources and causes of risk. In the TSQC model, the sources of risk are related to the three classes of software quality control parameters. Table 4-3 shows classes of parameters, specific examples of sources of risk within a class, and general attributes of those sources that may be the cause of risk in the predevelopment phase prior to and after the selection of a developer. The questions in appendix B illustrate more specifically the causes of risk.

The sources of risk to achieving software quality are the requirements and constraints on the program. Those requirements and constraints change over time. There are three major times when risks must be identified, which are described below.

a.   Predevelopment, prior to selection of a contractor

At this stage, all risks are due to Government-generated requirements, constraints on the Government, and constraints the Government may place on potential developers.

b.   After selection of a contractor

At this stage, more is known about the contractor's organization, technical and management process, and technical approach. These add constraints, eliminate some potential risks, and add new risks.

c. During development

During this phase, the behavior of the Government and the contractor can be observed and evaluated. Products, processes, and resources can be assessed to evaluate or predict the quality of final products, and to reassess risks.

Appendix B is a questionnaire that can be used to help identify potential risks at or during each of these phases. It is organized into risk areas that can be correlated with the risk identification phases shown in table 4-2.

Table 4-2. Risk Identification Phases and Risk Areas

Risk Identification Phase	Risk Area
Predevelopment prior to selection of a developer	Requirements Government Schedule and Budget
After selection of a contractor	Requirements Government Developer Schedule and Budget
During development	Requirements Design and test Maintenance planning Government Developer Schedule and Budget

There are other criteria that can be used to identify risk in addition to the questionnaire in appendix B. The following is a list of references that may be consulted to further identify risks:

a. SEI Software Contractor Capability Evaluation [HUM87]

b. Software Development Capability/Capacity Review [ASD87]

c.   Software Management Metrics [SCH88]

d.   Rome Laboratory Software Quality Framework [BOW85]

e.   Air Force Acquisition Management Software Risk Abatement Pamphlet [AFS88a]

f.   Top Ten Software Risks [BOE89].

None of these references address risks introduced by the Government, which are specifically addressed in appendix B.

For the phase prior to development and to the selection of a developer, table 4-3 shows very general sources and causes of risk grouped by class of quality control parameter. These risks are due to Government requirements and constraints. This table can be used, as shown later, to guide the selection of quality control techniques.

4.5.3.2   Assessing Risks

Figure 4-2 shows that risk assessment is the basis for selecting software quality control techniques and metrics. Risk assessment involves identifying those causes of risk that are known at the time of the assessment so they can be managed through a choice of software quality control techniques. At the same time, there are some risks that cannot be estimated because of a lack of adequate information that should have been available. These are the unknown risks in the diagram. Metrics, measures, or other information-gathering activities should be performed to determine whether these are valid risks. Other metrics and measures evaluate the effect of TSQC techniques on the known risks. These become the **Do** and **Check** activities of this PDCA cycle.

Table 4-3. Predevelopment Sources of Risk

Parameter	Source of Risk	Cause of Risk
Products	System Requirements SSS	Definition Difficulty Stability Clarity
Products	Interfaces ICDs	Correctness Completeness Adequacy

Process	Acquisition Process	Organizational Complexity
		Stability
		Completeness
		Management Controls
		    Contract Type
		    Checkpoints

Process	Requirements Analysis	Completeness Correctness
Process	Software Development and Test Process	Maturity

Resources	Program Office Personnel
	Government Facilities
	    GFE*
	    GFP*
	    GFI*
		Capability
		Capacity
		Reliability
		Availability
		Stability

Resources	Budget, Schedule	Availability Stability

* Government-Furnished Equipment, Government-Furnished Programs, Government-Furnished Information

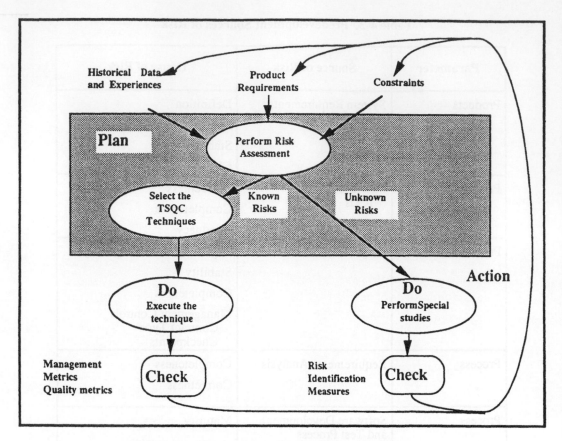

Figure 4-2. Risk Assessment in TSQC Planning

Appendix B is a checklist of questions to determine risks, grouped by source or area of risk. It covers risks in predevelopment and development phases, and can be used to identify and prioritize risks as follows:

a. A "Yes" response to a question indicates high probability that a risk exists for this program.

b. A "No" response indicates that it is unlikely that this cause of risk exists at this time. "No" responses must be reevaluated at later checkpoints, to see that the response is still valid.

c.   An "Unknown" response indicates that there is insufficient information to estimate the likelihood of the condition in the question, and that information should be known at this time.

d.   An "NA" response indicates that this question is not applicable to this program at this time. NA responses should be reviewed and changed if they become applicable.

A method of using the questionnaire to guide the selection of TSQC techniques is described below.

4.5.4   Selecting Software Quality Control Techniques and Activities

In the TSQC model, it is possible to select among techniques that can prevent or detect defects, or predict or assess quality. The following factors enter into the decision about the selection of techniques:

a.   Some techniques should always be used, although their level of use may vary.

b.   The choice of techniques must balance the requirements, risks, and constraints against the kinds of benefits the techniques can give.

c.   Some techniques are redundant or conflicting, so only one should be selected.

d.   Some techniques are complementary. They can be used together for the same or similar purposes, to increase the benefits of each.

e.   The techniques cannot conflict with contractual arrangements.

f.   Some techniques are only applicable during specific phases or activities or at certain events.

g.   Detective techniques should be used as early as possible to prevent defects from propagating.

h.   For programs with high risk, TSQC activities and checkpoints should not be too far apart in time.

Tables in this section and the prior section can guide a user to the relevant techniques in volume 2 of this report, which can then be studied in more depth. Undoubtedly, some iteration and refinement of the selections will be needed. Options in making choices are described below. The final choices should be documented in summary as part of section 5 of the TSQC plan, and at the individual technique level in section 6. The choices are not limited to the set in volume 2.

4.5.4.1   Using a Core Set of Techniques

Some techniques should be used on any mission-critical system, even if the system is small and is similar to one developed earlier. A recommended list is shown in table 4-4, along with the organization that must do each. Many on this list are described in volume 2; others are identified in DOD or service regulations, specifications, and standards.

Table 4-4. A Core Set of Quality Control Techniques

Technique	Performed By
RFP Review	Government
Configuration Management	Contractor and Government
Software Development Plan	Contractor
Training	Contractor and Government
Inspections	Contractor
Testing	Contractor and Government
Software Quality Assurance	Contractor
SPR Analysis	Contractor and Government
Management Metrics for Developer	Contractor and Government
Management Metrics for SPO	Government

4.5.4.2   Selecting Additional Techniques to Control Risk

As indicated above, the primary rationale for selecting software quality control techniques is the high risk of not achieving important system requirements. Figure 4-2 indicates that some techniques defend against **known** risks, and some techniques gather information to better assess **unknown** risks. Both choices of techniques can involve gathering information, as metrics, measures, or in other forms, such as special studies. In all cases, the extant regulations, specifications, standards, and other official guidance should be consulted in addition to the techniques in this guide.

Several approaches to selecting techniques for controlling known risks are given below. They all use information in this guide to select techniques from those in volume 2. Suggestions for other techniques can be found in sections 2 and 3 of this guide, and the books and reports referenced throughout the guide. One of the approaches below can be selected and used during predevelopment planning.

a.   Identify the known sources and causes of risk, and the classes of parameters involved, using table 4-3 as a guide. Review table 3-3 to select techniques from volume 2 that impact the relevant parameter classes and specific items.

For example, if the highest source of risk identified for a program using table 4-3 is "System Requirements" and the most likely cause of this risk is "Definition," since the system is new and the user has not been closely involved in similar systems, then table 3-3 identifies techniques that affect Requirements in the Product Column. These include, for example, Configuration Management, Government Reviews, IV&V, Prototyping, and Requirements Verification Matrix. Table 3-3 contains techniques that are applied before and during development. Table 3-1 shows when the techniques are applied. Volume 2 can be used to pare down the list of techniques to those that address requirements definition risks.

b.   Use the questionnaire in appendix B prior to the start of development. For each question answered "Yes" in the questionnaire in appendix B, use the risk area in which it is grouped to look in table 4-5 for techniques to be applied during pre-development that will impact those risk areas. Similarly, use table 4-6 to find techniques applied during development.

By consulting volume 2, reduce the list to those techniques that address the specific known risks within the area, as determined by individual questions answered "Yes" in an area. The same technique may be appropriate to several questions in the same or different areas. This approach could be used to weight the choice of techniques, but we do not advocate a strictly numerical approach, since the questions are not always independent of each other or of equal significance. In some cases, a "Yes" on only one question is important enough to merit a risk reduction technique in that area.

For example, use of the questionnaire might show that the problem with system requirements definition is that many users are involved in generating and approving the requirements, and that the requirements are unique to this program. This would lead to the same risk area in table 4-5, but the screening of relevant techniques in volume 2 might indicate that the largest risk reduction may be achieved by the use of prototyping during predevelopment.

Table 4-5. Predevelopment Quality Control Techniques versus Risk Area

Risk Area / Quality Control Technique	Requirements	Development & Test	Maintenance	Government	Potential Contractor	Schedule & Budget
Cause and Effect Analysis						
Configuration Management						
Government Reviews						
Independent Verification&Validation	x			x		
Inspections						
Performance Engineering	x					
Prototyping	x			x		x
Reliability Modeling						
Requirements Traceability						
Requirements Verification Matrix	x			x		
RFP Preparation and Review	x			x	x	x
SEI Software Capability Evaluation					x	
Software Audit						
Software Design Metrics						
Software Dev Cap/Cap Review					x	
Software Development Folders						
Software Engineering Environment	x			x		x
Software Engineering Exercise					x	
Software Engineering Prototype						
Software Management Metrics						
Software Quality Assurance						
SPR Data Gathering & Analysis						
Standards	x			x	x	x
Testing						

Table 4-6. Development Quality Control Techniques versus Risk Area

Risk Area / Quality Control Technique	Requirements	Development & Test	Maintenance Planning	Government	Developer	Schedule & Budget
Cause and Effect Analysis	x	x			x	x
Configuration Management		x	x			
Government Reviews	x	x	x	x	x	x
Independent Verification&Validation	x	x		x	x	x
Inspections		x				
Performance Engineering	x	x				
Prototyping	x	x		x	x	x
Reliability Modeling		x	x			x
Requirements Traceability	x	x			x	
Requirements Verification Matrix	x	x	x		x	
RFP Preparation and Review						
SEI Software Capability Evaluation					x	
Software Audit	x	x	x	x	x	x
Software Design Metrics		x	x			
Software Dev Cap/Cap Review					x	
Software Development Files		x	x		x	
Software Engineering Environment		x		x	x	
Software Engineering Exercise					x	
Software Engineering Prototype		x			x	
Software Management Metrics	x	x			x	
Software Quality Assurance	x	x	x		x	
SPR Data Gathering & Analysis	x	x	x		x	
Standards	x	x		x	x	x
Testing		x	x			

c.   In addition to the technique in item b, above, individual questions can be examined to see what would change the "Yes" to a "No" or an unknown to a "Yes" or "No."

It is not always possible to change a "Yes" to a "No"; e.g., if the number of SRS requirements is very large, there may be no way to make them fewer without changing the system, but it would be worthwhile to conduct a careful review of the requirements to see if they are all necessary, especially if there are considerably more SRS requirements than SSS requirements.

On the other hand, if the answer to the question "Are many users involved in generating and approving requirements and changes to requirements?" is "Yes," then the Program Office might schedule a review in which all users are required to resolve differences or lose the opportunity to affect the requirements. A demonstration or prototype might be used at that review to help users reach an agreement.

If the answer to the question "Are the specific functional, performance, and quality requirements unique to this program?" is unknown, then the program office might want to conduct a study, probably prior to issuing the RFP, to see whether this program presents potential risks with respect to technical feasibility, or place special emphasis on technical feasibility in the information required in response to the RFP.

4.5.5   Applying the Techniques

The selected TSQC techniques can be divided into two groups as a function of when they are implemented. This can be determined from tables 4-5 and 4-6 if risk areas are known, or from table 3-1 if the techniques are known. Some techniques must be implemented by the Government prior to completing predevelopment activities, e.g., those that affect the selection of the developer and the RFP package. These should be reviewed, refined in ways described below, and carried out during the predevelopment planning. Then the TSQC plan should be updated, as described later in this section.

Other techniques are applied after development has begun. These techniques should be entered into the draft TSQC plan and refined as described below until a final set is determined.

4.5.6   Refining the Selections

The list of techniques can be refined by reducing the number of techniques, tailoring them to focus on specific risks, and reducing the cost of a technique through choosing options for their implementation.

4.5.6.1   Reviewing Controls over the Developer

As a means of controlling quality, the Government can require the developer to use certain processes for management and development, to provide specified products, and to meet minimum standards for the resources used.

For example, requirements such as these might be levied on a developer.

   a.   The developer shall use a compilable Ada Design Language.

   b.   The development facility shall have at least one workstation for every three programmers, with the equivalent of 1.5 millions of instructions per second (MIPS) in processor speed.

   c.   There shall be a Chief Software Engineer with a minimum of 10 years' experience in designing and implementing similar systems.

   d.   The developer shall deliver, prior to the SDR, a timing and sizing report in accordance with the specified DID, and keep it current and available for review at all subsequent Government reviews.

In reviewing the set of requirements on the developer, the program office must be careful not to constrain potential developers unduly. Unless there is solid evidence that a software engineering technique or tool increases the probability of meeting a specific software quality goal of this system, or there is a need to conform to standards established for consistency among programs, the Government probably should not dictate the details of the developer's software engineering process. If the developer's organization is unfamiliar with the techniques or tools, the effects on cost, schedule, and quality may be negative. It may be better to choose a contractor with a method and tools that have proven to be beneficial to this organization on prior programs that had similar requirements.

For example:

   a.   The Government should not require object-oriented technology to be used on a program because it is believed to be the best design approach. Developers who propose using it should indicate how familiar they are with it and what evidence they have that it will work for them.

   b.   The Government should not require a contractor to use a specific CASE tool if the contractor is more familiar with a comparable one, unless that tool is a standard for all programs maintained by a Government organization.

Instead, the Government can establish criteria for reviewing the developer's proposed standards and practices, or impose minimum standards as described in earlier examples. Where Government policies, regulations, and standards may require the program office to impose some restrictions, it is the responsibility of the program office to tailor those restrictions to the risks associated with the development, and eliminate restrictions where they are unnecessary.

For example:

a.   For those parts of the system that utilize COTS software, Ada shall not be required, unit testing shall not be required, the test plan shall show how each package of COTS software will be tested, and a plan shall be submitted for the post-delivery support of the COTS software.

b.   The developer shall provide evidence of the extent of coverage of the software by the tests, but there is not a specific requirement to use a Performance Coverage Analyzer, so the developer can propose other methods.

4.5.6.2   Tailoring the Application of Techniques

Usually it is not practical to implement all of the TSQC techniques that are appropriate, because of the time and cost that would be involved. However, it is possible to control the cost of using TSQC techniques by varying their application through options described below. For the techniques in volume 2 of this report, information on these options is provided with the entry for each technique.

4.5.6.3   Selecting the Level of Application of Techniques

Many techniques can be applied at different levels that affect the cost of using them and the extent of their benefit. For lower risks or when insufficient resources are available, a lower level application of a technique may be better than no technique at all. The following are examples of ways that the level of application of a technique can be varied.

Informal versus Formal Use

Informal techniques can be less expensive, and not necessarily less effective. An informal technique may be one that is internal to the developer, i.e., not visible to the Government, or it may be visible but for information only, so the Government cannot act on it. Tests can be informal or formal in this context, as can other reviews and documentation.

A technique can be informal because its process is not documented with strict rules for its use, e.g., code reading versus formal inspections. The formality of a product is determined by how specifically its form, format, and contents are specified by the Government, how it will be assessed, who will assess it, whether it must be approved by the Government, and how changes to it will be controlled.

For example

a.   Peer reviews are usually internal to a developer's organization(s), although the results might be presented to the Government in metrics, such as number of errors found. The developer may choose to use formal inspections or informal peer reviews internally.

b.   Technical Interchange Meetings (TIMs) are informal reviews that can provide the Government with visibility and even allow joint developer/Government decisions, without elaborate formal preparation and formal documentation. They can be explicitly required as part of the contract either periodically, or to deal with specific areas of risk.

c.   "Formal Qualification Tests" can actually be informal, with the Government invited to witness the tests but not to formally approve them, when the system presents no risk at that level, or other testing will provide adequate information to the Government.

d.   Software Requirements Specifications may remain informal in terms of change control until they are authenticated, which can be late in the development. Then they will have strict change control.

Extent of Implementation

Many techniques have options that allow variations in the extent of their implementation and the consequent cost. For example, Software Problem Reporting can consist of few items or many. Management metrics can also consist of few or many data items. On some programs, several reviews, such as PDR and CDR, can be combined, or some documents listed in DOD-STD-2167A can be eliminated.

4.5.6.4   Selecting among Alternative Techniques

Some techniques are alternatives to others that differ in the effort required and the impact they have on quality. Depending on the risks, a lesser effort may be adequate. For example, selection of the contractor by review of the technical proposal may be sufficient on one program; while for another, where the size of the development or its cost is very large, the SEI SCE or SEE may be deemed worthwhile expenses. Volume 2 of this report references complementary or alternative techniques.

4.5.7 Planning Checkpoints

Checkpoints are those events and times when the developer provides information to the Government, and the Government responds to that information with an action. Section 3 of this report gave examples of different kinds of checking and information that the Government could require at checkpoints to control quality. Some checkpoints are determined by the Government, and others will be part of the developer's proposal or SDP.

In conjunction with each selection of a TSQC technique, the checkpoints must be planned when the results of using the technique will be analyzed, and corrective action will be planned based on the results. Planning also leads to the selection of information to be provided, in the form of documentation, metrics, and other types of products such as data from benchmarks or simulations, and demonstrations of prototype user interfaces.

Checkpoints serve the following purposes:

a.   Provide early visibility into the quality of the processes and resources, and the emerging products of the developer

b.   Provide a basis for predicting quality of the final products

c.   Provide information that can be used to verify that plans are being followed

d.   Provide information to allow replanning, including modifying system and software requirements, processes, and resources

e.   Provide a control point, e.g., when the developer may no longer make changes to a product.

The actions below are part of planning the use of checkpoints.

4.5.7.1   Planning the Acquisition Strategy

The Government's acquisition strategy defines the checkpoints, and the contractual conditions determine what replanning can be done at those checkpoints. A powerful software quality control technique a program office can use is to arrange the major sequence of activities and milestones during a system development to provide early opportunities to assess quality and adjust the quality control parameters to make improvements. While DOD-STD-2167A defines a standard set of activities with reviews as checkpoints, it does say that the activities "may overlap and may be applied iteratively and recursively." This gives the program office flexibility to select, often with the contractor, sequences of activities that reduce software quality risks.

The problems with the conventional waterfall model shown diagrammatically in DOD-STD-2167A are

a.   The primary form of products in the early phases is documentation, which can be difficult to assess, except as a manual, often subjective, review process.

b.   The interconnections and interdependence among documents, such as SRSs, for large and complex systems make analysis and assessment of document contents even more difficult.

c.   If it is difficult to discover defects through documentation, then the defects will remain in the system until it can be seen and tested. It is well-known that the longer defects stay in a system, the more expensive it is to correct them.

The Government and/or the developer can plan an overall development process that provides early, tangible, easy-to-interpret information for assessment of progress and the quality of the system and its software. Here are some ways.

a.   Prototypes during requirements analysis can show the user interface, including the sequence of actions and information available to an operator to perform a task. This enhances usability and correctness.

b.   A "build-a-little, test-a-little" approach might be used to demonstrate that the design is correct for support layers of a system before the rest of the system is designed. It can also demonstrate end-to-end connectivity for a small set of functions to show that the architecture and interfaces are correct.

c.   Testing support layers before mission-specific software is complete can demonstrate the bare system response time and resource use to aid in meeting performance requirements.

d.   Incremental development with block releases allows an assessment of the developer's ability to meet quality requirements within schedule and cost, but there is a real danger that this early performance may not be sustained as the system grows in complexity and size. However, it does have the advantage of producing an early operational capability.

e.   Evolutionary acquisition allows the requirements to evolve as the user experiences system operation, and takes the burden from the Government of specifying all ultimate requirements when there is no certain way to confirm them.

4.5.7.2   Planning Information Requirements at Checkpoints

Section 3 of this report showed examples of techniques that provide information at checkpoints. That information should be tailored to address the risks that are of concern. Other information can be obtained using questionnaires, such as those in the RSQF, the SEI SCE, the SDCCR, and in Government standards for reviews.

4.5.7.3   Reviewing and Refining Checkpoints

Some checkpoints should be scheduled and some information should be requested regularly, even for low risk programs, to ensure that conditions have not changed sufficiently to alter prior risk assessments. A subset of the Software Management Metrics combined with standard Cost Performance Reports should be adequate for programs where there is high confidence in the developer's capabilities, and the requirements are well understood, well stated, and stable.

To ensure that there is a reasonable number of checkpoints and that the right information is available, and to minimize the amount of information that a contractor must deliver and the amount of time spent in reviews and other program assessments, each selected checkpoint should be reviewed to see what risks it addresses, and what information is needed to address those risks. This is an example of the application of the GQM paradigm previously summarized in section 3. The goal is to reduce a set of risks. The questions address specific risks. The metrics at a checkpoint provide information to show the magnitude of the risk still remaining, as well as whether new risks have occurred. This review may lead to the elimination or addition of checkpoints as well as a definition of information. The following are some criteria for reviewing the selection of checkpoints and the information specified for the checkpoint:

a.   Are all "known" and "unknown" risks addressed, and addressed as early as possible?

If the highest risk is meeting quantitative performance requirements, and the first checkpoint for software is to review the SRSs, then it may be advisable to schedule an earlier checkpoint for reviewing the estimated performance of the system based on its design.

b.   Does the checkpoint address at least one "known" or "unknown" risk?

If there is a checkpoint for an FQT to perform CSCI-to-CSCI tests, but the design and major parts of the software have been used before and present very low risk, it could be cost-effective to test operational strings and eliminate the FQT.

c.   Is the information at the checkpoint adequate to assess the risks?

For example, if response time is a high risk requirement, presentation of the results from a simulation may not be adequate information to determine if the system and software design will meet the response time requirements. To assess risk, it may be important for the Government to see the input data used for the simulation, the confidence level of that data, and the assumptions that were made by the developer as the basis for estimating that response time requirements will be met. This is especially true of the assumptions about the load on the system, if this has not been precisely specified by the Government. This allows both the Government and the developer to agree on the current risk and to decide what additional risk control actions may be needed.

d.   Is the information provided at the checkpoint necessary or useful, and to whom?

If the information is only used by the developer, and has no value to the Government, then it should not be required to be delivered. For example, if the Government requires updated Ada Design Language (ADL) representations of the software design when the program office has no tools or resources for reviewing the ADL and the maintainers do not plan to use it, then delivering the ADL may serve no purpose. Instead, the Government might require analyses of the complexity of the software design to predict the reliability or flexibility of the software, and the developer might use an ADL to compute design complexity.

e.   Who can act on that information?

The Government should make sure that it can act on the information it plans to receive. That may mean changing its own products, processes, and resources, or those of the developer. The contract terms will affect the flexibility of both the Government and the contractor to act on the information. For example, if the results of benchmarks show the selected computers are not large enough or fast enough, whether different hardware can be selected and who will bear the cost are contract terms.

f.   Can the program office handle all the information it has required the developer to deliver?

If the Government will not or does not have staff to review the documents and other information, then the list of deliverables should be prioritized into those that are part of the final product, and those that are for risk management. The latter can also be prioritized and scaled down or reduced.

4.5.8   Documenting an Overview of the TSQC Process

When a selection of TSQC techniques has been made and the checkpoints determined, these decisions are summarized in section 5 of the TSQC plan. Initially, before selection of the developer and approval of the plans, the TSQC plan documents the process the Government intends to use for Total Software Quality Control and the limitations it plans to place on the developer's processes and checkpoints. It allows a high level presentation and review of the strategy that will be followed for Total Software Quality Control, and it contains the following information:

a.   Brief descriptions of the set of techniques that have been chosen for Government use

b.   A time line showing when each set of activities is scheduled to begin and end

c.   The set of techniques the contractor or developer will be required to use, placed on the same or a similar time line

d.   Dates of other important events, including dates for external milestones such as deliveries to outside organizations, and dates when the Government must supply information (GFI), programs (GFP), and equipment (GFE), also on the same or a similar time line

e.   Checkpoints or decision points, where actions may occur to change the plan or to select a planned alternative, placed on the same time line

f.   A brief description of the purpose of each checkpoint, including risks addressed, and actions planned

g.   A calendar estimate of the Government staffing that will be required to carry out the plan.

The plan should be reviewed at this level to see if the primary risks have been addressed and if the distribution of checkpoints allows for early and adequate checking and action to correct and improve development of quality for the final product.

4.5.9   Making Detailed Plans for TSQC Activities

As shown in table 4-1, section 6 of the TSQC plan describes each technique in more detail. The items to be included are shown in the table. Of special importance is the set of data or information that will be delivered by the contractor at checkpoints or generated by the Government, the thresholds at which actions will take place, and what those actions will be. Some of this descriptive information can be based on what is in volume 2 of this report. The detailed plans must be examined as the overview is developed. As a result, iterations may be made to consolidate, eliminate, and schedule techniques and checkpoints so the total set is effective and affordable. The details can be aggregated to determine the metrics that will be collected, and when they will be delivered. The actions for each checkpoint can also be aggregated across specific techniques to feed into the overview in section 5 of the plan.

4.6   UPDATING THE TSQC PLAN

Just before the start of development, and during development, changes occur that can affect the assumptions made in the TSQC plan. There are more constraints added as decisions are made and activities are completed that preclude prior options. Especially at checkpoints, but also whenever some unplanned but significant event occurs such as major changes in requirements or reductions in program office staff, the TSQC plan should be revisited and revised if necessary.

4.6.1   After Developer Selection

One major point when the plan should be revised is after the developer has been selected. There are new sources of risk, and some unknown risks may have been resolved. The developer is supposed to supply an estimate of risks and plans for managing those risks. This adds new information that can affect the constraints on the program.

At a minimum, the risks should be reevaluated, especially those that were not applicable at an earlier phase because the contractor had not been selected, and the overview (section 5) should be updated to show TSQC events and activities introduced by the contractor.

4.6.2   During Development

The Government and contractor performance during development can add more constraints and risks, or reduce and even eliminate risks. At a minimum, the TSQC plan should be reviewed at each checkpoint, and revisions made as follows:

a. Review the information at the checkpoint to take any planned action that will change requirements,and the Government's or developer's products, processes, and resources.

b. Update Quality Requirements (section 2), and Constraints (section 3) if necessary.

c. Review the risks, using the questionnaire in appendix B, for example, to see if the risks have changed. If there are changes in sections 2 or 3, the predevelopment risk assessment questions should also be reviewed. Section 4 of the plan should be updated if necessary.

d. Update the plan to eliminate unneeded techniques, add techniques, change the level of techniques, and adjust schedules and program office staffing requirements accordingly. Document the changes in sections 5 and 6 of the plan.

SECTION 5

SUMMARY AND CONCLUSIONS

5.1   SUMMARY

In this guide, we have presented a Total Software Quality Control model based on Rome Laboratory's Software Quality Framework, but extended to control the causes of quality defects and their sources. The sources of defects have been grouped into three classes: products, processes, and resources. Controlling software quality requires active choices on the part of the Government and the developer to control sources of defects by specifying constraints on their values, by checking that the constraints have been met, and by making adjustments in them, when necessary, to improve the quality of the end product. The basis for those choices is a continuous assessment of the risks to achieving software quality. A set of techniques is described in some detail in volume 2 to help in the selection of software quality control activities. Many other techniques can be found in section 3 of this report, in Government regulations, specifications, standards, handbooks, and guides, and in the other documents referenced in this guide.

5.2   CONCLUSIONS

This guide is only a beginning. It deals with the current status of software quality control based on reviews of what others have said and written, and on our own experiences. There is not enough empirical data widely available yet to back up the guidance we have presented, but our rule-of-thumb advice should be helpful if tempered with judgment.

Our views of the current status and future direction of Total Software Quality Control, based on the experiences we have had and the information we gathered for this guide, are summarized below.

5.2.1   What is the Current Status of Total Software Quality Control?

a.   We are quite certain that we know most of the potential sources and causes of risks to achieving software quality.

Software problems have been highly visible, and a multitude of studies have identified the salient causes.

b.   Not all sources of risk to software quality are in the software development process. Other major influences include the schedule, the budget, and the systems engineering process.

c.   We are beginning to understand how to reduce or control risks to some degree through preventive techniques coupled with early detection of problems.

5.2.2 What is Needed to Gain Greater Control over Software Quality?

a. We need more empirical data on the relationship between software development products, processes, and resources, and the quality of the software after it is delivered.

The developer, the maintainer, and the user of the software must integrate and correlate their data on quality to analyze causes and effects in controlling quality.

b. Managers who control funds must be convinced that collecting data is a worthwhile investment in future improvements as well as a means of controlling the current development.

c. Managers who control funds must also be convinced that producing quality software can save money, so they are willing to invest in tools, training, and process improvement.

5.2.3 What Can Be Done Now?

There are some promising trends that should improve our ability as buyers and developers to realize high quality software on time and within budget. The trend toward software process improvement, triggered by the SEI Capability Maturity Model [HUM89], is leading development organizations to measure and improve their processes and resources. This will lead to repeatability in processes within a developer's organization, and provide data that will increase the predictability and control of software cost, schedule, and quality for that organization. There is beginning to be evidence that software process improvement investments pay off quickly [HUM91].

The Government's role is to encourage and reward the use of mature processes by development organizations and their collection and analysis of data to control software cost and quality. The Government must also measure and improve its own process. As has been noted often lately, if the contractor has been assessed at a Level 4 in the SEI Software Capability Evaluation, and the program office is equivalent to a Level 1, then the program will suffer. We need to establish a maturity model and improvement process for Government organizations involved as buyers, users, and developers of software.

This guide is a first pass at collecting, from diverse sources, empirical data and experiences that can assist a buyer, customer, or manager in a development organization to make informed choices in planning how to control software quality. This guide is meant to evolve over time. It needs additional data and experiences, feedback, and refinement from users and other practitioners. Readers and users of the guide are encouraged to send their comments to the authors and to Rome Laboratory.

There are several areas where the guide can be extended now. More information can be added on the post deployment software quality control process, and on the use of metrics by and for the Government and industry. More consideration should be given to long-term improvement through the collection of data from programs and organizations.

LIST OF REFERENCES

[AFS86]   Air Force Systems Command, 31 January 1986, *Software Management Indicators*, AFSCP 800-43.

[AFS88a]   Air Force Systems Command and Air Force Logistics Command, 30 September 1988, *Acquisition Management Software Risk Abatement*, AFSC/AFLCP 800-45.

[AFS88b]   Air Force System Command/Air Force Logistics Command Pamphlet 800-5, 20 May 1988, *Software Independent Verification and Validation (IV&V)*.

[AFS90]   AFSC Pamphlet 800-51, 9 November 1990, *Software Development Capability*, Air Force Systems Command.

[ASD87]   ASD Pamphlet 800-5, 10 September 1987, *Software Development Capability/Capacity Review,* Aeronautical Systems Division.

[ATT90]   Attridge, W. S., E. R. Buley, March 1990, *The Software Audit*, MTR-10803, The MITRE Corporation, Bedford, MA.

[BAS89]   Basili, V. R., 1989, "Software Development: A Paradigm for the Future," *Proceedings of COMPSAC 89*, IEEE, New Jersey.

[BER84]   Bersoff, E. H., January 1984, "Elements of Software Configuration Management," *IEEE Transactions on Software Engineering*.

[BOE81]   Boehm, B. W., 1981, *Software Engineering Economics*, Englewood Cliffs, NJ: Prentice-Hall, Inc.

[BOE88]   Boehm, B. W., May 1988, "A Spiral Model of Software Development and Enhancement," *IEEE Computer*, pp. 61-72.

[BOE89]   Boehm, B.W., 1989, *Software Risk Management,* IEEE Computer Society Press, Washington, D.C., pp. 115-147.

[BOW85]   Bowen, T. P., J. T. Tsai, G. B. Wigle, 1985, *Specification of Software Quality Attributes—Software Quality Evaluation Guidebook,* AD-A153-990, RADC-TR-85-37, Volumes I, II, III, Rome Air Development Center, Air Force Systems Command, Griffiss Air Force Base, NY.

[CAR90]   Card, D. N., R. L. Glass, 1990, *Measuring Software Design Quality,* Englewood Cliffs, NJ: Prentice Hall.

[CHA90]   Charette, R.N., 1989, *Software Engineering Risk Analysis and Management*, McGraw-Hill.

[CUR81]   Curtis, B., July 1981, "Substantiating Programmer Variability," *Proceedings of the IEEE*, Vol. 69, No. 7.

[CUR88]   Curtis, B., H. Krasner, N. Iscoe, November 1988, "A Field Study of the Software Design Process for Large Systems," *Communications of the ACM*, pp. 1268 ff.

[DEM86]   Deming, W. E., 1986, *Out of the Crisis*, Massachusetts Institute of Technology Center for Advanced Engineering Study, Cambridge, MA.

[DEU88]   Deutsch, M. S., R. R. Willis, 1988, *Software Quality Engineering: A Total Technical and Management Approach*, Englewood Cliffs, NJ: Prentice-Hall, Inc.

[DOD88a]   DOD-STD-2168, 29 April 1988, *Defense System Software Quality Program*.

[DOD88b]   DOD-STD-2167A, 29 February 1988, *Defense System Software Development*.

[FAG79]   M. E. Fagan, 1979, "Design and Code Inspections to Reduce Errors in Program Development," *IBM System Journal*, Vol. 15, No. 3.

[FEI83]   Feigenbaum, A.V., 1983, *Total Quality Control*, McGraw-Hill.

[GRA87]   Grady R. B., September 1987, "Measuring and Managing Software Maintenance," *IEEE Software*, pp. 35-45.

[HEN81]   Henry, S. M, D. G. Kafura, September 1981, "Software Structure Metrics Based on Information Flow," *IEEE Transactions on Software Engineering*, Vol. 7, No. 5, pp. 510-518.

[HUM87]   Humphrey, W. S., W. L. Sweet, September 1987, *A Method of Assessing the Software Engineering Capability of Contractors*, CMU/SEI-87-TR-23, ESD-TR-87-186, AD A187230, Software Engineering Institute, Carnegie Mellon University, Pittsburgh, PA.

[HUM89]   Humphrey, W.S., 1989, *Managing the Software Process*, Reading, MA: Addison Wesley.

[HUM91]   Humphrey, W. S., T. R. Snyder, R. R. Willis, July 1991, "Software Process Improvement at Hughes Aircraft," *IEEE Software*, pp. 11ff.

[MAY90]   Mays, R. G., et al., 1990, "Experiences with Defect Prevention," *IBM System Journal*, Vol. 29, No. 1.

[MCC76]   McCabe, T. J., December 1976, "A Complexity Measure," *IEEE Transactions on Software Engineering*, Vol. 2, No 4, pp. 308-320.

[MIL85A]   MIL-STD-1521B, 19 December 1985, *Technical Reviews and Audits for Systems, Equipment and Computer Software*.

[MIL85B]   MIL-STD-483A, 4 June 1985, *Configuration Management Practices for Systems, Equipment, Munitions, and Computer Programs*.

[SCH87]   Schulmeyer, G., J. McManus, 1987, *Handbook of Software Quality Assurance*, New York: Van Nostrand Reinhold.

[SCH88]   Schultz, H. P., May 1988, *Software Management Metrics*, AD A196 916, M88-1, The MITRE Corporation, Bedford, MA.

[SCH89]   Schultz, H. P., July 1989, *Software Engineering Exercise Guidelines*, AD A212 510, M89-32, The MITRE Corporation, Bedford, MA.

[WAL89]   Wallace, D. R., R. U. Fujii, September 1989, NIST Special Publication 500-165, *Software Verification and Validation: Its Role in Computer Assurance and Its Relationship with Software Project Management Standards*, National Institute of Standards and Technology, Gaithersburg, MD.

APPENDIX A

QUALITY GOALS, QUESTIONS, METRICS, REQUIREMENTS

This appendix provides examples of the establishment of quality factor goals and the deduction of the product and process requirements by means of the Goal Question Metric (GQM) paradigm [BAS89]. The goals are qualitative statements of user desires. Based on the goals, a series of questions are posed whose answers help to quantify the goals. Associated with each question, a series of metrics is established, which in turn is used to establish system and software requirements.

Within this section, goals are denoted by the letter G, questions are denoted by the letter Q, metrics associated with the questions are denoted by the letter M, product requirements by the letters PR, and process activity requirements by the letters AR. The quality factors of efficiency, reliability, and integrity are shown in this example.

A.1 EFFICIENCY

Efficiency is by its nature a system-level quality factor and is determined by architectural considerations and relationships with elements external to the system, as well as the specific hardware and software components contained within the system.

Efficiency goals must be stated from a system perspective. The following are examples of system level efficiency goals:

G1—To be able to expand or modify the system without adding new hardware.

G2—To expand or modify the system at a minimum total life cycle cost.

Both these goals imply different criteria and measures of success. Goal 1 implies that a certain amount of spare hardware capacity must be delivered with the system. Goal 2 implies that additional hardware can be added at a later date and that the total life cycle cost is a driving consideration.

Associated with the two goals presented above, the following kinds of questions and metrics may be formulated:

Q1—What is the resource use of each architectural component under scenario xyz?

   M1—Measure the CPU, memory, and I/O use for each component or machine. First use estimates and then measured values.

Q2—What is the resource use growth potential of the system?

M1—Measure the CPU, memory, and I/O use of the system as a whole.
M2—Determine the impact on resource use of increasing the message load by 25 percent.

Q3—How much does the initial system (hardware and software) architecture cost?

M3a—Measure or estimate the initial cost for the architecture
M3b—Measure or estimate the cost for each expansion element
M3c—Measure or estimate the cost for modifying the architecture
M3d—Compare the cost to alternative hardware configurations

Associated with each metric, a series of product level requirements may be formulated. Examples of the structure of such requirements are presented below:

PR1—The software, executing under the environment defined in ...., shall use less than ...... percent of the CPU's delivered processing capability. The CPU processing use shall be measured over a ...... minute period. The definition of CPU use is provided in section .... of this specification.

PR2—The system shall be field modifiable to provide for 50 percent expansion of the mass memory storage capability. Software changes shall not be required to use the expanded capability.

In support of the attainment of the efficiency quality goals, a number of quality process requirements may be formulated.

AR1—The percent use of each architectural component of the system shall be reported at each Program Management Review (PMR).

AR2—An analysis of the growth limits of the architecture and of each individual processing component shall be presented at SDR.

AR3—An analysis of the expansion cost for each element shall be presented at SDR and at CDR.

A.2   INTEGRITY

Integrity goals deal with the ability of the system to minimize security failures.

System level integrity goals may take many forms.

G1—To prevent security-related failures due to unauthorized access to the system software or data.

G2—To capture security violation information, and to know when a violation has occurred and what has been accessed.

Associated with these goals, questions and metrics may be formulated:

Q1—How many security failures of the system related to unauthorized access to the software have occurred?

M1—Count the number of security-related problems that are traceable to software.

Q2—What access and security violation reporting mechanisms have been established?

M2—List the software requirement that addresses access control and reporting.

Q3—How have the violations occurred?

M3—List what data have been accessed and what software allowed the access.

Associated with each metric we may define product level requirements.

PR1—The number of security access problems attributable to software shall be less than ...... over a period of .... months. During this test period ..... independent people, appointed by the government, will attempt to violate the security mechanisms of the system.

Examples of quality process requirements include:

AR1—The Software Problem Reporting mechanism shall provide a means for indicating whether a particular problem affects the integrity of the system.

AR2—The number and cause of integrity-related problems shall be reported at each PMR.

AR3—The contractor shall formulate a plan for testing the ability of the system to prevent access to unauthorized personnel.

AR4—The functional security requirements shall be presented and reviewed at SSR.

A.3   RELIABILITY

Reliability of the system can be specified in a number of ways. It may be specified as mean time between failures (MTBF), as a failure rate, or as the probability of not failing within the mission time. The system-level reliability requirement is budgeted to the various system components. Recently, allocation or budgeting of a portion of the system failure rate to software has been given serious consideration. Software quality factor goals associated with reliability may take the following forms:

G1—To minimize the number of system failures attributed to the final delivered software.

G2—To minimize cost due to a system failure attributed to the final delivered software.

Associated with these goals, the following questions and metrics may be formulated:

Q1—How many failures due to software are detected during operational test?

M1—Count the number of system failures attributed to software during operational test.

Q2—How many software failures per unit time were detected during normal operations, after delivery?

M2—Determine the number of software failures per CPU hour during normal post-delivery operation.

Q3—How many defects remain to be corrected?

M3–Determine the deviation between the number of software failures detected and the results of applying the ____ reliability prediction model.

Q4—How much did the failure attributed to software cost the user?

M4a—Determine the cost in terms of dollars or time lost for each software failure.
M4b—Determine the average cost per CPU hour of the effect of software failures.

Associated with each metric, we may define product level requirements.

PR1—The number of software failures per CPU hour during operational test shall be less than ____.

PR2—The failure intensity of the software during the first year of operation shall be less than one failure per 1000 CPU hours.

In support of the attainment of the reliability quality goals, a number of quality process requirements may be formulated.

AR1—The contractor shall perform a cause/effect analysis upon all critical software failures. The criticality of a software failure is defined in _____. The cause/effect analysis shall suggest processes and resource changes for the remainder of the program that will help discover latent software defects.

AR2—The contractor shall use the software reliability model defined in _____. Data shall be collected to calibrate the model and the model shall be employed to predict when operational testing is to be complete and the number of latent (not yet discovered) software defects.

AR3—For each critical software failure, the cost impact shall be determined and a summary reported at each PMR.

AR4—The contractor shall track the software failure per CPU hour during the operational test period and during the warranty period. This data shall be reported monthly at the PMRs prior to FQT and quarterly after FQT.

AR5—Software failure information shall be documented in an SPR as defined in ......

AR4— The contractor shall track the software failures per CSU boot during the operational test period and during the warranty period. This data shall be reported monthly at the TIMs prior to FQT and quarterly after FQT.

AR5—Software failure information shall be documented in an SPR as defined in

APPENDIX B

RISK ASSESSMENT QUESTIONNAIRE

The following is an example of a questionnaire that can be used to assess risks and their potential causes before and during a development

B.1   RISK AREAS

Risks have been organized according to risk areas. The questions within each risk area are employed to provide a more complete definition of the risk area. The risk areas to be considered include:

a.   Requirements risk area

This area includes risks associated with the difficulty of implementing the requirements, the uncertainty in the requirements themselves, and the process by which requirements are derived, decomposed, and allocated. Depending upon the life cycle phase, this may involve system level requirements or software level requirements.

b.   Development and test risk area

This includes risks associated with the design, the development process, the test philosophy (both the developer part and the Government part), and the software development and test facilities.

c.   Maintenance risk area

This involves risks that impact the post deployment aspect of the life cycle. It involves the maintainability and adaptability of the software product resulting from the development phase as well as the maintenance process itself.

d.   Government risk area

This involves risks that exist because of the Government products, processes, and resources. These can usually be reduced by Government actions.

e.   Developer risk area

This involves risks that exist because of the developer's products, processes, and resources. These should be resolved by contractor actions. However, the actions to be taken to reduce the risks may be triggered by the Government.

f.   Schedule and budget risk area

The high level schedule is established by the Government and can only be resolved by the Government. The detailed schedule is developed by the contractor on the basis of the Government's schedule. If schedule risks exist, they must be resolved on the basis of a joint effort by both the contractor and the Government. This may sometimes involve changing the constraints and requirements imposed upon the system or modifying the schedule itself.

Budget goes hand in hand with schedule. The Government establishes the overall budget for the project and allocates portions to the developer based upon the bid. Both the Government and the contractor play important roles in establishing and managing their part of the overall budget.

B.2   USE OF QUESTIONNAIRE

Each risk area is described in the paragraphs below and is evaluated by answering the associated questions as either Yes (Y), No (N), Not Applicable (NA), or Unknown (UK). A question may be very applicable, but because of a lack of information, the answer is not known at the time of the evaluation. A question may not be applicable for a particular phase of a program but may become applicable as the program proceeds. If the answer is UK, this is a source of uncertainty and potential risk.

Each of the questions asks for an overall judgment. Minor defects in a process, product, or resource that are easily corrected should not cause the answer to a question to change. For example, if only 1 out of the 100 requirements is ambiguous and it can be easily corrected, one should answer N to the question "Are the requirements ambiguous?" However, if a large percentage of the requirements is ambiguous and a complete rework of the requirements document is necessary, then the answer to the question should be Y.

The questionnaire can be applied before and during development.

B.3   REQUIREMENTS RISK AREA

During the predevelopment phase of the life cycle, the system requirements, as contained within the evolving SSS and supporting documentation, pose a potential risk. Requirements that are unclear, constantly changing, or difficult to implement can result in an incorrect product being developed, a fragmented design, and a schedule that cannot be maintained. During development, the software requirements contained within the SRS and IRS are established. Risks associated with the SSS may still exist, and the more detailed software requirements may pose additional risk. The following questions help address this risk area:

a.   Are specific functional, performance, and quality requirements unique to this program (unprecedented)? Y__ , N__ , NA __, UK __

b.   Are the specifications of the requirements ambiguous? Y__, N__, NA __, UK __

c.   Are they expressed in terms that cannot be verified? Y__ , N__ , NA __, UK __

d.   Are the SSS requirements difficult to decompose into hardware, software, and human interface requirements? Y__ , N__ , NA __, UK __

e.   Is key Government-furnished information, which is necessary to determine the requirements, not yet available or not of good quality? Y__ , N__ , NA__, UK __

f.   Does the program lack a documented concept of operations? Y__ , N__ , NA__, UK __

g.   Are many different users involved in generating and approving requirements and changes to the requirements? Y__ , N__ , NA __, UK __

h.   Is there too little user involvement, which is likely to cause requirements to be changed late in the development? Y__ , N__ , NA__, UK __

i.   Does the system have a large number of interfaces to other systems? Y__ , N__ , NA__, UK __

j.   Are the number of requirements very large (requiring more than 30 people to implement)? Y__ , N__ , NA __, UK __

k.   Do specific requirements push the state of the art? Y__, N__, NA __, UK__

l.   Does the system have external interfaces to other systems that are not yet fully defined or are likely to change? Y__ , N__ , NA__, UK __

m.   Are the performance requirements (response time, throughput) very high and inflexible? Y__, N__ , NA__, UK __

n.   Does the system have multilevel computer security requirements? Y__ , N__, NA__, UK __

o.   Does the system have portability requirements between different operating systems and/or computer architectures? Y__ , N__ , NA__, UK __

p.   Do the software elements need to be reusable in another application? Y__ , N__ , NA__, UK__

q.   Does the system have very high availability or reliability requirements? Y__ , N__, NA__, UK __

r.   Must the system be fault tolerant? Y__ , N__ , NA__, UK __

B.4   DEVELOPMENT AND TEST

The design and test risk areas include risks associated with the design itself, the design process, and the test and evaluation process, as well as the development and test facilities. An immature design process, or one in which the tools are inadequate, can result in a poor software structure and the introduction of a large number of design and code defects. An inadequate test and evaluation process may result in inadequate test coverage and test procedures that do not adequately evaluate the ability of the software to satisfy its requirements. The development and test facilities provide the environment and contain the mechanisms with which quality is built into the product and the requirements are verified. The facilities must be of appropriate capacity so as not to affect the schedule, and must be appropriate for the product being developed. The following questions help address this risk area:

a.   Does the developer have an immature software development process (not used before, not well documented, not measured, less than Level 3 of the SEI SCE)? Y__ , N__ , NA __ , UK __

b.   Are the contractor's software development tools immature, poorly documented, or unreliable? Y__ , N__ , NA __ , UK __

c.   Does the developer lack experience with the software development tools and methods? Y__ , N__ , NA __ , UK __

d.   Has the developer presented the rationale for design decisions? Y__ , N__ , NA __ , UK __

e.   Does the design possess a large number of defects? Y__ , N__ , NA __ , UK __

f.   Has the design documentation been unacceptable to the Government? Y__ , N__ , NA __ , UK__

g.   Have a significant number of violations to the design and coding standards been discovered? Y__ , N__ , NA __ , UK __

h.   Have the test plans and procedures been delivered late or are they unacceptable to the Government? Y__ , N__ , NA __ , UK __

i.   Does integration testing occur at the end of the development? Y__ , N__ , NA __ , UK __

j.   Are the contractor's software development and test facilities late in availability, unreliable, or insufficient for the number of users? Y__ , N__ , NA __ , UK __

k.   Do the test facilities support only a subset of the capabilities needed to generate tests with realistic loads? Y__ , N__ , NA __ , UK __

B.5   MAINTENANCE PLANNING

Planning for PDSS must take place early in the program. An inadequate maintenance process can result in long delays in correcting defects, as well as the introduction of new defects as a result of the process itself. A low quality maintenance process may cause the structure of the software to deteriorate and introduce violations to the design and coding standards. The following questions help address this risk area:

a.   Was the maintenance organization not involved in planning prior to development?
Y__, N__, NA __, UK __

b.   Did the system requirements not include maintainability requirements?
Y__ , N__ , NA __, UK__

c.   Do no representatives of the maintenance organization attend reviews of software development? Y__ , N__ , NA __, UK __

d.   Do plans for maintenance and support of Government-Furnished Software (GFS) have to be formulated? Y__ , N__ , NA __, UK __

e.   Are some development and test tools and/or their documentation not deliverable to the Government? Y__ , N__, NA __, UK __

B.6   GOVERNMENT

Government personnel establish the overall plan for the project. They establish the constraints imposed on the contractor and the level of resources to be applied to the program. Both the experience level and the number of appropriate personnel must be considered in evaluating risk. As more organizations get involved in the predevelopment planning process, misunderstandings in communication may occur. This may result in misinterpretations and incorrect documentation of interfaces. The following questions help address this risk area:

a.   Does the program office lack managers with appropriate experience in software acquisition to understand risks and to perform risk management.?
Y__, N__ , NA __, UK __

b.   Does the program office lack technical staff with sufficient software engineering knowledge and practical experience to recognize risks? Y__, N__ , NA __, UK __

c.   Does the program manager have experience dealing with the type of contract?
Y__, N__ , NA __, UK__

d.   Are there many Government and potential associate contractor organizations involved in development? Y__ , N__ , NA __, UK __

e. Are the Government organizations remotely located from one another?
    Y__ , N__ , NA __, UK__

f. Do the product delivery schedules from the various associate contractors pose
    potential bottlenecks? Y__ , N__ , NA __, UK __

g. Are the responsibilities of the different Government organizations and associate
    contractors unclear? Y__ , N__ , NA __, UK __

h. Do plans still have to be developed for evaluating the contractor's processes and
    resources applied to the project? Y__ , N__ , NA __, UK __

i. Do checklists and procedures for verifying the quality of each of the formal
    deliverable products have to be developed? Y__ , N__ , NA __, UK __

j. Is the Government the integrator of the system? Y__, N__ , NA __, UK __

k. Does the Government have to furnish equipment, facilities, or software that are not
    yet available or may not be available when needed? Y__ , N__ , NA __, UK__

l. Is the type of contract appropriate to the requirements uncertainty or risk?
    Y__ , N__ , NA __, UK __

m. Has the Government been late in its obligations to the contractor in obtaining
    information or reviewing products? Y__ , N__ , NA __, UK __

n. Is the GFS or GFI undependable in quality? Y__ , N__ , NA __, UK __

B.7   DEVELOPER

During the predevelopment phase, the contractor has not yet been selected. After source
selection, new risks associated with the selected contractor may become apparent. The
following questions help address this risk area:

a. Does the contractor lack experience with the application area or the functional,
    quality, and performance requirements? Y__ , N__ , NA __, UK __

b. Does the contractor lack the training and experience with the technologies that will
    be required to build in quality, including language, operating systems, software
    engineering tools, standards, and methods? Y__ , N__ , NA __, UK__

c. Is the contractor's upper management unfamiliar with software development and
    the cost and schedule implications of attaining the specified level of quality?
    Y__ , N__ , NA __, UK __

d.   Does the contractor's management lack methods for tracking progress and quality and for identifying and managing risk? Y__ , N__ , NA __, UK __

e.   Is the number of experienced contractor personnel less than what was planned? Y__ , N__ , NA __, UK __

f.   Does the contractor have an immature (as defined in the SEI SCE) software development process? Y__ , N__ , NA __, UK __

g.   Are there many contractor and subcontractor organizations involved in development and are their responsibilities unclear? Y__ , N__ , NA __, UK __

h.   Does the prime contractor allow subcontractors developing software to use their own standards and/or development environment that differ from each other? Y__ , N__ , NA __, UK __

i.   Does the prime contractor lack a method of tracking the software development subcontractors' progress? Y__ , N__ , NA __, UK __

B.8   SCHEDULE AND BUDGET

An inappropriately short schedule may affect the ability of the contractor to completely implement and verify the software and thus negatively affect the ability of the system to satisfy its quality requirements. The major aspect to be considered is the credibility of the overall schedule.

Budgetary constraints affect the amount of time that personnel can apply to a program as well as the equipment and tools that can be applied to build in and verify quality. Both the size of the budget as well as the allocation of the budget should be considered. The following questions help address this risk area:

a.   Is the software schedule much shorter (greater than 15 percent) or is the software budget much less (over 15 percent) than predicted by a cost model? Y__ , N__ , NA __, UK __

b.   Is the schedule rigid with no allowance for slip? Namely, is slack absent in the schedule? Y__ , N__ , NA __, UK __

c.   Does the schedule contradict experience on similar programs, or has the Government failed to find similar programs for schedule comparison purposes? Y__ , N__ , NA__, UK __

d.   Has the schedule slipped steadily early in development? Y__ , N__ , NA__, UK __

e.   Has rescheduling reduced the time allocated for testing?

Y__ , N__ , NA __ , UK __

f.   Have SQA tasks been reduced to save time? Y__ , N__ , NA __ , UK __

GLOSSARY

ADL	Ada Design Language
AFLC	Air Force Logistics Command
AFSC	Air Force Systems Command
ASD	Aeronautical Systems Division
C^3	Command, Control, and Communications
CASE	Computer-Aided Software Engineering
CDR	Critical Design Review
CDRL	Contract Data Requirements List
CLIN	Contract Line Item Numbers
CM	Configuration Management
COCOMO	Cost Constructive Model
COTS	Commercial Off-the-Shelf
CPU	computer processor unit
CSC	Computer Software Component
CSCI	Computer Software Configuration Items
DID	Data Item Description
DOD	Department of Defense
DT&E	Development Test and Evaluation
ESD	Electronic Systems Division
FQT	Formal Qualification Tests
GFE	Government-Furnished Equipment
GFI	Government-Furnished Information
GFP	Government-Furnished Programs
GFS	Government-Furnished Software
GOSIP	Government Open Systems Interconnection Profile
GQM	Goal Question Metric
ICD	Interface Control Document
IFPP	Instructions for Proposal Preparation
I/O	input/output
IOT&E	Initial Operational Test and Evaluation
IRS	Interface Requirements Specification
IV& V	Independent Verification and Validation
MIPS	millions of instructions per second
MTBF	mean time between failures
NDI	Nondevelopmental Items

PDCA	Plan-Do-Check-Action
PDL	Program Design Language
PDR	Preliminary Design Review
PDSS	Post Deployment Software Support
PMR	Program Management Review
POSIX	Portable Operating System Interface
PQT	Preliminary Qualification Tests
RFP	Request for Proposal
RSQF	Rome Laboratory Software Quality Framework
RTM	Requirements Traceability Matrix
RVM	Requirements Verification Metric
SCE	Software Capability Evaluation
SDCCR	Software Development Capability/Capacity Review
SDF	Software Development File
SDP	Software Development Plan
SDR	System Design Review
SEE	Software Engineering Exercise
SEI	Software Engineering Institute
SEP	Software Engineering Prototype
SPR	Software Problem Report
SQA	Software Quality Assurance
SRR	Software Requirement Review
SSR	Software Specification Review
SSS	System/Subsystem Specification
SWA	Software Audit
TIM	Technical Interchange Meeting
TRR	Test Readiness Review
TSQC	Total Software Quality Control
UK	Unknown

☉U.S. GOVERNMENT PRINTING OFFICE: 1993-710-093-60194

PART I

Volume 2

Descriptions of

Individual Techniques

SECTION 1

INTRODUCTION

PURPOSE OF THE GUIDE

This guide is intended for Air Force personnel who are responsible for assuring that software in mission-critical systems attains and sustains a level of quality that is required for its effective use. Typical users of the guide will be in a program office, responsible for planning and overseeing the development of a system. Others concerned with the development of quality software may find it useful as well.

SCOPE OF THE GUIDE

The guide focuses primarily on the problems in quality control that are common to mission-critical systems with large amounts of software. These systems often have the following characteristics:

a.   Requirements are difficult to define.

b.   Meeting delivery schedules and budgets is as important as delivering quality.

c.   The software plays a key role in achieving system requirements.

d.   The software must meet rigid timing requirements.

e.   The system must have very high reliability; human lives may depend on its correct operation.

f.   The system must be operational virtually all of the time.

g.   The system may be embedded in another system that limits its size and accessibility for maintenance and repair, and increases the complexity of its external interfaces.

h.   The system must be easy to repair and modify quickly, for a long time after it is fielded.

These requirements place a heavy responsibility, often with high risk, on those who must assure the quality of a mission-critical system and its software. The methods and techniques in this guide may be useful but less essential for small software developments or systems where requirements are less demanding.

101

The guide addresses these questions about software quality control.

a.   How do you define software quality requirements?

b.   How do you plan for achieving software quality?

c.   How do you build quality into software?

d.   How do you predict or measure software quality?

e.   What actions can you take to improve software quality?

ORGANIZATION AND CONTENT OF THE GUIDE

This report provides tutorial information for those learning about software quality control as well as practical guidance on controlling software quality. The sources of this guidance are software engineering theory and practices; DOD and especially Air Force regulations, standards, and guidance; published reports and books; and our own experiences and those of our colleagues who have participated in the development and maintenance of mission-critical systems.

The guide is divided into two volumes. The first volume presents a quality control model, basic concepts of software quality control, a brief summary of techniques that have been used to control the quality of software, and guidelines for the selection of appropriate software quality control techniques for a program.

This second volume of the guide presents a more detailed description of selected techniques for controlling software quality. Each is described in terms of what it is, when and how it can be used, and what is known about its benefits and costs. This volume is a reference guide. Many of the quality control techniques introduced in volume 1 are described here in more detail. They are organized alphabetically for ease of reference.

Information on each quality control technique is organized as follows:

a.   **Description**—including background and other sources of supplementary information to allow the project office to decide whether to use the technique and how to apply it.

b.   **Purpose**—describes how the technique can help to control quality. Also included within this section are the major benefits anticipated from applying the technique.

c.   **Application**—describes when the technique may be applied within the software life cycle, by whom it is applied, and alternative uses for the technique when appropriate. Also described within this section are the checkpoints within the program where the effects of application of the technique are reviewed, and replanning and adjustments are initiated.

d. **Major issues**—include the decisions to be made when planning to apply the technique, and the limitations of the technique. This section also describes the caveats that must be considered prior to applying the quality control technique under discussion.

e. **Measurement and evaluation criteria**—include both the criteria for evaluating the project as well as the effectiveness of the quality control technique itself in terms of benefits gained and cost incurred.

f. **Activities** (implied by the technique)—in general, this section describes the planning that is necessary, the steps involved in the execution of the technique, and a description of the potential actions that can occur as a result of the application of the quality control technique.

g. **Related techniques**—quality control techniques are not all independent of one another. Some may be redundant, and redundancy may not be entirely bad. For highly critical systems, a large degree of redundant checking may be appropriate. Other techniques may be complementary; that is, one enhances the other. Finally, certain techniques may be incompatible with one another.

h. **Bibliography**—references to reading to supplement each brief description in this volume.

SECTION 2

CAUSE AND EFFECT ANALYSIS

Many of the software development and test processes rely on defect detection and correction through inspections, walk-throughs, reviews, and testing to achieve quality. However, reliance on detective techniques can be costly. Ultimately, one wants to use techniques that prevent defects from being introduced. The fewer defects that are created, the less rework is necessary and the less resources must be provided for the correction process.

Mays [MAY90] describes a process for defect prevention which is based upon a causal analysis of defects as a means to provide long-term process and resource improvement. It consists of four elements integrated into the development process (see figure 1).

  a. Causal analysis meetings to identify the root cause of defects and suggest preventive actions

  b. An action team to implement the preventive actions

  c. Kick-off meetings at the start of each stage of development to increase awareness of quality issues specific to that stage

  d. Data gathering and analysis to validate that the quality improvement actions are working.

PURPOSE

  a. To prevent the further introduction of defects into software products under development

  b. To provide data for long-term improvement of the processes and resources applied to the generation of a software product.

APPLICATION

Cause and effect analysis is applied by the developer using the developer's staff and the data they have collected to show how and why defects occur.

The level of application of cause and effect analysis can range from a complete analysis of all defects, with a large number of planned causal analysis meetings, to an analysis of a random sample of the defects, with a small number of causal analysis meetings. The following minimum level of activity is necessary:

a.   A kick-off meeting for each stage of development—this would occur prior to software requirements analysis, preliminary design, detailed design, code, test plan and procedure development, and software integration

b.   One causal analysis meeting for each development team at each stage

c.   An action team of at least three members for a development organization of 30 or fewer persons. A six-person team would be required for a development organization of between 120 and 150 persons.

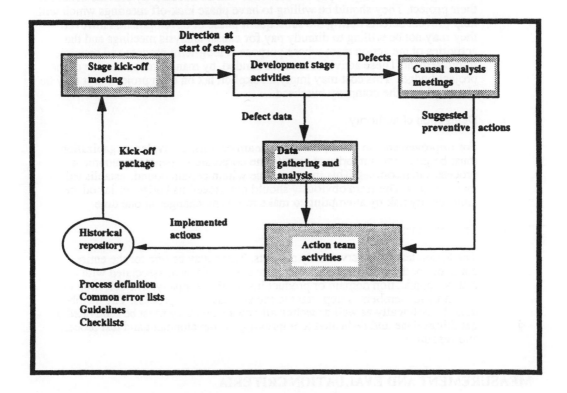

Figure 1. Defect Prevention

Expanded levels of application could involve integrating software quality assurance (SQA) activities with causal analysis by having a causal analysis meeting every time more than a predetermined number of defects are reported (for example, 20). The amount of effort to apply to causal analysis depends most strongly upon management's commitment to improving the quality of its software processes and resources.

MAJOR ISSUES

a.   Management commitment and funding

There is a continuing need for management support and funding for the cause and effect analysis process.

Individual project managers are responsible for getting their projects completed on time, within budget, and at a specified level of quality. Project managers are not, in general, willing to pay for activities that do not directly provide benefit to their project. They should be willing to have phase kick-off meetings which will help prevent defects during the subsequent phase of development. However, they may not be willing to directly pay for causal analysis meetings and the activities of the action team whose purpose is long-term process and resource improvement. These activities must be funded, by management, outside of the project budget. This cost may imply an explicit tax on each project, or it may be absorbed into the company overhead.

b.   Delegation of authority

For improvements to occur, the action team or some equivalent organization must be given the authority to modify the corporate software development process and resources. This must be done within certain bounds established by management. The team obviously should not exceed its budget or introduce unnecessary risk by attempting to make too many changes at one time.

c.   The action team

The action team can serve many projects. There may be one for the entire company or there may be a number of action teams each associated with a distinct application domain or product line of the company. The selection of action team members is important to the success of the process. The members must be politically as well as technically aware and they must be motivated to get things done and dedicated to improving the development and test process and resources.

MEASUREMENT AND EVALUATION CRITERIA

a.   This technique employs two major measurements or evaluations.

•   The data gathering and analysis part of this technique counts and analyzes defects detected during each stage of the development with sufficient detail to identify potential causes. For example, Software Problem Reports (SPRs) include the module in which the error occurred. Analysis can determine if a few modules are the source of many errors, and then those modules can be examined for the types of errors and why they occurred.

- The causal analysis meetings evaluate all or a sample of the defects to determine cause. This eventually leads to suggestions for preventive actions.

b. To determine the adequacy and effectiveness of the cause and effect quality control technique, one must

- Measure the improvement in quality over a number of projects by counting the number of defects categorized as follows:

    - Oversight defect—the developer failed to consider all cases and conditions.

    - Education defect—the developer did not understand some aspect of the product or the process.

    - Communications failure—the developer did not receive the required information or the information was incorrect.

    - Transcription errors—the developer knew what to do but simply made a mistake.

- Measure the cost to the project and to the corporation's overhead of performing the cause and effect defect prevention process.

ACTIVITIES

a. Planning

Implementing this technique is a corporate management decision. An individual project manager within a corporation cannot make the decision to initiate such a process.

Cause and effect analysis must be an integral part of the development and test process. The program plan must provide time in the schedule for phase kick-off meetings, causal analysis meetings, and interaction with the action teams.

Planning the cause and effect defect prevention process involves

- Selecting the members of the action team

- Providing a budget for the action team and the process itself

- Establishing the interaction between the projects, the action team, and SQA

- Deciding on the checkpoints within the program where phase kick-off meetings are to occur

- Deciding when causal analysis meetings are to occur

- Deciding the degree of management oversight into the process.

b. Doing

- Causal analysis meetings

The software development process is divided into a number of design, development, and test stages, such as requirement analysis, code and unit test, and computer software configuration item (CSCI) integration. At the end of each stage, a causal analysis meeting is held where each defect or group of defects is analyzed. At these meetings the following types of questions are addressed:

- What is the category or cause of the error?

- How was the error introduced?

- At what stage in the development or test process was the error created or injected?

- How can this type of error be prevented in the future?

- Is there a trend in the errors that indicates a broader problem?

- What went right during the development stage? What saved time?

- What went wrong during the development stage? What wasted time?

- How can the defect detection process be improved?

The emphasis of the meeting is on gathering preventive suggestions.

- Action team implementation

The action team is delegated the responsibility to ensure that preventive actions are implemented. They meet regularly to

- Review new actions that have been proposed by the causal analysis meeting

- Decide which ones are to be implemented

- Decide how to implement them

- Assign new actions

- Review the status of actions that are currently open.

• Kick-off meetings prior to each stage of development

The purpose of the kick-off meetings is to review the technical aspects of the upcoming development process and the steps necessary to achieve quality. Information presented during these meetings includes

- A description of the process for the upcoming development stage

- Input data available for use during this stage of development

- Examples of outputs from the upcoming stage

- Validation methods that will be used during the upcoming stage (e.g., inspections, reviews)

- A common error list of errors often produced during this stage

- Assignments

- Schedule to be followed.

• Gathering and analysis of defect data

During each development stage, defect data must be collected and analyzed to determine if the anticipated decrease in the number of defects in each category has occurred. This is used by the action team to help define future quality enhancement suggestions, such as modifications of processes or tools.

c.   Generating Actions

Preventive actions fall into the following categories:

- Improvements or refinements of the process

- Development or purchase of tools that support the development and test process

- Education actions to improve knowledge about products and processes

- Requirements changes

- Improvements in communications.

RELATED TECHNIQUES

Complementary

a. SPR data gathering and analysis

b. SQA

c. Software Development Files

d. Inspections.

BIBLIOGRAPHY

[MAY90]   Mays, R.G., et. al., 1990, "Experiences with Defect Prevention," *IBM Systems Journal*, Vol. 29, No. 1, pp. 4-32.

SECTION 3

CONFIGURATION MANAGEMENT

Configuration Management (CM) is an essential process for the development of any software system. It is the discipline of identifying the configuration of a system, at discrete points in time, for the purpose of systematically controlling changes to the configuration and maintaining the integrity and traceability of the configuration throughout the system life cycle.

CM is not responsible for the generation of change requests or the implementation of the changes. It provides the mechanism for controlling the change process.

In the parlance of DOD-STD-2167A [DOD88], the item to be controlled is called a CSCI. Software CM starts when a baseline of the CSCI is established. The elementary entity of software configuration identification is the Configuration Element (CE); each CE is a controllable entity. A CSCI baseline consists of a set of CEs. A baseline is a formal snapshot of the system at a specified time in the program.

CM consists of

a. Identifying and documenting the functional and physical characteristics of the configuration item

b. Controlling changes to the item and its documentation

c. Recording the configuration of actual items

d. Auditing the configuration item and its identification.

PURPOSE

a. To provide a uniform mechanism for controlling changes to an evolving software product and its documentation

b. To maintain and improve the quality of the evolving software product by preventing inconsistencies and defects from being introduced into the software and its documentation as a result of the change process.

APPLICATION

CM is performed by both the Government and the contractor during the life of a system.

111

a.   CM is performed by the contractor during the development process.

b.   CM is performed by the Government, with possible contractor participation, after the software product is released to the Government.

CM by the contractor is an important way to identify and control evolving versions of software and documentation. It is essential in coordinating activities such as integration of components, testing, repair or other modification of software and documentation, especially when multiple users and development organizations participate.

CM by the Government during development includes controlling changes to the functional and performance requirements of the System/Segment Specification (SSS). This can be done by chairing and participating as members of a Configuration Control Board (CCB) that approves requirements changes. Similarly, a developer may have a CCB that controls changes to software that do not affect requirements. When software or its documentation is released to the Government and accepted, then the Government must assume responsibility for configuration management of the software requirements, implementation, and related deliverables.

The results of the CM process are reviewed at Government reviews such as Program Management Reviews (PMRs).

MAJOR ISSUES

a.   Establishing the baselines and CEs to be controlled

Careful definitions of the baseline and the CEs of the baseline are necessary to control the cost and schedule impact of the CM process. The process can become overburdening if too many baselines are specified and/or too many CEs are incorporated into each baseline.

Three formal baselines are defined in MIL-STD-483A [MIL85]. We have included an expanded definition of the content of these baselines [DUN80].

- **Functional baseline**—describes the problem to be solved, and the product that will be deployed. The functional baseline is the basis for agreement between buyer and seller. In DOD-STD-2167A, the CEs of the functional baseline are the SSS and any referenced Interface Control Documents (ICDs).

- **Allocated baseline**—provides an apportionment to specific hardware and software of the functions to be performed. At this point, the CSCIs have been defined, and the authenticated Software Requirement Specification (SRS) and Interface Requirements Recommendation (IRS) form the CEs of this baseline.

- **Product baseline**—the software and its documentation after physical configuration audit/functional configuration audit (PCA/FCA). At this point, control of the CM process is passed from the contractor to the contracting agency. CEs of this baseline consist of the Version Description Document, the code, and supporting design, user, and maintenance documentation.

This list of baselines can be expanded to address the need for informal CM during the development process. These additional baselines may include

- Top-level design baseline, which is a description of the overall scheme for meeting the requirements of the allocated baseline. The preliminary design portion of the software design document forms the CE for this baseline.

- Detailed design baseline, which describes how the software will be built. The entire set of software design documents may form the CEs for this baseline.

- Developmental baseline, which is used to control the configuration during the implementation and integration process. The CEs for this baseline consist of the various data and code modules which constitute the CSCI.

b. Providing tools and automation

CM for a large development effort involving multiple releases of the software must be supported by automated tools that provide

- A mechanism for storing, maintaining, and retrieving source and object code and its supporting documentation

- A mechanism for automatically identifying all the elements of a configuration

- A mechanism to interface with the tools that build the deliverable software image

- A mechanism to maintain a historical log of the changes in the configuration by storing the incremental changes to each version, so one is able to recreate an old version

- A mechanism to maintain and access the CM records and logs.

MEASUREMENT AND EVALUATION CRITERIA

a. The CM process can provide information to evaluate the change activity and quality of a program.

- Plot the number of change requests received and the change rate as a function of time, to see if the system requirements and the software are stabilizing

- Determine the number of change requests in each of the following categories to see where improvements are needed in the development process

  - Changes due to requirements clarifications

  - Changes due to requirements additions or deletions

  - Changes due to defects in the code or its documentation

  - Changes to increase performance

- Determine the percent of change requests that receive final disposition.

b. To evaluate the quality of the CM process itself, determine

- The overall cost of the CM process

- The cost divided by the number of change requests handled

- The number of problem solutions that had to be reworked

- The time to close a change request

- Amount of delay in calling a configuration control meeting.

ACTIVITIES

a. Planning

- The developer should develop and document the Software Configuration Management Plan, usually as part of the Software Development Plan (SDP). The plan should contain

  - Description of the items to be controlled

    Definition of baselines

    Definition of the CEs for each baseline

- Organizational Structure

    The organization responsible for CM and its relationship to other organizational elements

    The participants in the CCB

    The role of the CCB manager

- Description of the CM activities

    Configuration identification

    Configuration control

    Configuration status accounting, audits, authentication.

- The Government should establish its CCB. Members of the CCB for formal CM should include representatives of the

    - User community

    - Buyer

    - Development contractor

    - Independent Verification and Validation (IV&V) contractor (if applicable).

    The CCB for informal CM should include representatives from the

    - Program office

    - SQA

    - CM organization (usually the chairman of the CCB)

    - Development organization.

b. Doing

The overall flow of the CM process is shown in figure 2. Change requests may be generated by any organization because deficiencies were detected, requirements have changed, or functional enhancements are necessary. Each change request is analyzed by the development organization if code already exists, or by the CCB if requirements documentation will change.

The result of the analysis is the generation of a formal Engineering Change Proposal (ECP). The analysis group may work with the generator of the change request to clarify the description and rationale for the change. The ECP is then submitted to the CCB, which either approves or disapproves the ECP. The personnel charged with analyzing the change cannot reject a change request. They only present the results of their analysis of change requests, and recommend action to the CCB.

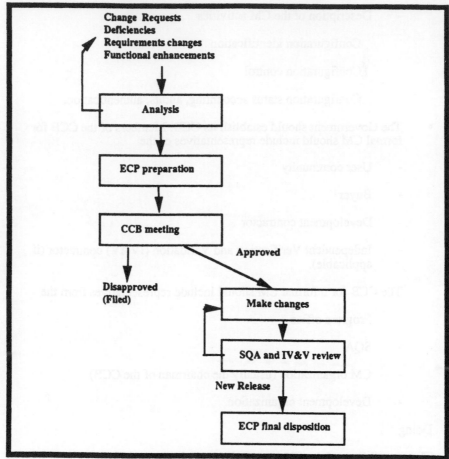

Figure 2. The CM Process

The CCB can either accept or reject the ECP. Disapproved ECPs are retained for future reference. Approved ECPs are submitted to the appropriate organizations to make the changes and perform verification. A contract change

organizations to make the changes and perform verification. A contract change is often required. SQA and IV&V (if part of the program) are used to verify the quality and technical aspects of the implementation. The result of this change is combined with other changes to create a new product release and an update to the configuration identification. After the new release occurs, the ECP is considered complete.

c. Auditing, record keeping, and generating reports

This part of the process is performed in parallel with the normal CM activities. It consists of

- Maintaining and making visible to management the official status of the software

- Verifying that the CM process is being performed according to plan

- Verifying that the documentation of each change request contains all the information required and is updated as required. An example of the record-keeping items for each change request can be found in the SPR report described in section 2.13 of Volume 1.

d. Generating actions

The result of CM actions may be

- Rejection of a change request for reason

- Acceptance of a change request for processing

- Approval of the implementation of the change

- Generation, validation, and release of new versions of software and documentation

- Modification of the details of the CM process itself.

RELATED TECHNIQUES

Complementary

a. SPR data gathering and analysis

b. IV&V.

BIBLIOGRAPHY

[BER84]   Bersoff, E. H., January 1984, "Elements of Software Configuration Management," *IEEE Transactions on Software Engineering*, Vol. SE-1, No. 1.

[DOD88]   DOD-STD-2167A, 29 February 1988, *Defense System Software Development*.

[DUN80]   Dunn and Ullman, 1980, *Quality Assurance for Computer Systems*, McGraw-Hill.

[MIL85]   MIL-STD-483A, 4 June 1985, *Configuration Management Practices for Systems, Equipment, Munitions, and Computer Programs*.

[SCH87]   Schulmeyer, G., J. McManus, 1987, *Handbook of Software Quality Assurance*, New York: Van Nostrand Reinhold.

SECTION 4

INDEPENDENT VERIFICATION AND VALIDATION

Independent Verification and Validation (IV&V) provides an independent evaluation of the software being developed and provides suggestions to improve the product, processes, and resources. The definitions provided by the IEEE-STD-729 are useful in understanding the role of IV&V [IEE83].

a. Verification is the process of determining whether or not the products of a given phase of the software development cycle fulfill the requirements established during the previous phase.

b. Validation is the process of evaluating software at the end of the software development process to ensure compliance with software requirements.

Major verification activities include

a. Concept definition evaluation

b. Requirements analysis

c. Design evaluation

d. Code evaluation

e. Document verification.

Validation activities involve

a. Testing

b. Installation and checkout activities.

All may be performed to varying degrees depending upon the criticality of the application. AFSC/AFLC Pamphlet 800-5 [AFS88] describes a method for determining the degree of IV&V applicable to a given program, and the specific activities that may be performed. This is more fully described below under IV&V Activities.

PURPOSE

a. To ensure software performs its intended functions correctly

b. To ensure the software does not perform any unintended functions

c.   To evaluate the quality of the evolving software products

d.   To uncover high risk defects early in the development process.

APPLICATION

IV&V is usually performed by a contractor working directly for the Government. The IV&V organization should not be associated with the development contractor. When applied during the predevelopment phase of a program, it provides an independent view of the system concepts and the request for proposal (RFP) package. The IV&V contractor, in particular, concentrates on the SSS and the ICDs. When performed during development, it can provide a detailed independent review of all development activities and products, starting with requirements analysis, and proceeding through formal test and evaluation.

MAJOR ISSUES

a.   The cost of IV&V can be high.

Depending upon the level or degree of application of IV&V, the cost can vary widely. National Institute of Standards and Technology (NIST) special publication 500-15 reports that IV&V can cost 10 to 30 percent of the development contract [WAL89]. The elements of IV&V cost include

- Personnel cost

- The sharing or duplication of development and test resources

- Cost of increased paperwork to provide written responses to IV&V defect reports and concerns

- Interaction of the development contractor and the IV&V contractor.

b.   Careful coordination of the IV&V role and the developer's role is needed.

An overemphasis should not be placed solely on an IV&V process to produce high quality products. The IV&V contractor must never assume the developer's responsibility for mission success, system safety, or other quality assurance practices. IV&V must complement and reinforce the developer's software engineering process; it should not duplicate it. In some cases, the IV&V contractor does not communicate with the developer directly to maintain independence, while in other cases the IV&V contractor reports results to the developer to give the benefit of independent feedback.

Therefore, careful planning is necessary to specify the role and activities of the IV&V contractor and the relationship to the development contractor prior to the start of development. NIST special publication 500-165 [WAL89] provides a comprehensive list of documents that can assist in the planning process.

c.   The level of the IV&V activities depends upon the needs of the program.

AFSCP/AFLCP 800-5 pamphlet [AFS88] suggests three possible levels of effort, dependent on the risk associated with the software and its criticality to the system.

- Level 3 tasks include

    - Evaluating software documentation

    - Participating in milestone reviews and formal qualification testing

    - Identifying critical requirements and design issues

    - Monitoring the development process and providing technical consultation

    - Evaluating critical test results

    - Performing selected audits.

- Level 2 tasks include

    - Performing all level 3 tasks

    - Analyzing selected critical functions

    - Performing spot checks on design performance

    - Independently testing critical code

    - Analyzing the developer's test results

    - Providing independent evaluation of all software change requests.

- Level 1 tasks include

    - Performing all level 2 tasks

    - Performing a structural and functional analysis of the requirements, design, and code

    - Developing alternative design proposals for critical design areas

    - Recoding key areas of the design

-    Conducting special tests in critical areas beyond the contractor's Formal Qualification Test (FQT).

d.   The IV&V role may duplicate the role of other SQA organizations.

For a discussion of whether IV&V is necessary, and how it adds to the assurance of software quality, see [GAO91].

e.   Automated tools may be necessary.

The IV&V process can be very tedious if not supported by automated tools. The tools are the same as those used by the developer and include

- Computer-Aided Software Engineering (CASE) tools to help determine the completeness and adequacy of the requirements

- Code analyzers

- Traceability tools to help determine the completeness of the SRS, design, and test cases

- Test coverage tools.

MEASUREMENT AND EVALUATION CRITERIA

a.   A wide variety of measures and evaluation criteria may be applied by the IV&V contractor to determine the quality of the evolving software product, such as

- Measure the number of defects detected during each phase of development and their severity.

- Determine the number of requirements that cannot be traced from the system to the software requirements documentation, and thence to the design.

- Determine the number of requirements that are not covered in the test cases.

b.   To determine the adequacy and effectiveness of the IV&V process itself

- Measure and track the cost of the IV&V effort versus plan.

- Measure the number of errors found only through the IV&V process per 1000 lines of code.

- Determine the cost of IV&V per defect found only by the IV&V process.

- Determine the impact on system performance of errors found only by the IV&V process.

- Determine the length of time from when an error is made until the IV&V team uncovers it.

- Determine what percent of the defects found by IV&V were also found by other organizations such as SQA, and the delay if IV&V had not found them.

- Determine the percent of IV&V recommendations that are acted on.

ACTIVITIES

a. Planning

- Determine whether the system warrants an IV&V effort based upon the criticality of the system. AFSCP/AFLCP 800-5 [AFS88] describes a method of criticality analysis that includes

  - Listing the software requirements

  - Identifying the potential impact or consequences of not meeting the software requirements on performance, safety, and cost

  - Estimating the probability of occurrence of not satisfying the requirement as frequent, probable, or improbable

  - Determining the overall criticality value for the system or its components as a combined evaluation of impact and probability of occurrence.

- Establish the magnitude or level of the IV&V effort; namely, define all the IV&V activities and their scope.

- Establish the organizational relationships among the Government, the IV&V contractor, and the development contractor.

- Place words into the prime contractor's Request for Proposal (RFP) package and into the contract to provide for interaction with an IV&V contractor.

- Establish the IV&V budget.

b.   **Doing**

- Select the IV&V contractor. The selection process should be independent of the prime contractor source selection process. Selection criteria include

    - IV&V experience

    - Application experience

    - IV&V tools and methods.

- The IV&V contractor then performs the activities as defined within the contract. The Government monitors and responds to the results of the IV&V activities.

c.   Generating actions

The result of IV&V actions may be

- To remove requirements, design, and code defects

- To suggest alternative design approaches

- To institute new test procedures.

The IV&V process may be terminated or redirected depending upon the cost and benefits accrued to date.

RELATED TECHNIQUES

The following techniques are partially redundant, but may be used along with IV&V, depending on the role of IV&V:

a.   Software Audit

b.   Government Reviews—Software Specification Review (SSR), Preliminary Design Review (PDR), Critical Design Review (CDR), Test Readiness Review (TRR)

c.   SQA

d.   Software Management Metrics.

BIBLIOGRAPHY

[AFS88]   AFSC/AFLC Pamphlet 800-5, 20 May 1988, *Software Independent Verification and Validation (IV&V)*, Air Force Logistics Command, Wright-Patterson Air Force Base, Dayton Ohio.

[IEE83]   Software Engineering Technical Committee of the IEEE Computer Society, 1983, *IEEE Standard Glossary of Software Engineering Terminology*, IEEE-STD-729-1983, New York: IEEE.

[GAO91]   Government Accounting Office, February 1991, *Space Shuttle—NASA Should Implement Independent Oversight of Software Development*, GAO/IMTEC 19-20.

[WAL89]   Wallace, D. R., R. U. Fujii, September 1989, NIST Special Publication 500-165, *Software Verification and Validation: Its Role in Computer Assurance and Its Relationship with Software Project Management Standards*, National Institute of Standards and Technology, Gaithersburg, MD.

SECTION 5

INSPECTIONS

Inspections are reviews of any software products that are done manually by teams of developers prior to software testing to detect and remove defects. An inspection usually reviews designs and code, but specifications, plans, and test procedures, or any intermediate product of software development, can also be inspected. Inspections can be informal or formal. The formal inspection process described by Fagan [FAG79, FAG86] is very structured both in the steps to prepare, conduct, and follow up on an inspection, and in the roles of people in the group who do the inspection.

Informal inspections, called "peer reviews" or "walk-throughs," have been used successfully for some time to find defects and to inform people working on related parts of a system about the interfaces and assumptions that have been made about their parts. Although they do not require as disciplined a process, and the investment in time and effort may be less, they are also found to contribute to the quality of software and the efficiency of detecting errors.

PURPOSE

Inspections can be used for the following purposes:

a. To improve the quality of software under development by detecting and removing errors early, before they propagate into later stages and become the basis for further errors

b. To increase programmer productivity and hence reduce time and cost for development by reducing rework later in the program

c. To assure adherence to programming and documentation standards

d. To assure other quality characteristics, such as maintainability

e. To provide data as input to cause and effect analyses that determine why errors and other defects are occurring and correct the causes

f. To identify defect-prone portions of the system that may require special handling.

Statistics on the benefits of inspections have shown that code inspections alone can be two to four times more efficient in finding errors than testing by execution [RUS91]. In an October 1991 article in the newsletter of a well-known software developer, the savings per code inspection was estimated to be $1000, compared with the cost of fixing six errors found and reported during testing. Fagan noted that the experience from inspections caused programmers to reduce the number of errors they made in subsequent design and code on the same project [FAG86]. He further cites examples ranging from 50 percent to over 90 percent of all defects being found by inspection, which, in turn, led to reductions in the cost of corrective maintenance.

APPLICATION

Inspections are performed by developers, usually peers of those who are developing the code. Initially, inspections were applied only to code; but, over time, the technique has been more widely applied to products of each stage or phase of development. The basic principle is that the output of each activity or operation during development should satisfy some exit criteria, and that inspection can find failures to meet those criteria as soon as possible after they have been introduced. This means that inspections can be applied to specifications, design, and code; i.e., any product, preferably as early as possible in the development process. Inspections have even been applied to code that has already been tested but found to be error-prone [FAG86].

A variation on the use of formal inspections for requirements specifications has been described in [MAR90.] A number of independent software development teams inspect the system requirements specification using checklists, and a moderator consolidates their reports of faults. Their independent teams found different faults by reviewing the documentation and meeting with the users. In an experiment, 84 percent of the faults found through the specification and design phases were found during requirements inspection. Ten independent teams were used, and 20 percent of the errors were found by only one team, whereas only 5 percent were found by all 10 teams. It would appear that the multiple inspections are justified for highly critical software.

The participants in formal inspections must be trained for the inspection to be effective. This, in turn, implies that there is a well-defined process with roles for people, checklists and criteria for the reviews, and standards for inspection reports. When the participants are themselves developers, they learn from the inspection process how to improve their own performance.

Although it is the developer who implements inspections, the Government may influence the use of inspections by requiring them, or favoring those who use inspections in the criteria for source selection.

MAJOR ISSUES

a.   Inspection is viewed as low-level, manual work. People think testing is easier and faster.

   •   People who have introduced inspections have indicated the necessity of motivating team members by showing what they can learn as well as the savings to the project from inspections. Over time, objections may disappear as benefits appear.

b.   Inspections are costly but perhaps not as costly as other methods of detecting defects.

- The cost of inspections is estimated to be at least 15 percent of development costs for code inspections alone. Inspections also consume time early in development when customers and managers are anxious to see tangible results from software being tested. Once again, the evidence of the effect of inspections must be presented by using the measures described below.

MEASUREMENT AND EVALUATION CRITERIA

Inspections are a source of information on the types of errors found, where in the software or its documentation they are found, how severe they are, and how many new errors are introduced in correcting errors. This information comes from recording the results of inspections. Among the measures that might be taken during inspections to evaluate the development process and products are the following:

a.   Number of defects found at each stage of development

b.   Number of errors found by inspection and otherwise per thousand lines of code

c.   Number of errors found in each unit, to identify error-prone units

d.   Number of errors found in fixes.

Inspections themselves can be measured to determine their cost and effectiveness, to improve the inspection process, and to aid in planning future inspections. Among the measures that can be applied are

a.   Time spent in inspection versus number of errors found

b.   Percent of all defects found (during and after delivery) by inspection

c.   Time spent per error detected in inspections versus testing

d.   Time spent on fixing errors found by inspections versus testing

e.   Number of errors present but not found by an inspection, and type of error

f.   Time spent in inspections versus size of documentation reviewed

g.   Number of people on the team versus number of errors found.

ACTIVITIES

a. Planning

Planning for inspections involves the following activities:

- Defining the stages or operations of the development process after which inspections will be performed, and defining the exit criteria for products that complete each stage

- Defining the inspection process, the roles of people, how many will be involved, and the training they will receive

- Correctly executing the inspection process.

b. Doing

The inspection process involves

- Preparing for an inspection by obtaining material to be inspected, arranging the availability of participants, assigning them roles, and training them

- Reviewing the material by the participants prior to the inspection meetings

- Finding defects in a disciplined way, without looking for solutions

- Verifying that all fixes have been made and that no new defects have been introduced.

The participants (usually three to six people) have the following roles:

- Author, who created the product, but is usually silent during the inspection

- Reader, who paraphrases the design or code (there may be more than one reader, but all must be familiar with the larger context of design or code being reviewed)

- Tester, who views the code from the testing viewpoint

- Moderator, who conducts the inspection, keeps the team working together using the inspection process, and records the results unless there is a recorder.

c.   Generating Actions

Following inspections, the inspection team or some other organization should see that the corrections are made, and that no new defects have been introduced. An analysis of the results of one or more inspections can reveal weaknesses in the development process, in the resources used for development, and in the products. Actions resulting from these analyses include

- Rejection of a product and rework so it meets inspection criteria

- Recommendations to improve training or tools to avoid recurring defects

- Changes to improve the inspection process.

RELATED TECHNIQUES

Complementary

a.   Testing

b.   Cause and Effect Analysis.

BIBLIOGRAPHY

[FAG79]   Fagan, M. E., 1979, "Design and Code Inspections to Reduce Errors in Program Development," *IBM Systems Journal*, No. 3, pp. 184-211.

[FAG86]   Fagan, M. E., July 1986, "Advances in Software Inspections," *IEEE Transactions on Software Engineering*, pp. 744-751.

[MAR90]   Martin, J., Tsai, W., February 1990, "N-Fold Inspection: A Requirements Analysis Technique," *Communications of the ACM*, pp. 225-232.

[RUSS91]   Russell, G.W., January 1991, "Experience with Inspection in Ultra-Large Scale Developments, " *IEEE Software*, pp. 25-29.

SECTION 6

PERFORMANCE ENGINEERING

Performance problems are often discovered late in the system development process and are often very expensive to correct. System performance involves an interaction between hardware and software running in a specified environment. The requirements for system performance are contained within the SSS. These are decomposed and allocated to the hardware and software elements of the system.

Performance engineering involves modeling the system and software to isolate those performance bottlenecks or load characteristics that can create problems during later stages of development. Prior to detailed design, analytical and computer-based models using the functional description of the system, as contained within the SSS and SRSs, are the basis for performance engineering. As the design evolves, the actual structure of the design is substituted for the functional representation, and actual measurement of execution time, overhead, and latency are made to update the model parameters.

Benchmarks of specific software modules are often used to compare or evaluate the effect of different design decisions. For example, benchmarks may be used to determine the relative performance of tasking in Ada and using processes in the operating system, or to compare the execution time for two different algorithms or two different communication protocols for accomplishing the same function. Benchmarks are also used to obtain reference points to scale an analytical or other computer-based model. Knowing the execution speed of a processor for a mix of instructions believed to be typical of the system's software is an important basis for performance estimates.

Performance engineering involves modeling, estimating, measuring, and predicting the following:

a. **Execution time**—the time it takes to perform a particular function. Execution time depends upon

- The algorithm being implemented

- The efficiency of the code generated by the compiler

- The operating system overhead

- The time absorbed by the library functions in the run time environment

- The amount of memory available for the programs and data, and the time for management of that memory.

131

b. **System response time or latency**—the time it takes the system to respond to a given input. The response may be indicated by a measurable output or a change in the state of the system. System response time is a function of

- Execution time for the sequence of software and hardware components (the threads) that are needed to respond to the given input

- The amount of time absorbed by other functions contending for system resources.

c. **Throughput**—a measure of the number of times or rate at which the system performs a set of functions. Throughput depends upon

- The frequency with which the various threads of the system are scheduled

- Other demands for system resources.

d. **Utilization**—the amount of each resource used under a specified load condition. There are three types of resources.

- **Computer Processing Unit (CPU)**—the processor capacity to perform more processing

- **Memory**—both the memory available for software and data while they are being used for execution of the software, and the secondary storage devices where they reside when not being directly accessed and used

- **Input/Output (I/O) bandwidth**—the capacity to transmit more information on buses and other communication lines within and among hardware components in the system, and communications lines entering and leaving the system.

Ultimately, one is interested in the reserve capacity of a system, which is a measure of the additional load the system can handle while still satisfying all of the system performance requirements. Reserve capacity is essential for future growth in functions and load on a system; utilization is related to reserve capacity. However, it is very difficult to measure reserve capacity since it depends on the specific nature of the load to be added. For example, even if a CPU has a measured utilization of 50 percent (the CPU is only operating 50 percent of the time over the scenario), there may not be sufficient reserve capacity to accommodate additional hard real-time functions.

Utilization is a function of

- The scenario or test system load specified for the system

- The performance of the various hardware elements

- The execution times of the various software elements involved in the threads used to process the scenario.

PURPOSE

a. During predevelopment, performance engineering provides a basis for establishing the system performance requirements and estimating the range of possible designs that could meet those performance requirements. This helps in determining the feasibility of performance requirements, and in evaluating offerors' proposals for technical approaches to meeting those requirements.

b. Performance engineering during development provides an early understanding of the performance issues and risks so that rational decisions can be made about the system architecture and the choices of hardware and software components.

c. Performance engineering provides early detection and correction of performance-related design problems.

APPLICATION

a. The Government must establish and state explicit performance requirements in the SSS. This involves a definition of the response times for various functions, and the load on the system that will be used to measure the throughput, utilization, and response time. Load times are usually expressed as scenarios of different kinds and amounts of inputs over a specified period of time. The Government must also specify the criteria by which the system will be evaluated against those performance requirements, i.e., what will be measured, how frequently, and how it will be scored.

b. Prior to development, performance engineering techniques such as analytical and computer modeling may be used by the Government or by contractors funded to perform studies to better understand performance risks, to determine that performance requirements are technically feasible, and to help in evaluating technical proposals during source selection.

c. Performance engineering techniques may be used by the developer and independently by the Government during the development phase to predict or detect potential performance problems prior to making critical hardware and software design decisions. Performance engineering is an important activity when the satisfaction of performance requirements is essential to the operation of the system, e.g., when the system interacts with or is even embedded in equipment that will not function properly unless processing times are met. These are "hard" or "real-time" performance requirements, with narrow tolerances.

d.   Performance engineering is used by the contractor to measure actual timing of the system and its components as a means to verify that requirements are satisfied and that the model is valid.

e.   The results of performance engineering activities are reviewed and evaluated at the following times:

   • During the generation of the SSS so appropriate system-level timing requirements may be established

   • When establishing the tasks within the Statement of Work (SOW) portion of the RFP so that performance risks may be reduced

   • At the System Design Review (SDR), SSR, PDR, and CDR. At these reviews, the results of performance modeling and benchmarking are presented

   • At PMRs, during test and integration, when actual performance measurements are presented and evaluated.

MAJOR ISSUES

a.   The Government must establish reasonable, technically feasible requirements, and state them clearly and completely.

The whole purpose of performance engineering is to meet Government-established performance requirements. To allow for future growth in system requirements, some performance requirements have been overstated, e.g., other systems that must provide the inputs could never meet the loads that have been levied as requirements for the system about to be developed. This makes unnecessary demands on a system developer and can increase the cost of system hardware as well as performance engineering activities and software development. The external work load and the range of variability must be specified in the SSS and reviewed as part of the RFP preparation and review process.

b.   Performance modeling and simulation can be costly and inaccurate.

Performance modeling itself can be an expensive activity if the model is very detailed. In some cases, an analytical model is sufficient to influence the design of a system. Other models are not only detailed and complex representations of the system under development, but they require exceedingly accurate data for their results to be accurate. One recent model for a system took 10 staff-years of effort to develop. Simulations can also take large computers and large amounts of computer time. The models themselves must be validated against some real data. As the system design evolves, the models may have to be reprogrammed to more accurately represent the system.

c.   Benchmark data do not necessarily scale up.

Benchmarks are often used to extrapolate the performance of a system by providing a reference point for a model. They are used to help select commercial-off-the-shelf (COTS) products such as compilers, operating systems, and database management systems, and to assist in making higher level decisions such as the hardware platform, the language to be used, and other characteristics of the hardware and software architecture.

Benchmarks are, by their very nature, a limited sample of the processing expected on a program. Since the number of variables affecting system performance is large and the number of sample points used in benchmarking often small, it can be difficult to deduce solid statistical facts. General conclusions based only upon benchmark data may be misleading. For example, a developer developed benchmarks with a standard mix of instructions to determine the speed of the processor as a basis for estimating performance of the system. When the system software was integrated, the processor speed, in millions of instructions per second, was one-fourth what the benchmark had shown, due to an entirely different mix of instructions in the actual application software. In another example, benchmarks to determine memory utilization were discovered to be far from the actual usage when the software was completed, and the decision to buy more hardware was difficult and expensive at that late stage because the computers were militarized. However, benchmarks do serve to point out the potential for performance problems or to serve as one of many inputs into the selection of COTS products and architectural design decisions. However, they should not be the only input to the decision-making process.

d.   The external work load must be modelled realistically.

A performance model generates performance data based upon its internal structure and a representation of the external environment. The external environment supplies the inputs used to drive the simulation of the system. It is very important that a realistic and controllable external work load be incorporated into the performance model before measurements of latency, throughput, and capacity are made. The ability to easily modify the external load strongly influences the ability of the model to contribute to answers of "what if" questions.

e.   The internal load must be modelled realistically.

The model must have representation of all of the system components that contribute significantly to the system performance. One source of performance problems is the operating system. A simplistic overhead of a flat percentage for the operating system has led to serious errors in both models and the consequent system design with serious performance shortfalls. If a multi-tasking environment is being modeled in one or more computers of the system, then the threads should not be measured in isolation. The significant threads that execute during a scenario should be activated to create realistic internal loads on the system. Other demands on the CPU, memory, and I/O resources need to be simulated to obtain realistic results.

MEASUREMENT AND EVALUATION CRITERIA

a.   To evaluate the performance of a system, measurements from both a model as well as the actual system should be employed. Prior to implementation, simulation and benchmark measurements can help to predict performance. Once an implementation is available, measurements should be made using the actual hardware and software, incorporating as many realistic internal and external loads as possible. Measurements performed on both the model and the real system include

   •   The execution time of the high frequency software elements

   •   The response time associated with threads selected because of their performance impact

   •   The throughput of the system employing a scenario consisting of multiple threads. Both nominal and worst case external and internal loads should be employed

   •   The reserve capacity of the system based upon throughput measurements and the individual thread measurements.

b.   The effectiveness of the performance engineering process itself can be judged by

   •   Evaluating and counting the number of performance problems discovered or prevented versus the cost of modeling and simulation

   •   Comparing the results of models with those obtained by running the actual system

   •   Comparing the results of different models (such as analytical and discrete event simulations) both as a means of calibrating them and to see which kinds of modeling are most cost-effective

   •   Determining the number of performance problems which were not detected by means of the performance engineering activities

- Comparing the cost of building a model or simulation to the validity of its predictions.

ACTIVITIES

a. Planning

- Define the performance engineering objectives. The objectives include specification of the system-level performance requirements to be incorporated into the SSS and the reduction of any risk associated with meeting the performance requirements.

- Define the external work load to be used as the basis for system and software performance evaluation and the measurement criteria.

- Define the tasks that the Government and the contractor are to perform to support the performance engineering objectives, and incorporate the developer's tasks into the SOW portion of the RFP package. These may include

  - Providing a model to predict performance

  - Providing the Government with timing and sizing reports

  - Providing the Government with the performance model, its assumptions, and the data necessary to run the model

  - Reporting the results of timing analyses at each PMR.

- Provide a budget for Government and contractor performance engineering activities.

- Integrate performance engineering activities into the overall program design and development schedule.

b. Doing

The developer should

- Define threads through the system

- Select tools and methods to apply

- Perform a quick analytical queuing model to identify potential bottlenecks

- Build a simple functional model incorporating the key threads that involve hardware and software elements

- Build an external environment generator

- Estimate and measure the building blocks of the system model

    - Similar applications and similar architectures may be used for comparative estimates

    - Benchmarks may be used to measure operating system and application-level primitive functions

- Run the functional model to establish functional performance goals

- As the design develops, substitute the hardware and software design elements for the functional elements; this may require a reorganization of the model

- Run the model and isolate potential problems

- Report performance problems to management by means of timing and sizing reports and at the PMR presentations

- Measure the timing of completed software elements and incorporate them into the model.

c.   Generating Actions

- Limit the use of features of the compiler, operating system (OS), and hardware facilities that absorb a lot of time.

- Change the compiler, hardware architecture (including processors, disks, and local area networks (LANs)), and the software architecture.

- Modify the performance requirements contained within the SSS and/or the budgets contained within the SRSs. This includes changes to allocations of functionality to architectural elements.

- Modify the design and algorithms to optimize performance.

RELATED TECHNIQUES

Complementary

a   RFP Preparation and Review

b.   Government Reviews

c.   Prototyping.

BIBLIOGRAPHY

[CLA89]   Clapp, J. A., October 1989, *A Case Study in Performance Engineering for Real-Time Systems*, M89-66, The MITRE Corporation, Bedford, MA.

[JAI91]   Jain, R., 1991, *The Art of Computer System Performance Analysis*, John Wiley.

[SMI90]   Smith, C., 1990, *Performance Engineering of Software Systems*, Addison Wesley.

SECTION 7

PROTOTYPING

Prototyping is a process of carrying out some small subset of a software development to learn more about technical risks, alternative technical solutions, and their costs and benefits. The subset may be limited to requirements analysis, user interface design, algorithm design, or use of a new software development environment or methodology. Some prototypes can be extensive enough to be working systems or subsystems with limited capability or capacity, used to test operational concepts or interfaces with other systems. For example, a prototype may be a mockup of user display screens to convey the format or capabilities of a proposed system. An engineering prototype may be the actual code needed for a communications protocol between two systems, to see if the existing system and the new system will be able to communicate and meet the required traffic load.

Most prototypes are detailed in the areas under investigation, and simplify or neglect other aspects of the final system. For example, "quick and dirty" prototypes do not have the quality that is desirable in operational software. If all that the prototypes demonstrates is screen formats, it may not even use the same programming language or environment as the actual system. For this reason, some prototypes are throwaways. Once they have provided the information needed to make a decision, the information and not the prototype is preserved. Other prototypes are software implementations that actually may be used as part of the delivered operational system.

PURPOSE

Most prototyping activities are to learn something to avoid early in a development or to control the risk of problems later in development.

a. During predevelopment, prototyping contributes to the operational concept for the system and the system-level requirements by providing examples of an executable model of the system, user interfaces, and interactions with the external environment.

b. During development, prototyping helps to define software requirements and refine system-level requirements.

c. Prototyping provides a preventive approach toward design since many of the problems associated with the interactions between the hardware, system software, COTS, reused software, and application software may be better understood prior to a firm commitment to the design and integration approach through selective implementations.

140

d. Prototyping provides a demonstration of the user interface to communicate with users and obtain early approval that the format, content, and mode of interaction will be satisfactory, thus eliminating the cost and schedule impact of rework.

e. Prototype implementation of critical algorithms can show the speed or accuracy that can be achieved as an input to decisions about detailed design.

f. A prototype can be used to understand and experiment with new technology and/or a new software development process prior to commitment to its use for the system.

g   Prototyping the performance aspects of a system is such an important topic to large real-time systems that it is covered separately under performance engineering.

APPLICATION

a. Prototyping techniques may be used by the Government in phases prior to development, such as concept/validation and demonstration/validation, to help establish the operational concept for the system, establish system-level requirements, assess technology, obtain concurrence from users on the user system interface, and assist in understanding the cost implication of various high-level requirements and design decisions.

b. The Government may ask the contractor to demonstrate the development process by performing a Software Engineering Exercise (SEE) or immediately after contract award by performing a Software Engineering Prototype (SEP). Both the SEE and SEP are prototype uses of the software development process and tools by a potential or selected developer team.

c. Prototyping may be used by the developer and the Government to refine requirements and the user system interface during development.

d. Prototyping may be used by the developer during the early stages of development as input to design decisions. Benchmarks, for example, can be prototypes of time-critical functions rather than synthetic workloads.

MAJOR ISSUES

a. Level of detail

The rapidity with which the prototype can be defined, implemented, and the results analyzed greatly influences its usefulness. A prototype must, by definition, emphasize certain aspects of a problem and ignore others. If the prototype is too extensive, it may take as long to implement as the system itself.

If the prototype is too superficial, it may not discover or solve significant requirements, design, or process problems. For example, showing a user a set of screens with sample data will not address whether it is possible to obtain the data on the screen within a reasonable response time.

To establish the level of detail of the prototype, the objectives or the problem being investigated must be clearly stated. These objectives are determined by the risks addressed by the prototype. For example, risks associated with a large number of diverse users may imply that a prototype of the user system interface be developed which emphasizes the interaction between the user and the system. It is better for the problems to surface at the beginning of a program and obtain concurrence with the user rather than wait for an implementation to find out that the user is not satisfied. Then, all factors that might contribute to meeting that objective must be accounted for in the scope of the prototype.

b.   Quality characteristics of the prototype

There is a trade-off between development speed and quality. The more stringent the quality requirements for the prototype, the longer the prototype development will usually take. The degree to which quality requirements are imposed on the prototype depends upon whether the prototype will be thrown away or whether it is planned to be used throughout the development or even incorporated into the final system. A prototype used to demonstrate a user interface may not have to be designed with high reliability if it is only going to be used once. On the other hand, if algorithm correctness or accuracy is an issue, the prototype should include all of the options that may occur in the use of that algorithm, or their effect should be well-understood before they are omitted.

c.   Throwaway versus retained

Some people view prototypes as implementations that avoid the rigor of a formal development and provide quick response to an operational need. However, many a so-called prototype has been fielded and put into long-term use. As long as the risks associated with this approach are recognized, the approach will be useful. Most of the risk lies in supporting and modifying the system, and in its reliability. In those cases that are most successful, the prototype provides a lesser capability than had been planned, but has acceptable quality. The prototype, available at a much earlier date than the full system, meets so many needs of the users that they cannot relinquish its use.

MEASUREMENT AND EVALUATION CRITERIA

a.   Since prototypes are developed to gain information, they should include measurements that provide that information. The measurements and evaluation criteria are associated with a prototype.

b. To judge the effectiveness of the prototyping process itself

- Count the number of problems discovered and corrected as a result of the prototyping process, e.g., the number of user comments received on a demonstration or working prototype, and the number of changes resulting in the requirements or design of the system or software.

- Determine and count the number of requirements, design, and software process risks and problems not addressed, but which could have been addressed by a prototyping effort.

- Determine the cost to implement a prototype and compare with the estimated or known costs of changing software later in the development if the prototyping had not occurred.

- Measure the delay to the program due to the prototype development versus the estimated delay if issues addressed by the prototype were not examined until later in the development.

ACTIVITIES

a. Planning

- Establish the prototyping objectives by defining the risks to be addressed by the prototyping activities, and what will be learned from the prototype.

- Define the tasks that the Government and the contractor are to perform to support the prototyping objectives. Incorporate the developer's task into the SOW portion of the RFP package. For instance, these may include

  - Providing a user system interface prototype

  - Providing a prototype of the critical algorithms to be implemented

  - Reporting the results of the prototyping effort at each PMR.

- Define the functional and quality requirements to be satisfied by each prototype.

- Define the level or degree of implementation of each prototype, including programming standards, documentation requirements, scope of the functionality, and review and approval required by the Government.

- Provide a budget for Government and contractor prototyping activities.

      •   Integrate prototyping activities into the overall program schedule.

b.   Doing

      •   Select tools and methods to implement the prototype.

      •   Build the prototype.

      •   Execute and evaluate the prototype results.

      •   Interact with the user, if necessary.

c.   Generating Actions

      •   Modify system or software requirements.

      •   Determine or modify design approaches.

      •   Modify the software development process.

      •   Modify the details of the algorithms to implement.

      •   Accept or reject the incorporation of new tools and approaches for incorporation into the software development process.

RELATED TECHNIQUES

a.   Complementary—Government Reviews

b.   Redundant

The following techniques are partially redundant, because they are equivalent to specific kinds of prototypes:

      •   Performance Engineering

      •   SEE

      •   SEP.

BIBLIOGRAPHY

[CLA87]   Clapp, J., 1987, "Rapid Prototyping for Risk Management," *Proceedings of COMPSAC87*, IEEE Computer Society Press.

SECTION 8

RELIABILITY MODELING

Software reliability modeling allows the prediction of the reliability growth of software as it progresses through integration and acceptance testing.

The quantification of software reliability requirements may be approached from both the user's and the developer's point of view. From the user's perspective, reliability is the probability that the software will perform according to its requirements in the user's environment for a given period of time. This definition of software reliability implies that software cannot fail unless it is executing.

On the other hand, a developer is concerned about avoiding defects in the code. The developer does not want to make mistakes or misinterpret requirements. A defect is a characteristic of the code that exists whether or not the software is executing, and may cause a failure when the program executes. Clearly, if the number of defects in the code is reduced, the reliability of the software is increased.

These two concepts, defect and failure, have led to two distinct approaches toward the definition, measurement, and verification of software reliability requirements.

a. The Rome Laboratory Software Quality Framework (RSQF) defines the measure of the reliability quality factor from the developer's perspective, in terms of defect density, that is, software defects per thousand source lines of code (KSLOC).

    This definition leads to a requirement that software be delivered with less than a specified level of defects per KSLOC. To verify that this requirement is satisfied may be difficult, since one has to estimate the number of defects remaining undetected in the code after some amount of testing has uncovered known errors. SAIC, under contract to Rome Laboratory, has developed a technique that enables one to estimate the initial defect density (prior to testing) in terms of selected characteristics of the application, the development environment, and the software itself [MCC87]. This initial estimate is then used to estimate the number of defects remaining in the software as errors are detected.

b. Software reliability modeling stems from an analogy with hardware engineering that measures "failure intensity," that is, the failure rate as a function of execution time.

    One of the first software reliability models was formulated by Jelinski and Moranda in 1972 [JEL72], who made the assumption that software behaves in much the same way as hardware, but with the failure rate decreasing as defects are detected and corrected. In 1975, John Musa [MUS75] modified this concept in two obvious but significant ways.

145

- He pointed out that the time variable in the Jelinski-Moranda model should be execution time (roughly equivalent to CPU time) and not "wall clock" time, since software can only fail while it is executing.

- He pointed out that the failure intensity of the software depends upon the environment in which the software executes because the frequency of execution of the various software functions depends upon the operational environment.

Under appropriate assumptions one could deduce a failure intensity from a defect density. For example, if we assume the following:

a.   Each defect results in a single failure.

b.   The rate at which SLOC are executed can be determined and is a constant.

c.   All SLOC are executed with equal probability.

Then the failure intensity, λ, can be expressed in terms of the defect density, D, and the execution rate of the machine upon which the software runs, E, as

$\lambda = DE$, where

λ = failure intensity = defects per unit time.

D = defects per KSLOC. This quantity would be expected to decrease with time as the software matures and defects are detected and corrected.

E = number of KSLOC executed per unit time.

Both defects and failures are important views of software reliability, and both have their benefits and shortcomings. The goal of all software reliability models is to use failure data obtained during software test and operation to estimate future behavior. The failure time data are used to estimate the parameters of the failure intensity, which in turn are used to statistically predict the future failure characteristics of the software. Software reliability models can provide insight into the amount of additional testing that must be performed to achieve a given level of reliability.

The basic definitions and relationships involved in all the reliability models are described below.

a.   T = the time interval over which the reliability is measured. If the system is designed to perform its mission over a specific time span, T may be the mission time.

b. $\lambda(T)$ = failure intensity. This is, in general, a time-varying function.

c.   R(T) = reliability = probability that the software will not fail in the time interval from 0 to T.

$$R(T) = e^{- \int_0^T \lambda(t) \, dt}$$

d.   F(T) = 1–R(T) = probability that the software will fail in the time interval from 0 to T.

e.   MTBF = mean time between failures. If λ is a constant, then the MTBF is a constant, $1/\lambda$. However, if the failure intensity, λ, decreases with time, as is the case with reliability modeling, then MTBF is not a constant, and is a function of T.

The differences in the various reliability models are found in the different formulations of the failure intensity function.

a.   Exponential $\lambda(t) = a \, e^{-bt}$

b.   Weibull $\lambda(t) = a \, t^{-c} e^{-bt}$

c.   Pareto $\lambda(t) = a \, (b+t)^{-c}$

d.   Gamma $\lambda(t) = a \, t \, e^{-bt}$.

Each of these failure intensity models is determined by a finite set of constant parameters (a,b,c). Reliability modeling uses the failure time data to estimate these parameters and then uses the failure intensity to determine the reliability, the MTBF, or any other statistic that is appropriate for determining the reliability of the software. A comprehensive description of many of these failure intensity formulations may be found in Musa's book, *Software Reliability* [MUS87], and in an article by Littlewood in the *Software Reliability Handbook* [LIT90a].

PURPOSE

a.   To determine the additional time to allocate to system-level testing and evaluation

b.   To determine the additional testing and computing resources needed for reliability growth

c.   To determine the probability of achieving a given system and software reliability and/or availability requirement.

APPLICATION

Reliability modeling is applied by the developer during integration testing. The results of reliability modeling and data gathering can be reported at the PMRs or at regular intervals.

MAJOR ISSUES

a.   Measuring the CPU hours between failures

The time at which a failure is noticed is often reported as part of the SPR. However, the amount of time the software has been running is seldom recorded. The system or software needs to be instrumented to record actual running time, or a special manual process is needed to change the normally reported "wall clock" time to CPU or execution time.

b.   Defining and maintaining the operational environment

Reliability modeling assumes that the software is executing in the same operational environment or on a standard load that is representative of that environment. In many situations the software possesses different modes of operation that may imply multiple operational environments. The operational environment may also change as the system progresses from one test phase to another. Incremental deliveries of software also change the operational environment, since new and modified functional capabilities must be tested with new tests.

c.   Validating software failure data

Not all software failures are of equal significance. Each failure report must be reviewed to determine whether or not it is to be counted in the reliability modeling effort. If the reliability requirement is phrased in terms of critical failure intensity, each failure must be reviewed to determine whether it is critical and should be incorporated into the failure intensity calculation.

Complications are introduced into the application of reliability modeling when multiple test stations or multiple field installations exist, since each may report a failure at different times caused by the same defect, or each may report different manifestations of the same failure.

d.   Selecting the appropriate reliability model

Many software reliability models exist [LIT90a]. They are differentiated by the form of the failure intensity. Multiple models may be used at the beginning of the reliability modeling process. Eventually, one must be selected and used for predictive purposes.

MEASUREMENT AND EVALUATION CRITERIA

a.   To establish the reliability prediction model, the failure intensity must be determined from measurements of the CPU time between software failures.

b.   To judge the ability of the model to predict reliability growth, a control chart should be developed in which the model prediction error is plotted as a percent deviation from actual. The data can be used to calibrate the model.

ACTIVITIES

a.   Planning

-    Formulate the reliability requirements in terms of a level of failure intensity to be obtained.

-    Define the methods to gather, validate, and analyze failure data.

-    Define the operational environment(s).

-    Select one or more reliability models.

b.   Doing

-    Failure time data is gathered as part of the normal test and integration process, and documented as part of the SPR process.

-    Each SPR is evaluated to determine whether and how the data will be used based upon the severity of the failure.

-    The failure data is entered into an appropriate database and maintained.

-    The reliability models are updated. The parameters of the various failure intensity models are reestimated, and the failure intensity is extrapolated to determine when testing or evaluation will be completed.

- The actual failure intensity measurements are determined and plotted for presentation.

c.   Generating actions

- Revise the test and integration schedule.

- Allocate additional resources (personnel and facilities) to the test and integration process.

- Accelerate the informal CM process and the defect correction process.

- Select a single reliability model.

- Terminate the reliability modeling process.

RELATED TECHNIQUES

Complementary

a.   SPR data gathering and analysis

b.   Testing.

BIBLIOGRAPHY

[JEL72]   Jelinski, Z., and P. B. Moranda, 1972, "Software Reliability Research," in *Statistical Computer Performance Evaluation*, edited by W. Freiberger, New York: Academic Press.

[LIT90a]   Littlewood, B., 1990, "Software Reliability Growth Models," in *Software Reliability Handbook*, edited by P. Rook, London and New York: Elsevier Applied Science.

[LIT90b]   Littlewood, B., 1990, "Modelling Growth in Software Reliability," in *Software Reliability Handbook*, edited by P. Rook, London and New York: Elsevier Applied Science.

[MCC87]   McCall, J., et al., 1987, *Methodology for Software Reliability Prediction*, RADC-TR-87-171, Rome Air Development Center, Griffiss Air Force Base, Rome, NY.

[MUS75]   Musa, J., 1975, "A Theory of Software Reliability and its Application," *IEEE Transactions on Software Engineering*, Vol. SE-1, No.3, pp. 312-327.

[MUS87]   Musa, J., et al., 1987, *Software Reliability—Measurement, Prediction, Application*, New York: McGraw-Hill Book Company.

[MUS87]   Musa, J. et al., 1987, *Software Reliability—Measurement, Prediction, Application*, New York: McGraw-Hill Book Company.

SECTION 9

REQUIREMENTS TRACEABILITY

System development begins with a specification of the functional and other system requirements, documented in the SSS. Regardless of the methodology employed, the responsibility for satisfying user requirements is eventually allocated to the various hardware and software components. Those requirements allocated to the software are further allocated to CSCIs, Computer Software Components (CSCs), and to Computer Software Units (CSUs).

For complex systems with many requirements, it is possible that some system-level requirements will be overlooked in the allocation process, and functions that are not requirements may be implemented. To reduce this possibility and to ensure that all requirements are addressed in the design and the test planning, a Requirements Traceability Matrix (RTM) is required by DOD STD-2167A and the Data Item Descriptions (DIDs) associated with it. The RTM may actually be a series of tables or graphical representations that show the association between system-level requirements and the Hardware Configuration Items (HWCIs) and CSCIs that implement them. As the design is completed, the traceability is extended to the CSCs and CSUs and from them back to the SRSs and IRSs. That association is bi-directional, i.e., from an SSS requirement to all the hardware and software components that implement it, and from each component to the system-level requirement it implements.

The information needed for an RTM becomes available as the system is designed. Therefore, it is documented at different points in the development process. The requirements traceability documentation should eventually contain the following kinds of information:

a.   For each system-level requirement contained in the SSS and ICD

   •   Paragraph number and unique requirement identification within the SSS and ICDs

   •   Description of the requirement

   •   Reference to the paragraph(s) in B-level documentation that implement this requirement.

b.   For all B-level (B1, B2, B5, SRS, IRS) requirements

   •   Paragraph number and unique requirement identification within the B-level documentation

   •   Description of the requirement

- Paragraph number and unique requirement identification within the SSS that this requirement implements

- Any B-level requirement not traceable to an A-level requirement should be designated as a derived requirement, and a rationale for its incorporation into the specification should be available.

c. Test information

- Test procedure identifier

- High-level description of the test procedure

- Identification of the B-level requirement it tests

- Traceability to special test requirements, if applicable.

PURPOSE

The requirements traceability documentation assures that software quality is being achieved by the system design, and assists in the planning of testing. The RTM allows assessment of quality criteria specified in the RSQF, as shown below.

a. Assess completeness of the software design.

b. Assess consistency of the software design.

c. Demonstrate traceability of the software design.

d. Ensure completeness of software test plans.

e. Assess the maintainability of the software by showing how localized or dispersed the implementation of a requirement is within the software components.

f. Assist in analyzing the effect of requirements changes upon the software design and test procedures.

APPLICATION

Information on requirements traceability is derived at many stages in the design of a system. The System Design Document contains an RTM for both HWCIs and CSCIs.

These data form the basis for generation of the individual RTMs associated with each CSCI documented within its SRS.

The RTMs in the SRSs are usually reviewed as part of the SSR. Test planning usually occurs between SSR and PDR. During this time, the information that relates test procedures and software requirements is generated. The high-level design is also formulated and the traceability between the software requirements and the high-level software design elements may be determined. Both of these levels of traceability are reviewed at PDR.

After PDR, the detailed design is produced. During this process, the traceability between the software requirements (and possibly their decomposition) and the CSUs is determined. The Software Design Document for a CSCI documents the traceability of requirements between the SRS and IRS and the CSU level of each CSC. This final level of traceability is reviewed at CDR.

While the developer is responsible for producing RTMs, an IV&V organization may also develop requirements traceability documentation as part of its independent review.

MAJOR ISSUES

a.   Depth of traceability

The effort applied to the traceability process can be tailored from program to program in the following ways:

- The level of design for which traceability is documented

    - The system specification requirements may be traced only to hardware and software or to individual HWCIs and CSCIs.

    - The CSCI requirements (contained within the SRS) may be traced further to high-level CSCs or to all the CSCs.

    - The CSC requirements may be further decomposed and traced to individual CSUs.

    - The CSCI requirements may be traced to only high-level test areas or they may be traced to individual test procedures.

- The precision with which requirements are traced

    - System-level functions or capabilities may be traced to hardware or software functions or capabilities.

- Each individual system-level requirement may be decomposed and traced to individual software requirements.

- System-level requirements may be traced to test threads that exercise a partially integrated hardware and software system.

Tailoring can be based upon the importance of specific requirements to mission success or the risk associated with those requirements.

b.   Automation

A database tool can greatly enhance the efficiency of generating and maintaining RTMs. A manual system is very prone to error especially when requirements, test procedures, and design are in the formative stages. An automated system will automatically check for internal consistency of the data, and simple sorting will show which requirements have not been traced. Once initialized, an automated database used by a requirements traceability tool is very easy to maintain.

The essential characteristics of such a tool include

- Ability to sort requirements by ID

- Ability to produce a traceability from the A-level specification to each individual B-level specification requirement

- Ability to produce a consolidated traceability of all A-level requirements

- Ability to trace each B-level requirement to one or more A-level requirements

- Ability to trace each B-level requirement to individual software elements

- Ability to reconstruct the decomposition of requirements

- Ability to trace each B-level requirement or set of requirements to specific test procedures

- Ability to sort the test procedures by the B-level requirement ID.

MEASUREMENT AND EVALUATION CRITERIA

a.   The content of the RTMs may be used to judge completeness of the evolving design and test process. The following measures may be employed at the appropriate points within the program:

- The percentage of SSS requirements traceable to HWCIs, CSCIs, user interface, and ICDs

- The percentage of SRS and IRS requirements traceable to verification or test procedures

- The percentage of SRS and IRS requirements traceable to CSCs and CSUs.

b. To evaluate the effectiveness of the application of RTMs, the following measures may be incorporated into the program:

- The cost or effort expended in generating and maintaining the RTMs

- The number and percentage of requirements determined to be nontraceable as a result of the RTM process. This includes SRS requirements not traceable to test cases, SSS requirements not traceable to SRSs, and SRS requirements not traceable to the software design elements.

ACTIVITIES

a. Planning

During predevelopment, the Government must establish the traceability requirements to be imposed upon the contractor. This is accomplished by tailoring DOD-STD-2167A and its DIDs in the following ways:

- Determine the degree to which traceability is to be performed. This includes the depth to which SRS requirements are to be traced into the design as well as the depth to which SRS requirements are to be traced into the testing process.

- Determine the form and mechanism by which traceability is to be presented to the Government.

- Determine if an automated database is required to maintain the traceability information, whether the Government is to have access, and how the access is to be obtained.

- Incorporate appropriate words into the RFP package to indicate the developer's responsibility.

- During source selection, the Government should determine if the developer understands the traceability requirements, has the appropriate mechanisms and tools in place, and will provide the appropriate training to personnel.

b. Doing

- During system requirements analysis, the developer must allocate the decomposed system-level requirements to the various HWCIs and CSCIs.

- During system requirements analysis, software requirements analysis, and software design, requirements traceability information must be generated for each CSCI in accordance with Government traceability requirements.

- As the development proceeds and the requirements and design change, the RTMs must be maintained in a timely fashion.

c. Generating Actions

As a result of generating and analyzing the RTM, the following actions may be taken:

- Defects in the RTMs must be corrected.

- The initial traceability from the SSS may indicate that the allocation of requirements between HWCIs and CSCIs must change.

- The results of traceability to software design elements may indicate that the design must be modified and extended.

- The results of traceability to the test cases may reveal the need to redefine the test cases or to incorporate additional ones into the test plan.

RELATED TECHNIQUES

Complementary

a. Requirements Verification Matrix

b. Government Reviews

c. Software Quality Assurance

d. IV&V.

SECTION 10

RFP PREPARATION AND REVIEW

The RFP package is a solicitation, offer, and award package that provides the basis for the competitive procurement of a system. The RFP contains a number of sections which are of particular relevance to the software aspect of a procurement.

a. Section B—Suppliers or Services and Prices/Cost—contains the Contract Line Item Numbers (CLINs) and the descriptions for the basic contract and the options that may be purchased by the Government.

b. Section C—Description/Specifications/Work Statement—either contains or references the SOW, the technical requirements (often contained in the SSS), and the Contract Data Requirement List (CDRL).

c. Section F—Delivery and Performance—contains the schedule for delivery of each CLIN.

d. Section L—Instructions, Conditions, and Notices to Offerors—contains the Instructions for Preparation Proposal Preparation (IFPP).

e. Section M—Evaluation Factors for Award—contains general and specific criteria for award in technical, management, and cost areas.

The quality of the content of these sections of the RFP often establishes the success or failure of a subsequent software-intensive project. Therefore, a review of the software aspects of the RFP is included as an important quality control technique.

PURPOSE

The purpose of the RFP review is to

a. Evaluate the software aspects of the RFP package

b. Reduce the propagation of defects, within section C of the RFP or in the referenced SSS and SOW, which can lead to confusion and to expensive rework in the future

c. Clarify section L and M of the RFP which provide a basis for evaluation of an offeror's proposal

d. Ensure that the requirements and schedule are feasible.

158

APPLICATION

The RFP review is conducted by the Government during the predevelopment phase of a program. Reviews should be done well in advance of issuing a draft RFP and after each major revision. Some feedback may come from potential offerors who review the draft RFP.

MAJOR ISSUES

a. A review of the software aspects of the RFP needs to be performed early in its development to allow time to make changes to improve it.

b. The RFP is a reflection of the procurement agency's interpretation of the user requirements. The program office is limited in the amount of discretion that it may exercise in the establishment of the requirements or the delivery schedule.

  • The reviewers must identify technical and schedule risks even if they cannot be changed by the program office. It is possible to require additional information from offerors, e.g., an SEE, or additional tasks, such as prototyping, to control those risks.

c. Because of potential software risks, reviewers familiar with software acquisition and technical issues should be used early in the formulation of the RFP and the associated acquisition strategy.

MEASUREMENT AND EVALUATION CRITERIA

The review of the major software-related portions of the RFP should be made using a standard set of checklists such as the following list, tailored and augmented to address particular issues in a program.

a. Technical requirements or SSS checklist

   The SSS provides the documentation of the requirements that the system must satisfy. It should be evaluated for the following:

   • **Non-ambiguous**: Every requirement or group of requirements (capability or function) must have only one interpretation.

   • **Unique Identification**: Each requirement and each group of requirements (capability or function) must be individually and uniquely identified. Conventionally, each requirement is indicated by the word "shall."

- **Correct:** Each requirement should be correctly stated. An error in the specification will be costly to correct after the contract is awarded.

- **Complete:** All essential requirements need to be included. Special attention should be paid to quantitative performance requirements.

- **Necessary:** The specification should not require unnecessary capabilities unless the user has agreed to accept the additional cost.

- **Feasible:** A judgment must be made whether the requirement or group of requirements can be implemented in a timely, cost-effective manner. If it is judged that some requirements are not feasible, they should be removed.

- **Verifiable:** Each requirement or set of requirements needs to be verified by test, inspection, analysis, or demonstration. Vague words such as "minimize" or "reasonable" may be appropriate as guidance but should not be used within requirements statements, since there is no way to verify that those kinds of requirements have been met.

- **Reference consistency:** Unique and identifiable names must be employed when referencing external interface data. The use of different names for the same item of information or the use of the same name for multiple pieces of data may lead to errors in the interpretation of the requirements and the system that is implemented.

- **Requirements consistency:** The individual requirements stated in the SSS must not conflict with one another.

- **Quality requirements:** Any performance, design, or adaptation quality factor requirements need to be formulated in a verifiable fashion.

- **Timing and sizing requirements:** In specifying a real-time command and control system, one needs to explicitly specify the sizing and timing requirements of the system and the conditions under which they will be verified. If they are not specified, they may not be delivered.

- **Special Test Requirements:** Any requirements to perform specific tests under specified loads or scenarios with specified test equipment must be stated. These special test requirements are not meant to be the test plan; they represent requirements that the test plan must satisfy.

- **Human Interface Requirements:** The human interface requirements must be clearly stated.

b.   SOW and CDRL checklist

The SOW describes the activities and the CDRL the deliverable products to be produced during the execution of the project. They should be reviewed for

- **Development Activities:** The SOW should be reviewed to verify that all the activities deemed necessary to be performed by the contractor are described. Government standards, such as DOD-STD-2167A, can provide a basis for appropriate constraint. These standards are understood by both the Government and the offerors and impose a degree of consistency in the development and documentation of the software.

- **Deliverable Products:** Each of the required deliverable products appears in the CDRL. This list should be reviewed for completeness and consistency with the SOW. Every product should require a task to generate it. If the product is not in the CDRL, it does not have to be delivered.

- **Formal Government Reviews and Audits:** The formal Government reviews and audits, specified within the SOW, need to be reviewed for content and schedule. The content of these reviews is often selected as a subset of MIL-STD-1521B and modified appropriately during the contract on the basis of PMRs.

- **Quality Control Activities:** The SOW should describe the quality control activities required to be performed during the course of the program. They may include those described within this document or those specifically formulated for the program by the developer. These quality control activities should be reviewed for their applicability, cost, the measurements to be taken, the method of analysis and presentation, and reports to be generated. The quality control techniques specified must be consistent with the type of contract issued.

c.   Schedule evaluation checklist

The elements of the program schedule are contained within a number of portions of the RFP including the CDRL and section F, and are sometimes detailed within the SOW.

- The schedule for all activities and products needs to be clearly described within the RFP.

- The reasonableness of the schedule needs to be evaluated based upon the size and difficulty of the development.

d.   Sections L and M Checklist

These sections of the RFP describe to the offerors the information required within the proposal, and the criteria against which the contract is to be awarded. Section L is usually referred to as the IFPP. If the proper information is not requested from the offerors in the IFPP, then it will be very difficult to make a sound determination during the source selection process. The content of these sections of the RFP is dependent on the type of contract. A fixed-price contract would tend to focus on cost. A cost plus fee contract for a large software development should, as a minimum, request the offeror to provide a description of

- **The technical approach to the problem:** This should describe the major technical issues that need to be resolved and the way in which the contractor proposes to address these issues.

- **The software development approach:** This should describe the proposed software development methodology, the tools to be used in support of the methodology, and the experience of the company and personnel in applying the tools to the methodology.

- **Risk management:** The contractor should be asked to identify the current program risks, their priority, and the proposed method to resolve them. The contractor should also be asked to describe the mechanisms that will be used to continue to identify and resolve risks.

- **The quality control techniques:** The contractor should describe the quality control techniques that will be used, when they will be used, and the specifics about how they are going to be applied.

RFP REVIEW ACTIVITIES

a.   Planning

The plan to review the system and software aspects of the RFP package should be established prior to development of the RFP package itself. The main part of the planning process involves the generation of checklists for review of the major sections of the RFP, as previously described. The plan should prioritize the various evaluations described in this guide and indicate the degree to which each evaluation will be performed; this may range from a complete detailed analysis to a spot check.

b. Selecting the review team

The review team should be independent of the personnel involved in the generation of the RFP package. It should contain personnel with expertise in both the contractual and technical aspects of the RFP.

c. Doing

The review should follow the checklists. In addition, the parts of the RFP must be checked with each other for consistency, so that the work to be done and the products to be generated are consistent with the requirements and the deliverable products, and so the information supplied by the offerors is complete enough to make the evaluations defined in the RFP.

d. Generating Actions

On the basis of the review, a series of actions may be generated. These may include

•   Revising requirements (part of section C or the SSS)

•   Revising the acquisition strategy

•   Revising parts of the RFP

•   Revising the schedule

•   Changing the type of contract because of the perceived uncertainty or risks

•   Recommending that the RFP package be released.

RELATED TECHNIQUES

None

SECTION 11

SEI SOFTWARE CAPABILITY EVALUATION

The Software Engineering Institute (SEI) has defined a procedure to assess the ability of an organization to control and improve its software development process, and its capability to use modern software engineering technology [HUM87]. It was developed by the SEI to provide objective and consistent assessments of different organizations during a source selection and within the same organization at different times to measure improvement.

The Software Capability Evaluation (SCE) is one form of that procedure to use during source selection. We will use the term SCE to include all uses of the SEI procedure to assess the capability of an organization.

The SEI is revising the SCE. This description is based on the current status. Those who plan to use it should consult the SEI for updates.

The SCE consists of a questionnaire and procedures to validate the responses and produce a score. The questionnaire is publicly available. There are about 100 questions which are answered "yes" or "no." They cover three areas of the developer's procedures.

a. Organization and resource management

b. Software engineering process and its management

c. Tools and technology.

A trained team conducts an on-site visit to the organization to make sure that the questions were understood, and to verify the answers by interviewing people, reviewing products, and seeing demonstrations from several projects.

The final score resulting from an analysis of the answers to the questionnaire is the level of maturity of the developer's software process. It is based on a capability maturity model that has five levels of process maturity [HUM89]. They are

a. Level 1 (Initial): There is no consistency in the developer's software development process. There will likely be cost, schedule, and quality problems. The results are dependent on the skills of the specific people who are involved.

b. Level 2 (Repeatable): The organization has standard practices for managing its activities including cost estimating, scheduling, requirements changes, code changes, and status review.

c. Level 3 (Defined): At this level, the organization has increased focus on software engineering. It has software engineering standards and methods. It holds design and code reviews. There are training programs for programmers and review leaders. An important qualification at this level is to have a software engineering process group that focuses on evaluating the process.

d. Level 4 (Managed): The software engineering process is reasonably well-controlled at this level. Data are gathered and used to make decisions. Projections, such as the expected rate of errors, can be made with reasonable accuracy. Tools are used to support the design process.

e. Level 5 (Optimized): This level is characterized by a high degree of control over the process and the ability to improve and optimize it by analysis of data to find the causes of problems.

PURPOSE

The primary purpose of an SCE is to help in the selection of a developer who is likely to perform software development within the estimated cost and schedule, and deliver a product with required capabilities and quality. Its proposed use in source selection has motivated developers who compete for Government software developments to improve their capabilities. The results of assessments using the SCE can allow the Government to learn what level of capability is realistic to expect or require from industry.

When used as an assessment of the maturity of a developer's process of software development, the SCE can show where improvements are needed in a developer's software engineering and management processes.

APPLICATION

a. The SCE can be used by the Government to assess an offeror's software development process as part of source selection. It can indicate to the program office whether an offeror has an acceptable level of software engineering technical and management capability.

b. The SCE can be used by the Government during a development to assess a developer's weaknesses, and help find causes of software development problems.

c. The SCE can be used by the Government to evaluate the improvement in a development process during a long development. In this case, the contract might contain terms to assure that improvements are made in the deficient areas. Incentives might be tied to the achievement of improvements.

d. The SCE can be used by a developer at any time to assess its own strengths and weaknesses and to measure its progress.

An example of how an organization has moved from level 2 to level 3 is in [HUM91].

MAJOR ISSUES

These issues relate to the current version of the SCE. Proposed revisions aim to correct some of these problems.

a.   Five levels is a coarse quantification of the general capabilities of an organization. It may not truly represent the suitability of a developer to perform the work for a specific program.

The level alone should not be used as a disqualifier of an offeror. The responses to individual questions can be a better indicator of risk areas than an offeror's capabilities.

b.   The SCE evaluates a general set of capabilities, not the specific capabilities that may be required for a program.

The SCE does not address all of the capabilities of an organization and its staff that may be important for a specific program. For example, it does not ascertain that the people in the organization are familiar with the application and have built similar systems before, or that they are familiar with specific technology needed by the program. It should be supplemented with this and other information, such as how well the offerer manages subcontractors, if that is relevant.

c.   Rigid adherence to the responses to "Yes/No" questions can be misleading.

Each series of questions within the SCE has a major objective. The developer may be able to achieve this objective without applying methods suggested in the questionnaire. For example, it is not necessarily bad if a developer does not estimate the code size as long as there is a method to accurately estimate the effort and schedule of a program.

Many of the questions are subject to interpretation. The intent of the questions needs to be clearly understood by the evaluation team prior to applying the questionnaire and meeting with the developer.

d.   The consistency of the SCE scores depends on the capabilities of the review team.

The implementation of the SCE requires an evaluation team that is experienced in software acquisition and trained in the methods of the SCE. It is also highly sensitive to the members' skills in conducting the on-site visit. The ability to interview people and elicit significant information is a skill that requires experience. Otherwise, the results of an assessment can be inconsistent among teams.

e. The scoring based on a set of prior projects may not consider recent improvement.

More weight might be given to more recent experiences if they represent systematic and lasting improvement.

MEASUREMENT AND EVALUATION CRITERIA

a. The maturity level of a developer's process is judged by evaluating the responses to a questionnaire. An investigative team verifies the responses by an on-site visit and review of evidence from several projects; it then scores the results to arrive at a maturity level.

b. The effectiveness of the SCE process can only be judged over the long term by correlating the quality of the software products with the SCE maturity level.

   • Determine the cost of the SCE process and the savings from improvements based on the evaluation.

   • For a long process, evaluate improvement in the development process over the duration of the project.

ACTIVITIES

The activities described below assume that the SEI SCE is used during source selection to evaluate offerers.

a. Planning

   • Determine whether the SEI SCE is appropriate. AFSC Pamphlet 800-51 [AFS90] discusses the use of this technique and a related technique, the Software Development Capability/Capacity Review (described elsewhere in this volume). The following factors might enter into the decision to use the SEI SCE for a program:

      - If the software is highly critical in terms of its reliability requirements

      - If the software engineering requirements are technologically challenging

      - If a developer has been selected for reasons other than its software engineering capability.

- Choose and train an evaluation team

  The SEI recommends five people who have at least seven years' experience with software product development and management. They should know software development technology, and about the specific program and application domain as well.

  The team training takes about two and one-half days. The course includes instruction in the methodology for administering the SCE and team-building training.

- Put words in the RFP

  The RFP must notify offerers to prepare for the questionnaire and for an on-site visit. The intended use of the results, e.g., as part of source selection criteria or in the subsequent contract, must be spelled out. The SEI expects to provide model documentation for this.

b.   Doing

- Select projects for on-site review

  The developer provides profiles of six to eight projects. The government selects four, usually in different stages of development, for which the questionnaire will be answered, and which will be reviewed during an on-site visit.

- Assess and score the questionnaire

  The assessment data are gathered through questions answered by the offerers. Initially, the scoring process is fairly mechanical. To qualify for a particular maturity level, a developer must have "yes" answers to 90 percent of the required questions for that level, and to 80 percent of all questions for that and prior levels. The responses can show inconsistencies and areas requiring further investigation and clarification during the on-site visit.

- Visit the site

  The on-site visit is for fact-finding. Back-up material on projects and demonstrations can be requested to validate the level initially assigned by the scoring. Key people may be interviewed. The team spends three days at the site, including analysis time. The developer is involved for a total of two days.

- Analyze and provide feedback

  The team formulates findings and informs the offerer's management, who is allowed to refute them and to tell their plans for improvement. Results of all assessments are prepared for the source selection organization.

- Give feedback to the SEI for long-term improvement of the SCE vehicle.

  The SEI wishes to make improvements to the SCE based on experiences in its use. They wish to be informed of results whenever the SCE is used. They can also assemble data across projects and organizations to show the state of the practice in the industry.

c. Generating Actions

- If the SCE reveals that an offerer's software development process maturity level is a level 1, the offeror may be eliminated from consideration.

- If the SCE reveals areas that require the developer to provide information for closer monitoring or require the developer to make improvements, this should be written into the contract.

- The program office might focus its quality monitoring activities on those areas in which the SCE showed the developer to be weakest.

RELATED TECHNIQUES

a. Complementary

- SEE

- SEP

b. Redundant—Software Development Capability/Capacity Review.

BIBLIOGRAPHY

[AFS90]   Department of the Air Force, 9 November 1990, *Software Development Capability Assessment*, AFSC Pamphlet 800-52.

[HUM87]   Humphrey, W. S., W.L. Sweet, September 1987, *A Method of Assessing the Software Engineering Capability of Contractors*, Software Engineering Institute, Carnegie Mellon University, Pittsburgh, PA.

[HUM89]   Humphrey, W. S., 1989, *Managing the Software Process*, Reading, MA: Addison-Wesley.

[HUM91]   Humphrey, W. S., T. R. Snyder, R. R. Willis, July 1991,"Software Process Improvement at Hughes Aircraft," *IEEE Software*.

SECTION 12

SOFTWARE AUDIT

The Software Audit (SWA) grew out of the observation, gathered by MITRE Red Teams over a period of time, that there was a high degree of correlation between the existence of major software problems and earlier inadequacies in the system engineering and requirements allocation [ATT90]. These software problems often caused schedule slips and cost overruns that resulted in delivered software below acceptable quality limits. The Software Audit consists of a review by an independent team, not supporting the program, of a set of key aspects of the system status at the time that system engineering has been completed and software development is about to begin. The aspects of the system to be reviewed are described below in the section entitled "Measurement and Evaluation Criteria." Continuation into the software design phase can be made contingent on passing all the criteria evaluated by the SWA.

PURPOSE

a.   To assess whether the developer has performed the requisite requirements analysis and system engineering and is well-prepared to continue into the software preliminary design phase

b.   To determine whether the developer has a sound Software Development Plan (SDP) and is prepared to use the development methodology and tools defined therein

c.   To assess the developer's understanding of the technical issues, including timing and sizing, of the program.

APPLICATION

The SWA is performed by a Government team coincident with the SSR. It may be performed again at a later date if the developer fails major portions of the audit.

MEASUREMENT AND EVALUATION CRITERIA

The SWA evaluates eight criteria with a pass or fail score. These scores are then considered and weighed according to their importance for the specific program, and an overall pass/fail recommendation is made in addition to individual pass/fail scores.

171

The individual SWA criteria are discussed below.

a.   The adequacy of the mapping from the System-Level Requirements to the SRSs
     The developer should be able to exhibit a Requirements Traceability Matrix that
     shows how each requirement in the SSS (i.e., each "shall") is traced to the
     requirements documented in the SRSs. In addition, derived software
     requirements should be identified with the rationale for their existence.

     The developer will fail this aspect of the SWA if significant gaps or errors exist
     in the allocation of system-level requirements to the SRSs, or if a disciplined
     traceability methodology is lacking.

     The developer will also fail if allocations of critical system requirements were
     made to previously developed software including commercial-off-the-shelf
     software (COTS), and especially operating systems and database management
     systems, if there is an inadequate basis for believing this software will perform
     as needed. The SWA team should look for developer testing of such software,
     or published data to verify its functionality and performance.

b.   The completeness of the external system interface requirements definition

     The interface between each CSCI and each applicable external system should be
     well-defined by the time the SSR is held. These interfaces will be documented
     and the external interfaces should be completely defined at both the functional
     and protocol level.

     A large number of undefined external interfaces will cause the developer to fail
     this portion of the evaluation. Even a few gaps, if they are particularly critical to
     the system, may have the same result. In addition, if the developer's external
     interface requirements demonstrate a gross misunderstanding of the system
     interfaces, a failure will be indicated.

c.   The consistency and completeness of the functional requirements decomposition

     The developer should have completed the allocation of the SSS functional
     requirements by the time of the SSR. The software requirements for each CSCI
     should be defined and documented in the SRSs. There should be consistency in
     the requirements descriptions in all of the SRSs.

     Major gaps in the software requirements will suggest weakness in the
     developer's understanding of the functional requirements, resulting in failure
     relative to this evaluation criterion. If an operational concept exists, there should
     be consistency between it and the complete software requirements described in
     the SRS, or failure will result.

d.   The elimination of ambiguity from the definition of the user-system interface
     (USI) and the adequacy of the supporting analysis

USI requirements must be specified in a way that users will understand. Screen designs are a good means of describing what functions will be provided, and they can also be used to illustrate guidelines and design rules the developer will follow in describing the USI. Some contracts will require the guidelines and design rules to be delivered for Government approval, such that they will also form the basis for USI testing. For some systems, interactive prototyping will be necessary to describe requirements unambiguously in adequate detail.

Failure in this evaluation area will result if there is no identifiable basis for, or if there is inadequate detail in, the description of the USI requirements. The shortfall must be obvious and imply major areas of ambiguity. The developer should be able to show that functional requirements come from the SSS or from a more detailed analysis of user tasks. In addition, the developer should show that any selected development tools can support the style and size of the proposed USI.

e.   The completeness of the timing and sizing requirements, and the adequacy of the supporting analysis

By the time of the SSR, the developer should have identified the system's critical timing and sizing requirements, addressing both the software and target hardware. Depending on the nature of the system and programming language, this may include requirements on the compiler as well as the applications code. If COTS or previously developed software plays a significant role, it must be allocated a portion of the time line, memory, and all other storage media; key timing performance estimates should have been validated by appropriate benchmarking on the target hardware. The developer should also address contingency planning in the event the actual requirements significantly exceed estimates.

If the developer has no plan or disciplined methodology for estimating and measuring timing performance at the SSR and continuing throughout the development, or if critical software functions have not had timing and sizing requirements allocated, then the developer will fail this evaluation area. Even if the allocations exist, failure will still result if there is no basis for the allocations through supporting benchmarks or analyses.

f.   The consistency of the software test concept with the software structure and SDP

The developer's approach to testing should support the software implementation plans described in the SDP and the software architecture of the system. The approach should reveal the logical rationale for and relationships between unit tests, thread tests, integration tests, and FQTs. It should describe whether FQTs will be organized CSCI by CSCI, or cumulatively built up functionally across several CSCIs.

The SWA team will be looking for assurance that the interdependencies of the test approach concept and the planned software structure have been recognized by the developer. Furthermore, the SWA team will assess the developer's plans for test resources, including time, facilities, tools, and people.

g.   The implementation of the SDP

All too often, the developer's SDP, once submitted and approved by the Government, is not properly used by the development team. Therefore, it is important that the developer install and test the procedures and tools specified in the plan, and that the development team be trained accordingly. Ideally, the developer's team will be experienced, having used the planned process on prior software developments.

The developer will fail with respect to this evaluation area if the procedures and tools are not demonstrably in place. The developer also will fail if his software development management team does not demonstrate knowledge of and commitment to the SDP.

h.   The adequacy of the corporate peer review

Prior to the SSR, the developer is required to hold an internal peer review of the project to ascertain readiness for the SSR. The results of this internal review are expected to be briefed to higher level management prior to the SSR. The intent is to encourage increased developer management attention to the state of the project relative to schedule and quality, and to avoid holding the SSR before the developer is ready. Later, the SWA team and the Government Program Manager will receive this briefing.

The SWA team will assess the developer's internal peer review for thoroughness and objectivity. The SWA team also will assess the understanding by the developer's management of the complexities of the program. The developer will fail this evaluation area if the developer cannot show the review was held, or if the reported results are at gross variance with the subsequent findings of the SWA team.

ACTIVITIES

a.   Planning

- The SOW for the contract will include appropriate language indicating that the developer is required to support the SWA by performing a peer review and by responding to inquiries from the SWA team.

- Approximately 45 days prior to the scheduled SSR, the Government should select the SWA team, usually consisting of a team leader and two or three other experienced personnel.

- The SWA team leader will meet with the Program Manager and other Government representatives to define and implement the detailed steps leading to the SWA; this includes coordination with the developer. The SWA team will also plan its own review and evaluation activities, and establish a schedule for accomplishing its objectives.

b. Doing

- The SWA team will review existing documentation including the contract, SOW, System Specification, SDP, SRS, IRS, System/Segment Design Document (SSDD) (if available), and the SSR package.

- The SWA team will interview appropriate members of the program office and support technical staff. These interviews will focus on program description and status, including any areas of concern.

- The SWA team will review the developer's Peer Review briefing regarding readiness for the SSR.

- The SWA team will attend the SSR, but as a passive observer rather than a critical reviewer. The SSR will be a primary information source for determining the developer's understanding of the system requirements and approach to accomplishing the software objectives.

- The SWA may, after SSR, request specific information from the developer which they feel was not adequately covered by the documentation or the SSR presentation. This may result in a visit to the developer's facility to evaluate development facilities and receive additional data.

- Within two weeks after the SSR, the SWA team will consolidate its findings and prepare a briefing summarizing the results. This briefing will be informally presented to the Government staff and then formally to the Program Manager.

- In those situations where the developer fails the SWA, the briefing will be given to the higher level Government managers. If requested by the Program Manager, the SWA team briefing may be given to the developer.

c. Generating Actions

On the basis of the SWA, a number of actions may be generated. These may include

- Correcting specific discrepancies found

- Revising requirements of the SRSs

- Recommending redo to parts of the SSR

- Recommending specific actions to perform in the failed areas and a plan for the SWA team to revisit and/or review the revisions prior to continuing with software development or at PDR.

RELATED TECHNIQUES

Complementary—Government SSR.

BIBLIOGRAPHY

[ATT90]   Attridge, W. S., E. R. Buley, March 1990, *The Software Audit*, MTR-10803, The MITRE Corporation, Bedford, MA.

SECTION 13

SOFTWARE DESIGN METRICS

A software design represents one of the first handles we have on the quality of software. The design can serve as a predictor of the quality of the final product and is, in fact, a major determinant of its quality. The challenge of software metrics is to relate attributes of the design that can be measured objectively to the level of quality that will be achieved in the software when it is completely implemented.

Design metrics are measures of the software design made from some formal representation of the high-level design, the detailed level of design, or even the code itself. Design metrics can be simple counts, such as the number of connections among components or the number of lines of code in a component, to very complex computations involving combinations of measures.

Early design metrics were derived from principles of software engineering, such as modularity, that were believed to lead to desirable qualities in software such as flexibility, maintainability, and reliability. The metrics were measurable approximations for these more abstract principles. Human cognition, an imprecise science concerned with how much complexity a human mind can comprehend and remember, became part of the basis for the metrics. Overly complex software, according to this approach to design metrics, would lead to a higher probability of error in the software, take longer to implement, and cause more difficulty to maintainers trying to find errors as well as make modifications.

Many design metrics are concerned with the structure of software, that is, how the software is partitioned into components and the nature of the dependencies among components. These dependencies can be caused by control connections; e.g., one component uses another for processing or must synchronize with its operation. Other dependencies are caused by data connections, such as sharing the same sources of information or serving as a source for information used by other components. Design metrics are also concerned with the internal structure of components, such as the sequence and number of accesses to data. The number of dependencies among components, their type, and their strength can be correlated with how much of the total design a person must understand to implement a specific portion, or repair or modify the software in response to new requirements.

Other design metrics evaluate the "difficulty" of the software by measuring the number of distinct paths or decisions made within the software, or by counting the number of operators and operands that are referenced. Difficulty may be inherent in the requirements themselves. However, there are theories about distributing the difficulty among the modules of the system. Examples of more popular design metrics can be found in [MCC76], and [HEN81]. Card proposes a combination of design metrics that measures system complexity in terms of specific kinds of control and data connections, and module complexity in terms of decisions within the module as well as uses of the data [CAR90].

177

While the original design metrics were based more on intuition than on empirical evidence, many attempts have been made in recent years to correlate design metrics with actual data on the resulting quality of the software. Card [CAR90] provides a review of current software design metrics and the published empirical evidence of the value of the metrics.

PURPOSE

There are a number of distinct reasons to employ software design metrics.

a.   To identify parts of the software likely to have a high number of errors

b.   To predict the effort for the remainder of the development

c.   To predict the maintainability of the software

d.   To enforce design, coding, and testing standards established to ensure high quality

e.   To aid in the planning of software testing.

APPLICATION

Software design metrics are applied at various stages in the development of the design. Usually, the top-level design is defined and documented early in the development, since it is the blueprint that allows teams of people to work in parallel, refining and detailing parts of the total software design. Design metrics can be presented for Government review at regular intervals, such as PMR, or as part of a major review, such as PDR and CDR. Sometimes the Government imposes limits on design metrics, such as the size or complexity of a module, to reduce the probability of errors or increase the potential maintainability of the software.

MAJOR ISSUES

a.   Validity of most design metrics

Many rules of thumb exist within the software industry related to design and coding standards that presumably increase product quality. These have been translated into metrics that include

•   Limiting the size of a software module to between 50 and 200 SLOC

•   Minimizing the data coupling between software modules

•   Limiting the span of control of a module to 7 ± 2

•   Maximizing the internal strength or cohesion of a module

- Limiting the McCabe complexity of the system structure or module structure [MCC76].

Some of these rules have been shown to reduce the number of software defects under specific conditions. For others, the correlation between the rules and quality has been difficult to establish. For example, Card [CAR90] reports data showing that module size, per se, does not affect fault rate. Design metrics must be chosen with care and backed up with evidence that they are relevant to the specific program.

b.   Role of automation

Automation may help reduce the cost of collection and analysis as well as provide a higher quality analysis. Tools exist or can be developed to reduce the labor in gathering and analyzing metric data, provided the design itself is formally and rigorously represented, usually in a design language or graphics created by a CASE tool.

c.   Dependence on design methodology and design language

Different design methodologies may have different models of "good" design heuristics that help decide which metrics should be used and how they should be assessed. Similarly, a language such as Ada may require different design metrics from FORTRAN or C, when these languages are used to represent the design of the software.

MEASUREMENT AND EVALUATION CRITERIA

a.   Measuring the design and code

The references cited below all give measures and design metrics based on them. These include

- Count of number of modules

- Count of fanouts per module, that is, the number of calls from that module to others

- Cyclomatic complexity based on a directed graph of control paths (or decision points) within a module

- Number of data elements used by a module.

      b.   Judging the effectiveness of the software design and code metrics

The effectiveness of design metrics should be determined over many programs by:

- Counting the number of defects in the final code and documentation and comparing them with the values of design metrics to determine new acceptability thresholds for the metrics

- Measuring the cost and effort involved in gathering, analyzing, and reporting the metrics.

ACTIVITIES

      a.   Planning

- The Government and the developer should decide which, if any, design and code metrics the developer should report. Metrics should be selected that have validity based on the latest empirical data.

- Incorporate into the SOW and put on contract the relationship between the developer and the Government with respect to analysis and presentation of metrics.

      b.   Doing

- Prior to development, the developer should implement a plan for gathering and analyzing metrics data.

- During development, the metrics are presented at the appropriate internal review and Government reviews.

      c.   Generating Actions

As a result of the analysis of the metrics, the design of the software architecture or individual components may have to be changed.

RELATED TECHNIQUES

      a.   Redundant—Some Software Management Metrics are design metrics.

      b.   Complementary—Design and coding standards.

BIBLIOGRAPHY

[BEL81]   Belady, L.A., C.J. Evangelisti, 1981, "System Partitioning and its
            Measure," *Journal of System and Software,* Vol. 2.

[CAR90]   Card, D.B., R.L. Glass, 1990, *Measuring Software Design Quality,"*
            Englewood Cliffs, New Jersey: Prentice Hall.

[HAL77]   Halstead, M.H., 1977, *Elements of Software Science,* New York: Elsevier.

[HEN81]   Henry, S.M., D. G. Kafura, September 1981, "Software Structure Metrics
            Based on Information Flow," *IEEE Transactions of Software Engineering,*
            Vol. 7, No. 5.

[MCC76]   McCabe, T. J., December 1976, "A Complexity Measure," *IEEE
            Transactions on Software Engineering.*

SECTION 14

SOFTWARE DEVELOPMENT CAPABILITY/CAPACITY REVIEW

The Software Development Capability/Capacity Review (SDCCR) is a technique that evaluates an organization's capability to develop software for a particular system, as defined in the RFP [ASD87]. It is an integral part of the source selection process for full-scale development of mission-critical systems. The SDCCR has been used at the Aeronautical Systems Division (ASD) since 1983. The offerors are required to respond to the RFP with information on the software development tools and methods they propose to use on this specific development, with examples of their use and data on tool performance. A team of experienced technical experts and a contracting officer reviews the offerors and their subcontractors. The evaluation includes an in-plant review at an offeror's facilities using a predefined set of open-ended questions. The results of the SDCCR are used to select the developer, and the selected developer's process is incorporated into the contract.

An AFSC pamphlet [AFS90] shows how the SDCCR and the SEI SCE can be used during source selection. The primary differences between the two are the emphasis of the SDCCR on evaluation of an organization relative to a specific software development project, the inclusion by the SDCCR of an evaluation of the offeror's capacity in terms of available personnel and other resources, and the SDCCR's output, which is an assessment for source selection rather than a score on the maturity of the organization's process.

PURPOSE

The SDCCR has three objectives, as stated in ASDP 800-5 [ASD87].

a. To give the acquisition management team an understanding of the offeror's software development process

b. To assess the offeror's capability and capacity to perform that process to the program's requirements and within program baselines

c. To obtain a contractual commitment by the offeror to follow that process.

APPLICATION

The SDCCR is applied by a Government team during source selection prior to issuing a contract for the full-scale development of a mission-critical software-intensive system. It could be applied to a Demonstration/Validation phase software development if the software is considered critical to the success of the system.

MAJOR ISSUES

The following are some of the issues related to the use of the SDCCR:

a. The results of the SDCCR are highly dependent on the qualifications of the team. They must include senior experts in the technology and the application areas, as well as a contracting officer.

b. The SDCCR uses open-ended questions that allow for a wider range of answers, which can provide a more complete picture of each offeror but make it more difficult to provide consistency in reviews of different offerors.

c. The SDCCR does not guarantee that the personnel who are available will work on this program in adequate numbers and with adequate skills.

MEASUREMENT AND EVALUATION CRITERIA

The offerors and their subcontractors are measured in the following areas:

a. Software development management approach

    This includes ability to manage subcontractors, as well as organizational structure, configuration management, and quality assurance.

b. Management tools

    This includes contract work breakdown structure, software work package definition, and cost estimation.

c. Development tools

    This includes the development tools, standards, and facilities.

d. Personnel resources

    This includes the availability as well as the capability of personnel.

e. Ada technology

    This includes methods, tools, and personnel for developing Ada software.

ACTIVITIES

a.   Planning

- Determine whether the SDCCR is appropriate. AFSC Pamphlet 800-51 [AFS90] discusses the use of this technique and a related technique, the SEI SCE (described elsewhere in this volume).

- Select a team leader and the review team. Plan schedules for the reviews. This is one of the most important steps because of the dependence of the results on the ability of the team members.

- Identify how results of the SDCCR will be used in source selection.

- Incorporate into the RFP package information on the process that will be used, and information the offerors must supply, as well as the relevance of the SDCCR to the award process.

b.   Doing

- Ask the offerors to submit information on tools, methods, standards, practices for software development, and examples of where these have been applied on recent programs.

- Request each offeror to support an in-plant review, and identify the date.

- Review proposals for completeness of the requested information and its quality. Formulate clarification requests for the in-plant review. Tailor predefined questions or formulate new questions for the review.

- Perform the in-plant review, which is the most important part of the assessment process. The primary basis for the review is a predefined set of questions, listed in [ASD87], which the offeror can answer formally or informally. The review team records the responses. Each review takes one and one-half to two working days. Additional time may be required if facilities or demonstrations are viewed.

- Analyze results and compare results to predefined standards for evaluation.

c.   Generating Actions

- Follow through on the commitment made by the developer during development, by working with the developer to apply and improve the software development process and resources.

RELATED TECHNIQUES

a.   Complementary

- SEE
- SEP

b.   Redundant—SEI Software Capability Evaluation.

BIBLIOGRAPHY

[AFS90]   Department of the Air Force, 9 November 1990, *Software Development Capability Assessment,* AFSC Pamphlet 800-52.

[ASD87]   Department of the Air Force, 10 September 1987, *Software Development Capability/Capacity Review,* ASD Pamphlet 800-5.

SECTION 15

SOFTWARE DEVELOPMENT FILES

Software Development Files (SDFs), also called Software Development Folders, are repositories for information about each software unit under development. Each file contains information related to a unit that will help someone else understand the unit and check its status.

An SDF usually includes the following kinds of information:

a. Current listing

b. Change history

c. Software Problem Reports (open and closed) that affect this unit (or group of units)

d. CSU design

e. CSU test cases

f. CSU test results

g. Any other information that might help a software engineer understand and modify a CSU, including design trade-offs, alternate designs, constraints, etc.

PURPOSE

The primary purposes of maintaining SDFs are the following:

a. To facilitate audits, inspections, reviews of progress, and analysis of problems related to a unit

b. To help SQA organizations determine whether standard development procedures are being followed and to provide checkpoints where signoffs can be required to complete each development step for the unit

c. To support configuration management of the latest versions of a unit.

APPLICATION

SDFs are applicable throughout software development and software maintenance. SDFs should be established as soon as design activity begins. The SDFs are usually maintained by the technical staff and reviewed by their managers and by independent reviewers such as the SQA organization. In addition, the Government or an IV&V contractor may periodically review SDFs for indications of progress and the quality of the development process and products. The DID (DI-MCCR-80030A) for the SDP states that the format, contents, and maintenance procedures for the SDFs should be documented in the SDP delivered to the Government.

MAJOR ISSUES

a.   The maintenance of SDFs can be costly for large systems.

The Government has the option of requiring their use. Most organizations find them necessary and useful to retain control over their software at the lowest level while it is under development.

b.   Delivery of SDFs to the Government should be considered.

The program office should consider requiring formal delivery of SDFs, particularly if software maintenance is to be performed by someone other than the development contractor.

MEASUREMENT AND EVALUATION CRITERIA

The SDFs can be the source of information for management and quality metrics for a program. At the unit level, the SDFs can indicate

a.   Number of units designed, coded, and tested

b.   Which units have completed stages of development

c.   Number of defects found, types of errors, and in which units

d.   Whether software standards and procedures are being followed.

A monthly audit of 5 to 10 percent of the SDFs (depending upon the size of the acquisition and the resources available) should be conducted to see that the information in the SDFs is current.

ACTIVITIES

a.   Planning

In preparing the RFP, the program office must decide on the requirements it will impose on offerors to disclose their plans for maintaining SDFs and what level of formality will be required during development for the Government audit of SDFs and for the delivery of the SDFs. The RFP must reflect these decisions.

b.   Doing

The developer establishes and maintains the SDFs. The program office or its inspection teams may audit the SDFs periodically.

c.   Generating Actions

The developer should take action to change procedures or rework software if a disproportionate number of defects is being found during unit development within specific units or across all units.

RELATED TECHNIQUES

Complementary

a.   Cause and Effect Analysis

b.   CM

c.   Software Management Metrics

d.   SQA

e.   SPR Analysis.

SECTION 16

SOFTWARE ENGINEERING EXERCISE

The Software Engineering Exercise (SEE) is a test given to all offerors during source selection. It requires them to do some portion of a software development for a small specification. They should perform software engineering tasks and generate products in accordance with their proposed software development process, using members of their proposed development team. The exercise problem typically addresses one or more software technical risk areas on the program, such as concurrent processing and coordination, timing, or the use of Ada. The exercise must be designed to be performed and evaluated quickly, to minimize the schedule impact.

PURPOSE

The philosophy behind the SEE is that the software development process and the developer's personnel are major contributors to the quality of the final software product. Government insight into the process and the resources applied will enable a more considered choice during source selection, and reduce the risks associated with the development process and resources. A demonstration is a better way to gain that insight than documented plans, especially when the technology or tools are relatively new.

The SEE allows an evaluation of each offeror's software development process, including the requirements analysis approach, design methods, facilities and tools, and documentation. It provides an opportunity for the offeror to revise the SDP as a result of the exercise.

The SEE has also proven to be an effective tool for training the Government team that will oversee the software development.

APPLICATION

The SEE is performed as part of source selection. It is specified by the Government, and is performed after responses to the RFP have been received. The exercise is performed by all offerors, usually within one month with about five people. It is then evaluated by a Government team, and the results are part of the source selection.

MAJOR ISSUES

    a.   The SEE is costly.

        Experience has shown that from 6 to more than 18 staff-months of Government time and each of the offeror's time and effort (about 5 to 6 people for one month) are expended on the exercise. The effort is concentrated in a 2-month period for the Government and a 1-month period for the offeror, which must use its own funds. The cost to the Government is high because a team must devise the exercise, validate that it is clearly stated, and determine that it can be done in the allotted time. The Government team must also anticipate the range of solutions, and be prepared to evaluate them. The cost to the Government increases with the number of offerors since the submission of each must be evaluated and an on-site visit made to each. If the risk is high because of new technology, or it is essential to have a technically qualified developer, the investment can be worthwhile. For example, the SEE was used to ascertain Ada capability for the programs that were early users of Ada.

b.   The performance of the team on the SEE does not guarantee the same performance will be achieved during the development.

There is no guarantee that the same team will work on software development for the program, although key members should be retained.

c.   Small problems do not necessarily scale to large ones.

The SEE is a small test problem. Sample documentation, design, and code are produced and executed. Success on a SEE does not necessarily translate into success in a large development program. The SEE does not fully exercise the offeror's management structure. The coordination among a large number of personnel and organizations does not, in reality, take place during the SEE. Personnel work very hard and intensely on the SEE for a short period of time to obtain results. The same level of intensity may not exist during a long development process.

d.   Source selection sensitivity limits interaction and feedback.

The rules established for the source selection process do not allow a free and open dialogue between the offeror and the Government. The Government may only query the offeror concerning specific items raised in the proposal by means of the Clarification Request (CR) Deficiency Report (DR) process. The Government is not allowed to probe into areas not raised by the offeror. This can potentially limit the Government's ability to fully understand the offeror's software development process and may result in a low evaluation if a particular area considered important by the Government is not addressed by the offeror.

e.   Subcontractor performance is not evaluated.

The SEE helps in the selection of a contractor but it may not reveal the software engineering capability of subcontractors who may perform the development of critical software.

f.   Either the SEE or the SEP should be considered.

The SEE is performed during predevelopment and can influence the selection of the developer. The SEP (described elsewhere in this volume) is performed after source selection. The Government, rather than the developer, pays for the exercise during an SEP, but it allows more interaction between the Government and the developer to resolve development methodology issues.

MEASUREMENT AND EVALUATION CRITERIA

a. The SEE is used to evaluate the offeror based on the products delivered and on the presentations made during an on-site visit. Criteria such as the following might be used:

- Product evaluation

  - A description of the system architecture

  - A description of the software architecture for the sample problem

  - The conclusions and documentation resulting from the requirements analysis of the problem specification

  - Design documentation, including requirements traceability

  - Program design language, code listings, and cross-reference listings.

- On-site visit

  - Management approach

  - How well team members understand what they have done and why they have done it

  - A demonstration of the execution of the code developed (if required by the SEE).

b. The effectiveness of the SEE as a quality control technique can be judged by

- Documenting the problems discovered by the Government during the dry run, and observing whether other more significant problems occurred after development that were not revealed by the offeror's SEE

- Measuring the effort expended by the Government in preparation for the SEE, including the dry run versus the ability to recognize potential weaknesses in an offeror's software development process that might disqualify the offeror or might require special treatment if the offeror wins

- Documenting the concerns that arose about the offeror's SEE performance, and determining whether these concerns were addressed during the development or whether they remained.

ACTIVITIES

a.   Planning

- **Prepare the draft problem specification.**

  The first step in conducting a SEE is to develop the exercise problem. The problem may require the offerors to analyze performance requirements, illustrate their design method, and use the software engineering tools, methods, and techniques contained in their SDP. The draft problem must be relevant to the software risks of the system being acquired, and be restricted enough to allow requirements analysis, design, and possibly some coding to be accomplished in the allocated time.

- **Prepare inputs for the RFP package.**

  It is necessary to state in the RFP that a SEE will be conducted as part of the source selection process and to describe what it entails. It is also necessary to include the criteria to be used in evaluating an offeror's response.

- **Dry run the problem.**

  It is recommended that the SEE process include a dry run of the exercise by the Government prior to its specification to the offerors. A Government team would be created, tools obtained, and the exercise performed under the same conditions and rules as the contractor. This activity can improve the quality of the exercise by identifying potential problems that may be addressed by clarifying or changing the specification of the exercise, SOW, schedule, or other contractual documents. The dry run has also been found to be an effective way to train the Government team in current software engineering practices and tools.

- **Prepare detailed evaluation criteria.**

  Prior to evaluating each offeror's results, the Government should develop its own checklist of more detailed items to be used to evaluate the delivered documentation during the on-site visit.

- Prepare the SEE package.

  Detailed instructions for the SEE are normally given to the offerors upon submission of their proposals. This allows the offeror to complete the proposal prior to starting the SEE. The SEE packages should contain

  - The problem specification

  - The products to be delivered to the government

  - The schedule to be followed

  - The definition of the briefing to the Government

  - Instructions that the offeror use the tools and methodologies contained within the SDP and a team consisting of people who would be involved in the actual development if the contract is awarded to that offeror.

b. Doing

- The offerer performs the SEE.

  Upon receipt of the SEE package, each offeror must complete the work within the specified period of time (usually one month).

- The Government performs the on-site visit and the product evaluation.

  The Government will employ its evaluation criteria and detailed checklists, developed previously, to evaluate the offeror's results of the SEE.

c. Generating Actions

- The SEE evaluation is used as one of many inputs to the source selection process. A very poor SEE could disqualify an offeror.

- Poor performance in a particular aspect of the SEE may result in changes to the contract to provide additional Government insight into the problem area as the contract proceeds.

- Lessons learned from a SEE may result in changes in the SOW.

RELATED TECHNIQUES

Redundant

a. SEP

b. SEI SCE

c. SDCCR.

BIBLIOGRAPHY

[FIT89]　Fitzgibbon, J. P., 1989, "Lessons Learned in the Preparation of a Software Engineering Exercise (A Life Raft at SEE)," *Seventh Annual National Conference on Ada Technology*, pp. 58-66.

[HUF89]　Huff, G. A., S. M. Maciorowski, November 1989, *The CCPDS-R Software Engineering Exercise*, MTR-10544 (ESD-TR-89-303), The MITRE Corporation, Bedford, MA.

SECTION 17

SOFTWARE ENGINEERING PROTOTYPE

A Software Engineering Prototype (SEP), in principle, is very similar to a SEE, but is administered after contract award. A small portion of the system requirements are selected and described in a mini-system specification. The specification, accompanied by a set of instructions, is delivered to the contractor at approximately SDR. Requirements for conducting and documenting the SEP are also identified in the SOW for the program. The contractor is required to perform requirements analysis, preliminary design, and detailed design; and, after each of these phases, the contractor is required to deliver the associated requirements document and portions of the software design document. The activity is expected to last 90-120 days. The prototype products can be specified to be reusable in the system development.

Since the SEP is administered after contract award, a free and open dialogue with the contractor is achievable. The actual tool suite and development team will perform the prototype activities and prepare the documentation. This is not assured with the SEE, since it is conducted before contract award. Also, the open dialogue and delivery of documentation permit an early concurrence on the content of an SRS with the possibility for tailoring that data item if necessary. This increases the duration and scope of the SEP exercise, the software development methodology, and the tool suite to a greater extent than a SEE, and it should accurately demonstrate the contractor's ability to use the selected methodology and tools. At the end of the prototype, a "lessons learned" briefing and a written report are presented by the contractor, which should be the basis for a mutual agreement on the development approach between the Government and the contractor, and should allow the Government team to focus attention on those areas identified as problematic or containing moderate-to-high risk. Also, because the SEP results are not source selection sensitive, the Government can use the lessons learned from one program on other similar programs.

PURPOSE OF THE SEP

a.   The major objective of the SEP is to reduce risk by providing the Government an early assessment of the contractor's capabilities, and insight into the software development approach.

b.   As a result of the execution of the SEP, the Government and the contractor may discover and isolate new risk areas that deserve additional attention.

c.   The SEP reduces the amount of rework associated with CDRL deliveries by obtaining a firm understanding, at the beginning of the program, about the organization and content of the products that are expected to be produced.

APPLICATION

The SEP is performed by the contractor after contract award, and starts around the time of SDR.

The results of the SEP are reviewed

a.   After the SEP planning process

b.   At each SEP milestone, such as SSR, PDR, and CDR.

MAJOR ISSUES

a.   The SEP delays the initial schedule.

The SEP is usually scheduled for a 3- to 4-month period. This will necessarily delay the development and initial delivery of the software requirements documentation. However, the overall schedule, rather than being delayed, may be accelerated. One of the purposes of the SEP is to reduce the rework due to misunderstandings between the contractor and the Government, and to work out process and product issues early in the program.

The work performed on the SEP is intended to be reusable during the remainder of the program. The learning curve associated with adjusting to new tools, methodologies, and to the interaction with the Government would be necessary even without a SEP; the SEP just accelerates the learning curve process. In addition, the documentation produced as a result of the SEP can be used as a starting point for the development of the complete documentation.

b.   Small problems do not necessarily scale to large ones.

The SEP, like the SEE, is a small test problem. Success on a small sample SEP problem does not necessarily translate into success in a large development program. The SEP, however, does take place over a 3- to 4-month period rather than the shorter 1-month period for the SEE, which allows a larger problem to be addressed in more detail.

MEASUREMENT AND EVALUATION CRITERIA

a.   The SEP is used to evaluate the contractor based on the sample products delivered and on interactions between the Government and the contractor during their technical interchange meetings held during the period of the SEP. The following kinds of items associated with the SEP are reviewed by the Government in an interactive, cooperative fashion:

- A description of the system architecture

- A description of the software architecture

- The SRS and IRS

- The Software Design Document (SDD)

- A test plan, test procedures, and test reports

- PDL, code listings, and other listings produced by the compiler

- The software requirements analysis, development, and test processes

- The CM and SQA process.

b.   The effectiveness of the SEP as a quality control technique can be judged by

- Measuring the effort expended by the contractor and the Government in the performance of the SEP

- Documenting the issues that arose during the SEP and how they were resolved

- Determining how well the development is being performed and what significant problems did not surface during the SEP. This will allow the Government to judge the predictive power of the SEP, and can lead to long-term improvement of the SEP process itself

- Reviewing the lessons learned document prepared by the developer.

ACTIVITIES

a.   Planning

- Prepare inputs for the RFP package.

It is necessary to state in the RFP that a SEP will be conducted as part of the contract and to describe what it entails. The RFP instructions for the SEP should include

- Requirements that the facilities, tools, and methodologies used on the SEP be the same that are planned for the full-scale development, and be documented in the SDP

- Requirements that the personnel and organizational structures be the same as those planned for the full-scale development

- A CDRL for all the products to be delivered during the SEP

- The schedule to be followed by the SEP.

- Identify the risk to be addressed and prepare the mini-specification

  The first step in conducting a SEP is for the Government to develop the mini-specification. The mini-specification should address major software risks, and be restricted enough to allow requirements analysis, design, coding, and testing to be accomplished in the allocated time.

  The mini-specification is to be delivered to the contractor around the time of SDR along with a reiteration and elaboration of the instructions for developing the SEP, originally specified in the SOW.

- Prepare SEP evaluation criteria and checklists.

  As part of the Government's preparation for the SEP, evaluation criteria and a detailed checklist associated with each deliverable and process demonstration need to be developed.

b. Doing

- The contractor performs the SEP.

  Upon receipt of the SEP package the contractor will perform the SEP activities over the specified time period.

- Perform the SEP evaluation.

  The Government will employ its evaluation criteria and detailed checklists developed previously to evaluate the results of the SEP. Evaluations will also be performed based upon interactive meetings with the contractor and by demonstration by the contractor of his requirements analysis, design, test, CM, and SQA processes.

- Generate lessons learned.

As part of the SEP, the contractor is required to prepare a paper describing the lessons learned during the SEP. This will allow the Government and the contractor to adjust their approach toward the development. It will also allow the Government to adjust and modify approaches toward future developments on other programs.

c.   Generating Actions

- The SEP evaluation is used as a preventive quality control technique. As such, the plans for resolution of any organizational, process, or technical problems should be documented as action items and resolved early in the full-scale development. This will save cost and ultimately improve the schedule.

- Poor performance in a particular aspect of the SEP may result in changes to the specification, the SOW, or the contract.

RELATED TECHNIQUES

Redundant—SEE.

BIBLIOGRAPHY

[SCH89]   Schultz, H. P., July 1989, *Software Engineering Exercise Guidelines*, ESD-TR-89-199, Electronic Systems Division, AFSC Hanscom Air Force Base, MA.

SECTION 18

SOFTWARE MANAGEMENT METRICS

A set of Software Management Metrics (SMM) were originally devised at the request of an Air Force Electronics Systems Division (ESD) general who wanted a uniform way to obtain the status of major software developments for which he was responsible. The SMM documented in [SCH88] can be used to measure the progress of a software development effort compared with its plan, to indicate areas where there may be problems with the quality of the product or schedule, to indicate some of the probable causes, and to forecast where problems may occur. These metrics are often referred to as the ESD management metrics.

The SMM were primarily chosen to measure a small number of parameters that affect the cost and schedule of a software development effort. A basic assumption of the metrics is that a deviation from the plan or from required or expected performance will result in a change to the overall software development schedule (most likely a slip) and/or a change in the quality of the final products. It is for this reason that SMM are important for controlling quality during development. The SMM can reveal that the size or difficulty of the effort has increased, that the time allocated for an activity such as testing has decreased, or that the people doing the work are not as experienced as was planned.

A similar set of management metrics was defined by the Air Force Systems Command in [AFS86]. A correspondence between the ESD management metrics outlined above and these AFSC management indicators is summarized in table 1. Details of metrics within the categories shown sometimes differ. Since we have had more experience with the ESD metrics than the AFSC indicators, the remainder of this section will be oriented toward the ESD management metrics.

PURPOSE

a. To provide a high-level overview of the status of a program

b. To provide indicators of potential risks that could affect schedule, cost, and quality of software products and possible sources of those problems.

APPLICATION

Some subset of the SMM should be used on almost all software developments where it is important to know answers to the following kinds of questions:

a. Will the developer be able to deliver the software on schedule with the required quality?

b. Has the size of the effort grown without an adjustment in schedule and staffing?

c. Have the plans changed in ways that may affect the quality?

d. Is the development progress consistent with the development schedule?

e. Are the resources consistent with the plans?

Table 1. ESD Management Metrics and the AFSC Management Indicators

ESD Management Metrics	AFSC Management Indicators
Software Size	Included in Requirements Definition and Stability
Software Personnel (includes only developer's personnel)	Software Development Manpower (also includes program office personnel)
Software Volatility	Requirements Definition and Stability (also count of ECPs, number of requirements traceable and testable)
Computer Resource Utilization	Computer Resource Utilization
Design Complexity	Not included
Schedule Progress	Similar to Cost/Schedule Deviations
Design Progress	Part of Software Progress
CSU Development Progress	Part of Software Progress
Testing Progress	Part of Software Progress
Incremental Release Content	Not included
Not included	Software Development Tools

Schultz [SCH88] presents a summary of the the coverage of the SMM during development. This is shown in figure 3. The metrics appropriate to each stage of development are usually presented at the PMRs attended by the developer and the

Government. The metrics are also reviewed at the major Government reviews, as shown in figure 3.

The raw data for the SMM are generated or collected by the developer. The analysis and presentation of the metrics are usually performed by the developer. However, the Government may choose to perform additional analyses of the data to gain other insights into the status and progress of the software.

MAJOR ISSUES

a. Determining what to measure

The Government program manager must establish which data to measure and the metrics that should be presented at developer and Government management reviews. This should be done during predevelopment so that the appropriate wording may be incorporated into the SOW and the CDRL.

Metrics should be selected based upon anticipated and actual risks. They may be used to help determine whether a risk exists. For example, if one is concerned with the stability of the requirements, then the Software Volatility metric or the corresponding AFSC Requirements Definition and Stability indicator should be employed. If the system has an abundance of spare CPU, memory, and I/O capacity, one needn't go through the effort and expense to define, estimate, and measure resource utilization factors.

b. Application of the Metric

Once a metric is chosen, the degree of application of a particular metric must be determined. For example, program size may be collected for the total software or for each individual CSCI, CSC, and CSU. Personnel information may be estimated and gathered for the entire program or for each individual work breakdown activity and program phase.

The determination is a function of the budget and the anticipated use of the metrics. It is wasteful of resources to collect data without planning how and why they are to be used.

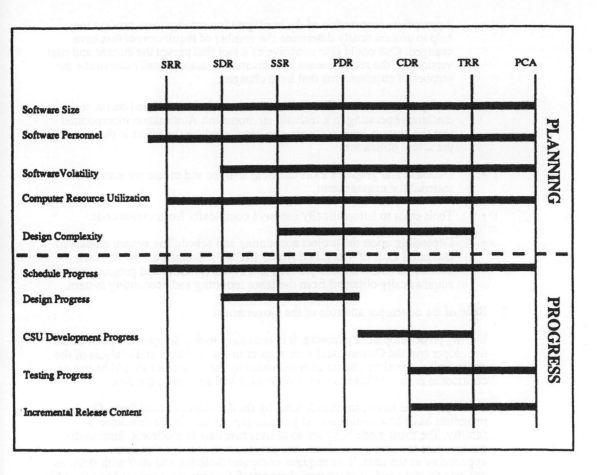

Figure 3. SMM Coverage

c. **Role of automation**

The frequency of collection and the degree of analysis depends upon the budget allocated to the process. Automation may help to reduce the cost of collection and analysis as well as to provide a higher quality analysis. Tools exist or can be easily developed to reduce the labor in gathering and analyzing metric data in the following areas:

- Actual software size may be automatically determined from source files. Comments may easily be eliminated from the count.

- Appropriate automation of the configuration management process may help to automatically determine the number of requirements that have changed. One could also conceive of a tool that parses the current and past versions of the requirements specification to automatically determine the number of requirements that have changed.

- Computer resource utilization must ultimately be measured on the real machines operating in a realistic environment. Automation incorporated into the system-level software can greatly reduce the effort in determining the actual utilization.

- Database and graphics tools can help analyze and create presentation material for management.

- Tools exist to automatically measure complexity from source code.

- Depending upon the project accounting and scheduling system employed, Budgeted Cost of Work Performed (BCWP), Budgeted Cost of Work Scheduled (BCWS), and planned and actual schedule and progress may be automatically obtained from the labor reporting and accounting system.

d. Role of the developer and role of the Government

During predevelopment planning, it is necessary to decide upon the roles of the developer and the Government with respect to the reporting and analysis of the management metrics. The metrics delivered by the contractor should be put on contract to ensure effort is spent in collecting and analyzing the data.

Some programs have graphs delivered by the developer in final form. Other programs have had on-line access to management data in the developer's facility. The third mode has been to deliver raw data in electronic form to the government for storage, analysis, and presentation in ways that seem appropriate at the time. This requires computer facilities and staff with skills to analyze the data and produce useful reports. Some program offices have found it useful to be able to analyze data themselves as an integral part of understanding what is happening and why. Standard reports can be more efficient to generate, on the other hand, and easier to compare across programs.

The SMM must be examined, interpreted, and integrated with the management process of both the developer and the program office in order to be effective. As stated in [SCH88], "The successful use of the metrics depends on the program manager's enforcement of a serious technical review of the data collected for each metric. The metrics graphs are a tool for escalating the discussion of important progress and status indicators to both Government and developer senior managers." To facilitate that discussion, some program managers include assessments of the metrics on the agenda of their PMRs with the developers. The best uses seem to be when both the Government and the developer have delegated responsibility to a specific person to produce and examine reports from the metrics.

e. Establishing the norms and thresholds

Most of the SMM are presented in graphical form to aid in observing trends as well as for comparing with plans. The basis or norms used for comparison may be the original program plans, updated program plans, or results from similar programs. When the deviations of actual program measurements from the norms exceed a threshold then management action is indicated. The establishment of norms and thresholds must be based upon experience from other similar programs. The plans themselves should be reviewed for reasonableness. Unfortunately, these norms and thresholds may be difficult to determine. For example, is a 10 percent growth in the estimated size of the software from SSR to CDR normal or is it cause for concern? Does a 5 percent change in the number of the software requirements between PDR and CDR mean that the schedule is going to slip? The answer may be different for each development organization and each program.

Only a limited amount of data has been gathered across multiple programs, and statistically significant norms have not been established. At a minimum, one can look at trends, extrapolate, and forecast whether plans will be met. If not, then replanning is necessary.

MEASUREMENT AND EVALUATION CRITERIA

a. Measurement of the program

The SMM consists of the following groups of metrics:

*   Software Size

    This is the primary parameter of COCOMO [BOE81] and other models to estimate the development effort. If the size grows, and other parameters such as official schedule and staffing are not adjusted, there is a danger that the deliveries will be late and that the quality will be less assured.

*   Software Personnel

    This is the largest cost driver in the COCOMO model. This metric deals with the experience levels of people and also their turnover rate, which is equivalent to measuring their length of time on the project. It can also be an indicator of morale problems, management problems, and quality problems if people do not have the necessary skill, familiarity with the program, or the necessary experience.

- Software Volatility

  This metric tracks the total number of requirements and counts the number of changes. If the requirements are changing, then the job is changing. "Requirements creep" is a common occurrence, where additions are made slowly over time, as users and developers review the detailed design of the software. Changes in requirements cause rework and can cause instability in design which in turn affects quality. The later in the development these changes occur, the more likely is the occurrence of rework and quality problems.

- Computer Resource Utilization

  This metric tracks changes in the estimated and actual utilization of the CPU, memory, and I/O of each of the target computers and the communication hardware. This is directly related to the quality of product. Planned spare capacity allows for growth during development and Post Deployment Software Support (PDSS). A shortage of CPU, memory, or I/O capacity often causes the code to become more complex and difficult to maintain.

- Design Complexity

  This metric is based upon the complexity measure defined by McCabe [MCC76]. Although there are no totally validated metrics to predict product reliability from a design, some experimental evidence suggests that there is a correlation between design complexity and the number of implementation defects (the more complex, the more defects). This metric could also indicate where testing effort should be concentrated.

- Schedule Progress

  This metric assumes that the work breakdown structure includes software work packages. It provides a view of the overall software schedule derived from estimates of the BCWP, the BCWS, and the planned number of months in the software schedule. If the software is behind schedule, quality will be sacrificed unless the schedule is lengthened and/or the requirements are reduced.

- Design Progress

  This metric evaluates the developer's ability to maintain progress during the initial software development phases. It tracks the development of the SRSs and the SDDs. The metric at a particular point in time is determined by the number of system-level requirements incorporated into the SRSs and the number of SRS requirements incorporated into the SDD.

- CSU Development Progress

  This metric tracks the progress of the design, code, unit test, and integration of the CSUs of the software. Comparisons are made between the actual and planned progress. Significant deviations affect the overall schedule, with the potential decrease in the quality of the final product, and may indicate which CSUs have quality problems leading to delays.

- Testing Progress

  This metric assumes that testing is done at the CSCI level. Two separate types of metrics are employed. Testing status tracks the progress of CSCI and system testing against the plan. The SPR tracking focuses attention on the number of open and new SPRs and the SPR density (cumulative number of SPRs per 1000 SLOC). Significant deviations in the test schedule affect the final delivery and may indicate a substantial quality problem. The number of open SPRs and the SPR density provide an indication of the amount of work remaining to be completed. Both test status and SPR status may provide a caution that the quality of the software product and its documentation may not be sufficient.

- Incremental Release Content

  This metric tracks the schedule and number of CSUs per release in order to monitor the developer's ability to preserve schedule and functionality in each planned release. A shortfall in the planned number of CSUs in early releases may indicate an off-loading of functionality to later releases. This affects schedule and may indicate a quality problem. An increase above plan in the number of CSUs in later releases may be an indication that the system is getting more complicated and the amount of code is growing.

b. Judging the effectiveness of the SMMs

The effectiveness of the SMM may be determined by

- Counting the number of risks uncovered as a result of the application of SMM

- Counting the number of action items resulting from the analysis of the SMM

- Collecting the cost and effort involved in gathering, analyzing, and reporting the SMM.

ACTIVITIES

a. Planning

- Select an initial set of SMM based upon risk.

- Incorporate metrics measurement, preparation, and analysis activities into the SOW and metrics as deliverables and put on contract the relationship between the developer and the Government with respect to analysis and presentation.

b. Doing

- Prior to development, the developer should implement his plan for gathering and analyzing metrics data.

- During development, the SMM are presented at the appropriate Government reviews and PMRs.

c. Generating Actions

As a result of the analysis of the SMM, the development program may be affected in a number of significant ways.

- Design and/or test activities may be rescheduled.

- Requirements may be reduced.

- Additional or different resources may be applied to the program, including personnel and facilities.

- Schedules and cost estimates may have to be revised.

- The system architecture or specific components of the architecture may have to be changed.

RELATED TECHNIQUES

a. Redundant

- Reliability modeling may produce similar estimates on defect density.

- Software Design Metrics may use Software Complexity as a measure of design quality.

- The SPR status portion of Testing Progress may be part of SPR data gathering and analysis. It may also be incorporated into the CM process.

b. Complementary

- SQA may be the responsible organization for gathering and analyzing management metric information.

- The IV&V organization may be tasked with collection and/or analysis of SMM data.

- The software engineering environment may incorporate the tools and mechanisms for gathering and maintaining the SMM data. It may also be the platform for hosting the automated tools used for analysis of the SMM data.

BIBLIOGRAPHY

[AFS86]   Air Force Systems Command, 31 January 1986, *Software Management Indicators*, AFSCP 800-43.

[BOE81]   Boehm, Barry W., 1981, *Software Engineering Economics*, Englewood Cliffs, NJ: Prentice-Hall, Inc.

[MCC76]   McCabe, T. J., December 1976, "A Complexity Measure," *IEEE Transactions on Software Engineering*.

[SCH88]   Schultz, H. P., 1988, *Software Management Metrics*, ESD/TR-88-001, ADA196916, M88-1, The MITRE Corporation, Bedford, MA.

SECTION 19

SOFTWARE QUALITY ASSURANCE

"Software Quality Assurance" refers to a set of software quality control activities performed by the developer to assure the quality of deliverable and nondeliverable software, its documentation, and the processes used to produce the deliverable software [ANS81]. The term is also used to designate a group within the developer's organization, usually independent of the developers themselves, that performs those activities. There are many definitions of SQA that vary in the strength of SQA's role in establishing standards and in seeing that the development organization follows those standards. Traditional SQA organizations check conformance to standards for processes, procedures, and documentation that have been defined for a project. There is an assumption that adherence to these standards will assure quality. SQA functions do not usually include an in-depth review of the technical content of the products. In some organizations, the role of SQA groups is becoming larger, encompassing more involvement in establishing standards and in technical review activities.

PURPOSE

    a. To provide an independent review of the software development process, its products, and the resources applied

    b. To check for conformance to the selected standards for products and their documentation, and for procedures used for software development

    c. To reduce the cost of correcting defects during test and integration by finding the defects during requirements, design, and code reviews.

APPLICATION

SQA is performed by the contractor during all phases of development starting with requirements analysis. Software quality assurance plans should be submitted for Government review. DOD-STD-2168 contains information that should be included in SQA plans. Some people advocate putting such plans on contract [MUR88].

Findings can be reported to higher management through a separate reporting chain from the development manager, whenever serious deviations in quality occur that require action. Reports from the SQA organization can also be part of formal reviews.

MAJOR ISSUES

a. Establishing the standards and practices for evaluation

To be effective, the SQA process needs to be institutionalized within an organization with checklists developed on the basis of experience across many projects. The standards against which the software products, processes, and resources are to be judged must be known and understood by the developers and the SQA team prior to the development. Without these checklists, the SQA process is undefined and cannot be considered under control.

b. How much control is given to SQA?

Care must be taken in the application of SQA so as not to create a bottleneck in the schedule when SQA recommendations are not prioritized with other required actions. The responsibility and authority of the SQA organization must be clearly established. This includes

•   Who receives reports and reviews them?

•   Can it approve or disapprove products or procedures?

•   How independent is its reporting chain?

•   What is its relationship to other quality assurance activities such as IV&V, Configuration Management, and testing?

c. Finding personnel with the necessary qualification for an effective SQA team

Experience with the software development process, the products, and the resource requirements is critical to an effective SQA organization. The caliber of the personnel assigned to the SQA process is often below that of the developers because SQA is not treated as an important or skilled job. They often lack experience in the development process and perform only the mechanical aspects of the SQA process.

d. Tools and methodologies

The detailed checking of all the products produced by the development organization may be tedious and time-consuming. To be cost-effective the SQA process needs to be supported by automated tools and methods that perform the mechanical and record-keeping part of the SQA process. Without a large degree of automation, the checking is often inadequate and many defects go undetected.

MEASUREMENT AND EVALUATION CRITERIA

a. To evaluate the quality of the evolving software product, the resources, and the processes applied

   • Evaluate the products against preestablished SQA checklists.

   • Consider applying the Rome Laboratory Software Quality Framework (RSQF) quality criteria score sheets for the quality requirements.

   • Count the number of defects found in each product and compare with the experience from other projects (if available). Statistical techniques such as histograms may help in the presentation and analysis of defect data.

   • Verify that the resources applied to the program are in accordance with the SDP.

   • Verify that the processes applied to the program are in accordance with the SDP.

b. To evaluate the effectiveness of the SQA process itself

   • Determine the cost of the SQA process as a percent of the software development effort. Compare with experience on other programs (if available) or to the program management plan.

   • Determine the number of defects found by the customer and not by SQA.

   • Determine the number of defects found as a result of SQA activities.

ACTIVITIES

a. Planning

   • Establish the SQA resources (personnel, budget, schedule, tools).

   • Establish the SQA checklists for each product, process, and resource to be reviewed.

   • Establish the responsibility and authority of SQA for approving and disapproving products, processes, and resources.

b. Doing

The SQA process is performed in parallel with the development process. The products, processes, and resources reviewed include

- All the deliverable documents defined in the CDRL

- The design, code, and unit test procedures

- The processes and resources as defined within the SDP.

c. Generating Actions

Possible actions of SQA include

- Approve or disapprove the release of a product.

- Approve or disapprove procedures, including test plans, procedures in the SDP, and CM procedures.

- Indicate where there are deviations from defined plans, procedures, and products.

- Modify the SQA process and resources themselves if indications suggest that they are ineffective or too costly.

RELATED TECHNIQUES

a. Complementary

- Cause and effect analysis

- SPR data collection and analysis

- Government reviews

- Internal design and code reviews.

b. Redundant techniques

IV&V is performed by an independent outside agency, while SQA is performed by an independent internal agency of the contractor.

BIBLIOGRAPHY

[ANS81]   ANSI/IEEE STD. 730-1981, 13 November 1981, *IEEE Standard for Software Quality Assurance Plans*, 345 East 47th Street, New York, NY 10017.

[MUR88]   Murine, G.E., 1988, "Integrating Software Quality Metrics with Software QA," *Quality Progress*, pp. 38-43.

SECTION 20

SOFTWARE PROBLEM REPORT ANALYSIS

Software Problem Report (SPR) analysis is a process of systematically gathering and analyzing software problem information. SPRs record information such as defects that are found, when and where they occurred, their cause, how they can be fixed, and when the fix has been verified. They can also be used to record changes that are needed in requirements and in documentation. DOD-STD-2167A contains a detailed description of Problem/Change Reports as a required part of the DID (DI-MCCR-80030A) for an SDP. Table 2, at the end of the section, lists items that can be recorded as part of an SPR.

PURPOSE

a. It allows the Government and the developer, independently or together, to monitor the efficiency and quality of the development, testing, and error correction processes, to estimate the reliability of the final product, and to predict when the testing will be completed.

b. It can allow the developer to isolate those products, processes, and resources that are particularly trouble-prone so improvements can be made.

c. SPR data collected during the PDSS phase allows correlation of the quality of the delivered product with the development process that was used, in order to identify improvements in an organization's development process.

d. It can provide information to a configuration management group, such as a Configuration Control Board, that must decide if the requirements must be changed or if the problem is caused by a defect in documentation or code.

e. It provides data for other quality control techniques including reliability modeling, cause/effect analysis, CM, SQA, and process completeness metrics.

APPLICATION

SPR data are collected by the developer. Data analysis can be performed by the developer during all phases of development starting with system requirements analysis through the PDSS phase. The SPRs can also be used by the Government to gain visibility into the status and quality of the development or maintenance process and the final product. Traditionally, SPR data have been collected after the software has been placed under configuration control during software integration, system test, and PDSS activities. SPR analyses, particularly from testing results, are usually an important part of reporting at PMRs. If the development has problems, the SPR analyses may be reported more frequently, especially when they are being used by the Government to monitor progress in testing.

MAJOR ISSUES

a. How much data should be collected and how much data should be presented to the Government?

- The more data collected, the more it will support trouble shooting and analyses of causes of problems; e.g., by recording which system components have problems, it is possible to locate "hot spots" responsible for the bulk of problems.

- The Government may not wish to see all of the data unless there are problems with the status of the software.

b. With what "normal" values should SPR analyses be compared?

- A common use of SPRs is to predict when the software will be "finished," with an acceptable level of errors remaining. SPRs show error density, rate of error discovery, remaining open errors, and other data that have been used to forecast completion. For example, if the literature says that there are x errors per thousand lines of code, then some projects assume that they will be done when x errors per thousand lines of code have been found. This approach obviously has flaws.

- An organization must develop its own "normal" values with which to compare SPR status information and to make predictions. SPR data from prior systems can be used to provide a basis for normal data.

c. Should SPRs be standardized by the Government across programs so data can be gathered to form normal curves?

If all programs reported the same data, the data could be combined to provide average or normalized data for programs that are similar in application and software development approach.

d. In what form should the data be delivered to the Government?

The SPR data should be maintained in an electronic form (ideally a database) usable by both the contractor and by Government personnel for analyses.

MEASUREMENT AND EVALUATION CRITERIA

The evaluation criteria to be employed are dependent upon the purpose established during the planning process. A list of measures that can be taken, using SPRs, can be found in

[IEE88]. The following are some examples. In each case, evaluation criteria must be specified based on past experiences or trends.

a. To evaluate the quality and efficiency of the test and integration process

   •   Plot the number of new SPRs detected during the test and integration period on a regular basis.

   •   Plot the cumulative number of open SPRs detected during the test and integration period on a regular basis or for each build.

   •   Plot the number of closed SPRs on a regular basis.

b. To isolate the cause of problems in particular development phases and activities, determine the number and percent of problems caused within each of the development phases (requirements, design, code, test, and integration).

c. To isolate trouble-prone requirements or capabilities, measure the number of problems associated with each set of requirements, functions, or capabilities.

d. To identify trouble-prone resources that need improvement, the number of problems associated with the specific personnel resources, or facility and tool resources needs to be identified and counted.

e. To identify trouble-prone products that need improvement, including software modules and documents, the number of problems associated with each identifiable product or software element needs to be counted and a histogram generated to isolate the most error-prone.

f. The efficiency and quality of the defect correction process may be determined by measuring

   •   The distribution ages of the open SPRs: 0-30 days, 30-60 days, 60-90 days, and over 90 days. This type of measurement may indicate that an improvement in the correction process is necessary or that some of the older problems are not important and should be eliminated. It may also reveal that the outstanding older problems are very difficult and that more resources should be applied to fix them.

   •   The SPR histogram as a function of priority of open SPRs (see table 2)

   •   The number of SPRs that result from fixes.

g. Each SPR should be checked to verify that the data reported are complete and correct. A process and organizational responsibility and authority needs to be established for this data verification process. Specific items to be checked include

- Missing data

- A problem description which describes the solution to the problem rather than the cause of the problem

- Improper identification of the source of the problem.

ACTIVITIES

a. Planning

- Define the objectives of SPR data gathering and analysis for the Government, and then specify reporting requirements in the RFP package. Examples of objectives include

  - To track test and integration quality growth, and predict system and software reliability

  - To isolate the cause of problems to particular development phases and activities within the program phase, such as CM, SQA, design reviews, unit test, etc.

  - To isolate trouble-prone requirements or capabilities

  - To identify trouble-prone resources that need improvement (in this context resources include personnel, facilities, and tools)

  - To identify trouble-prone products that need improvement, including software modules and documents

  - To measure SPR trend information, including the number of open and closed SPRs by priority, as a means of forecasting time to complete.

- The plan by the developer for SPR data gathering and analysis should also

  - Define the data to be collected (see table 2)

  - Establish the media and tools used to maintain the data

  - Define the measurements and analyses that are to be performed

  - Establish the responsibilities for data reporting, verification, and analysis

- Define how data is to be presented

- Establish when the data is to be presented.

b. Doing

- The execution of the SPR data collection and analysis process

  - Documents the problems in a timely fashion

  - Enters the SPR data items into an appropriate database

  - Validates the data for correctness

  - Analyzes the data according to the plan

  - Generates reports and presents them at planned reporting periods.

c. Generating Actions

As a result of the SPR analyses, a number of actions may be suggested.

- Resources could be concentrated on the most error-prone products.

- Processes and resources could be modified to prevent problems in the areas discovered to be problem prone.

- A more realistic schedule may be formulated for the remainder of the program.

- Requirements may be changed by the Government.

RELATED TECHNIQUES

Complementary

a. Cause and Effect Analysis

b. CM

c. Reliability Modeling

d. SMM

e. SQA.

BIBLIOGRAPHY

[IEE88]   IEEE Computer Society, 1988, *A Standard Dictionary of Measures to Produce Reliable Software*, IEEE.

Table 2. SPR Data Elements

a. Identification

 * System, subsystem, build, or project ID

 * Unique problem ID

 * Originator of problem report

 * Date problem reported

 * Identification of the test or review being performed

 * Identification of the test configuration or document being reviewed

 * Identification of the operational software configuration, mode and/or state (if applicable).

b. Problem description—this includes the description of the symptoms of the problem.

c. Problem classification as either

 * Code or data problem

 * Documentation problem

 * Design problem

 * Requirements problem.

d. Priority of the problem

 * Priority 1—Prevents the accomplishment of a mission-essential capability or jeopardizes personnel safety.

 * Priority 2—Adversely affects the accomplishment of a mission-essential capability so as to degrade the performance to a significant degree, for which no alternative work-around solution is known.

 * Priority 3—Adversely affects the accomplishment of a mission-essential capability so as to degrade the performance to a significant degree, for which an alternative work-around solution is known.

Table 2. (Concluded)

- Priority 4—An operator inconvenience or annoyance, which affects a required operational or mission-essential capability.

- Priority 5—All other problems.

e. Identification of the origin or cause of the problem

f. Description of the solution to the problem

g. Identification of the software element (CSCI, CSC, CSU), the document, the requirement, the test procedure, etc., that must be corrected

h. Individual assigned responsibility for problem resolution

i. Status, such as

- Problem reported but not acted upon

- Problem being reviewed by the Configuration Control Board, date completed

- Problem being investigated and start date

- Solution and (if applicable) test approved and date

- Solution implemented and date

- Test or documentation review successful, and date accomplished

- Anticipated date and identification of new release of code or document

- Problem closed and date of closure.

SECTION 21

STANDARDS

Standards are formal definitions of processes, products, and resources. Good standards capture good practices and good designs, and make them goals for each new situation in which they can be applied. This should lead to high quality products without faults caused by repeating bad practices from the past or reinventing faulty solutions.

There are many kinds of standards that should be considered for a software development. Process standards define how to do something. Product standards describe what a product should do and may specify how. Product standards are technical standards.

Standards are defined by Government organizations or commercial organizations for widespread use. Individual organizations can develop their own standards. The following are examples of standards.

a. **Interface standards,** for example

   - International Standards Organization Open System Interconnection (ISO OSI) Reference Model standard [DAY83], which defines a seven-layer model for connecting a communicating subsystem

   - Specific LAN communication protocol standards, such as IEEE Standard 802.3 Ethernet [IEE85].

b. **Language standards,** which include

   - Ada [ANS83]

   - ANSI standard FORTRAN [ANS78].

c. **Process standards,** such as DOD-STD-2167A [DOD85]

d. **Documentation standards,** as represented by the various Government DIDs required under Government contract; for example

   - System Segment Specification   DI-CMAN-80008A

   - Software Requirements Specification   DI-MCCR-80025A

   - Software Design Document   DI-MCCR-80012A

e. **Operating system standards,** such as POSIX (this standard is currently in draft form [IEE91])

223

     f.   **Electronic media and format standards,** such as

- MIL-STD-1840A [MIL88], which specifies a nine-track tape format

- Computer-Aided Acquisition and Logistics Support (CALS), which is being developed to standardize the format for electronic media documentation.

    g. **Standards created and adopted by a specific organization,** such as

- **Design standards,** which specify the design methodology such as Object Oriented Design (OOD) and functional decomposition

- **Coding standards,** which specify how to apply the language constructs

- **Test standards**, which specify what is to be done during testing and how it to be accomplished.

PURPOSE

Standards can be used to provide consistency across programs in the practices of organizations that manage the development and maintenance of Government systems by requiring that certain practices be followed. Technical standards can also provide consistency in the design and implementation of software in systems. This can lead to more efficient reuse of prior technical solutions, reuse of software components, and increased interoperability among systems.

    a. **Interface standards** foster interoperability among systems that communicate using standard protocols. They enhance the ability to replace software and hardware components, without disrupting an entire system, by meeting their interface standards.

    b. **Language standards** define the exact syntax and semantics of language constructs so that a program written in a standard language can be compiled by different compilers and produce equivalent results.

    c. **Process standards** increase repeatability so that the results of applying a process become more predictable and the process can be controlled as it is used. **Design, coding, and test standards** are examples of process standards that can eliminate the occurrence of error-prone practices. Process standards allow people to be trained and become proficient in their use, since the standards stabilize the process definition.

    d. **Documentation standards** establish a common vocabulary and define the format and content of documents.

e. **Operating system standards** provide definitions of the hardware and software interfaces for many of the system services provided by an operating system. They allow software to be used with more than one implementation of an operating system, e.g., on different hardware platforms with little or no modification.

f. **Electronic media and format standards** allow for the contractor and the Government to communicate and deliver documents in a machine-readable form. This eases configuration control and allows for the application of automated analysis tools.

APPLICATION

Different types of standards are applicable to different phases of the development process.

a. **Interface standards** to operators and other systems are normally specified by the Government during the precontract phase of the life cycle. Standards used by a specific program can be selected by the Government, the contractor, or both. Military and commercial standards may be selected when they are required for interoperability or consistency among systems. The contractor must adhere to these standards either in the purchase of COTS items for the system or in the design of the interfaces of the system to be developed. Standards for internal interfaces are usually specified by the contractor as part of the design process and are used to allow hardware and software components to communicate.

b. **Language standards** are usually specified by the Government and constrain the developer to employ compilers that adhere to the standard.

c. **Process standards** can be specified by the Government and define the activities to be performed by the contractor during the development process. Normally, a developer specifies the development process and shows that it is a standard by providing documentation (in the Software Development Plan and Software Standards and Procedures Manual).

d. **Documentation standards** are specified by the Government and are used by the contractor to define the format and outline of the document contents.

e. **Operating system standards** may be specified by the Government or contractor and used to either purchase a compliant COTS operating system or to develop a new design.

f. **Electronic media standards** are specified by the Government or proposed by the developer and used by the Government and the contractor to deliver and store deliverable products.

g. **Design, coding, and test standards** are normally specified by the contractor, and are used to constrain the design, coding, and test process. On occasion, the Government may specify a subset of all of these standards.

The results of applying standards are reviewed at the normal Government formal reviews. If DOD-STD-2167A is used, these would occur at SDR, SSR, PDR, and CDR. After the CDR, it becomes very costly to change the standards applied to a program. Internally, a developer's SQA organization checks for conformity to standards. An IV&V organization may also check for conformance to standards.

MAJOR ISSUES

a. Standards may be moving targets.

Standards, by definition, must be applied in a consistent fashion over many programs. Standards in a constant state of change cannot be considered standard. The fast-moving evolution in hardware and software engineering technology tends to make standards obsolete before they are fully accepted and applied by the development community. For example, DOD-STD-2167 was modified to DOD-STD-2167A within three years of its introduction. During this period, contractors were just beginning to learn how to apply the standard. The first time a standard is applied it may tend to increase the cost of a project since an extra effort is required of the contractor to utilize, interpret, and enforce the standard.

b. It is costly to verify COTS compliance to a standard.

Ada has a set of tests and an organization to certify that a compiler adheres to the Ada language standard. This organization and the application of the certification process is costly and is supported by the Government.

Other standards do not have a corresponding certification process and organization. The ISO specifies and maintains the OSI standard. However, neither the ISO nor the Government maintains an organization to certify products. The Corporation for Open Systems (a not-for-profit organization) will certify conformance to a particular specification but will not guarantee interoperability. This is left to the product developer. The users of COTS products are therefore dependent upon the integrity and reputation of the contractor with regard to standards compliance.

c. Process and documentation standards are often subject to interpretation.

Unless a process and documentation standard has been used many times by the Government and the contractor for similar applications, multiple interpretations are possible. These may lead to program delays while compromises are negotiated between the differing parties.

d. The system response time may be affected.

Technical standards by their very nature are designed to provide an agreed-upon generalized approach to design issues. The application of these general approaches may adversely affect the response time of the system. The use of standard operating system mechanisms for inter-task communication may be considerably slower than a specially implemented one. A standard communications protocol may be considerably slower than a specially designed one. The specification of standards must consider the performance impact.

e. Some standards must be tailored

Process standards and documentation standards, such as DOD-STD-2167A are defined to cover a broad spectrum of situations and are intended to be tailored to fit the needs of specific programs. Both the Government and the developer must contribute to the tailoring, or unnecessary expense may be incurred.

MEASUREMENT AND EVALUATION CRITERIA ACTIVITIES

The following are examples of the kinds of metrics that can be used to measure and evaluate the use of standards:

a. To evaluate the design of a system

- Number of formal military or commercial standards used as external protocols or interfaces to other systems

- Number of formal military or commercial standards used as internal protocols or interfaces among components within the system

- Number of uniquely defined interfaces selected versus publicly available standards.

b. To evaluate the development process

- Number of formally defined process standards available and used by the developer

- Extent of training given in these standards

- Percent of total effort spent checking conformance to the standards.

c. To evaluate the standard

- Number of implementations of the standard available

- Number of organizations adopting the standard

- Number of changes to the standard and frequency of change.

ACTIVITIES

a. Planning

- Define the process, documentation, electronic media and format, language, and operating system standards.

- Define the interface standards that the product under development must satisfy. External standards, such as network standards, may be dictated by requirements for interoperability among systems.

- Evaluate the cost, schedule, and performance impact of employing the chosen standards.

- Incorporate words into the SOW, which require the contractor to formulate and apply design, code, and test standards, and words that indicate if the Government must approve all standards.

b. Doing

- Apply the standards.

c. Checking

- Verify that COTS hardware and software satisfy the applicable standards.

- Verify that the standards are being adhered to. SQA can significantly help in this area by using the standards as a basis for judging quality.

- Validate that the product under development adheres to the specified interface standards.

d. Generating Actions

- On the basis of a review of the number of violations of standards, additional training for personnel may be appropriate.

- If the standards are very difficult to apply or the benefits are not considered to be worth the effort, then the standard may be modified or eliminated entirely. However, this is a dramatic step and the changing of standards during a program must be based upon sound reasoning. The purpose of standards is to foster consistency, and changing the definitions contradicts this.

RELATED TECHNIQUES

Complementary techniques

a. The SQA process can be used to verify that the product satisfies all specified standards.

b. The IV&V process can be used as an independent check that the final software product satisfies all specified standards.

c. Design and code inspections can verify that the design and coding standards are being utilized.

BIBLIOGRAPHY

[ANS87]   ANSI x.3.9, 1978, *Programming Language Fortran.*

[ANS83]   ANSI 770x3.97, 1983, *Programming Language Pascal.*

[ANS83]   ANSI/MIL-STD-1815A, February 1983, *Reference Manual for the Ada Programming Language*, Government Printing Office Report 008-000-00394-7.

[DAY83]   Day, J.D., and H. Zimmermann, December 1983, "The OSI Reference Model," *Proceedings of the IEEE*, Vol. 71, pp. 1334-1340.

[DOD85]   DOD-STD-2167A, 29 February 1988, *Defense System Software Development.*

[IEE85]   IEEE, 802.3, 1985, *Carrier Sense Multiple Access with Collision Detection*, New York, ICCC.

[IEE91]   IEEE, March 1991, *Draft Guide to the POSIX Open Systems Environment*, IEEE, 345 East 47th St., New York, New York 10017.

[MIL88]   MIL-STD-1840A, 1988, *Automated Interchange of Technical Information.*

SECTION 22

TESTING

Testing, unlike many other methods of checking quality which consist of reviewing documents, involves evaluating the software product by running part or all of the system. Testing can tangibly demonstrate quality factors such as correctness, reliability, survivability, usability, and efficiency.

Tests range from informal testing by the contractor, through formal qualification and acceptance testing involving the program office, to formal operational testing involving users and independent test organizations. Not every program uses every level of testing for every part of the system.

Software can be tested against its specifications, as documented in SRSs, and/or against system requirements, as specified in the SSS. The tests can be performed in simulated or real environments. The decision depends on how important each level of testing is to assuring the quality of the system.

Many Government programs define a set of test levels encompassing low-level software testing through operational system testing.

a. Low-level unit testing and CSC integration testing is performed by the contractor to detect and correct software defects in individual components or aggregates.

b. Preliminary Qualification Tests (PQTs) are performed by the contractor to verify that each CSCI satisfies the software requirements as specified in its SRS. PQTs employ Government-approved test procedures. These tests do not necessarily require Government witnessing and they do not require Government approval.

c. Formal Qualification Tests (FQTs) are the official mechanism for approval of CSCI tests. Approved test procedures are usually required, as is Government witnessing and approval of the test results.

d. Development Test and Evaluation (DT&E) involves testing the system with all its hardware and software elements integrated. These tests are usually carried out at the contractor's facilities and require Government-approved test procedures, as well as Government witnessing and approval.

e. Initial Operational Test and Evaluation (IOT&E) expands the DT&E test to operational testing in the field, usually with operators from the user organization. These tests also require Government-accepted test procedures, Government witnessing, and approval. After the approval of IOT&E and the resolution of any outstanding software, documentation, and test issues the

DD250 form is signed. This represents the official turnover of the accepted software to the Government.

Often these levels are extended to encompass the principles of

a. Early and continuous integration

b. Thread testing.

PURPOSE

The purpose of testing is to verify, through execution of the software, that the software does the following:

a. Performs its functions correctly

b. Meets its performance requirements

c. Detects specified errors and recovers properly

d. Does not perform functions that were not specified.

APPLICATION

Both the Government and the developer participate in the testing of software. Usually Government testing is performed at the end of a development or prior to release of a version of the system to the Government. However, the Government can be involved in the developer's testing in the following kinds of ways:

a. Specifying the requirements to be tested, including test conditions and test scenarios

b. Reviewing and approving the contractor's test plans and procedures

c. Reviewing and approving the Requirements Verification Matrix that determines how each requirement or set of requirements will be verified (verification may be performed by means of inspection, test, analysis, or demonstration)

d. Providing test equipment, facilities, and operators

e. Providing operational scenarios or other requirements for the contractor's tests.

The developer must perform some internal tests and some for the Government. Developers must also document test plans, procedures, test cases, and test results. The Government will witness and approve or disapprove tests, depending on the results.

MAJOR ISSUES

a. The amount of independence of testers from developers affects results.

- Testers require objectivity and independence to assure that test cases are complete and results are correctly interpreted. Each level of testing, from units to the system, can have a different testing organization with increasing independence. For example, programmers might perform unit testing of their own units, while a separate development team might handle software integration and testing. The Government should review the developer's plan and agree with the level of independence of testers.

- The Government also has testing organizations with differing degrees of independence from the program office and the user organization. At some point, the user must be well represented in the testing plans, process, and results.

b. The schedule for testing can be planned to reduce the risk of finding serious design problems late in the development schedule.

- Since testing reveals the achievement of some quality factors that cannot be easily verified by other methods, it is important to start performing testing early in the development phase to allow time to correct defects.

    "Build a little, test a little" is an example of early scheduling of testing, particularly integration testing. The testing of incremental builds accomplishes incremental testing.

- Early integration testing can reveal design errors.

    Integration testing finds errors involving more than one software component. These could be design errors involving interfaces, timing problems, and other interactions among the components.

    Early integration and testing of software that provides services to application software, such as scheduling and synchronization of processes, can provide timing and functional behavior information that is useful in designing application software. This is especially true if the support software is off-the-shelf, and its performance and functionality cannot be easily changed.

- It is better to test difficult parts of the system first. Testing easy parts can give a misleading impression of progress.

c. The level of testing and time at which software is tested can be chosen to lower effort and cost without sacrificing quality assurance.

- When a requirement has been allocated completely to a single software unit (CSCI down to CSU), it might be best to test it at that level. This would also be true if it were difficult to control test conditions at the subsystem or system level. Critical algorithms might be an example in which testing could be done for more cases in a stand-alone mode. Otherwise, testing might be done at a higher aggregation of configuration items.

- Testing of reused software and off-the-shelf software (nondevelopmental items) might be at a reduced level from newly developed software, provided there is assurance that the software has been tested thoroughly in previous uses and has not been modified.

- Performance coverage analyzers (automated test tools) can help to show how completely the software was tested by a given set of test cases. This approach focuses on executing paths through the software as opposed to executing test cases representing all possible variations on a set of requirements.

- Thread testing is often preferred to testing at the CSCI level. Each thread represents an end-to-end requirement (from input to output). It allows a demonstration at the requirements level that the software operates correctly. It can use less driver software than CSCI-level testing and it follows more easily into DT&E testing. The decision will depend on the structure of the software architecture, and whether strings can be as thorough in testing operational capabilities as CSCI-level testing.

d. Test facilities and tools affect the efficiency of the developer's testing process and the thoroughness with which the software can be tested by the developer.

- For many mission-critical systems, there is an operational environment that contains equipment, such as sensors and their controllers, with which the software must interact. Often the Government supplies the equipment, but if that equipment is not available to the developer to use during testing, then its behavior must be simulated. This is especially true when the equipment is expensive, has limited availability, or has not yet been produced. The longer the software must operate in a simulated environment, the more likely that interface or design errors may be found late in the development phase. If the interface has been wrongly defined, then the software usually has to be changed rather than the equipment.

- Sometimes large numbers of equipment are needed, and only a small number are supplied to the developer. In this case, the results of testing on a small number may not extrapolate to correct performance and functionality for the total system.

- If there are not sufficient computers or capacity in the test facilities for those who use them for testing, then the testing operation becomes a bottleneck or causes one. This can happen when test facilities are shared by those who perform development, integration, or configuration management, or who make repairs to tested software.

e. Regression testing can affect the thoroughness of retesting and the cost of testing.

The Government and the contractor must agree on the strategy that will be used for testing and the amount of regression testing that will be performed. This issue becomes especially important when tests are conducted on increments of software that are then modified before the next set of tests. How much of the prior software must be tested again needs to be established as part of the test plan.

MEASUREMENT AND EVALUATION CRITERIA

a. Testing can serve several purposes, as described above. The measurements that are taken will depend on the purpose of the test.

- Some tests measure functional and operational characteristics. Measurements identify deviations from the specifications for those requirements and the seriousness of those defects. The results can determine if the software is acceptable to the Government.

- Some tests measure or predict reliability and availability. These tests are usually performed over some period of time, and the results are statistically analyzed (see Reliability Modeling) to give measures such as mean time between failures, and mean time to recover.

- Some tests measure response time, system capacity, and throughput. These tests are concerned with the processing time consumed by the system and the load it can handle so that these kinds of measurements must be made.

b. Some measurements evaluate the testing process itself. For example:

- Measurements of the paths covered in the software indicate how thoroughly it has been tested.

- Measurement of the rate at which defects are repaired or problems resolved are other measures of the development process that use the results of testing (see Software Problem Reports).

ACTIVITIES

a. Planning

- The Government should specify, usually in the SSS, its requirements for verification and validation of specific system capabilities. Each major test should be identified—the conditions for testing, the program phase of testing, the period of testing, and the number of items to test—according to the DID for the SSS (DI-CMAN-80008A). The Government should also specify the criteria for passing tests.

- The Government must plan the level of involvement it will have in witnessing and approving tests and test plans, as discussed above.

- The Government must plan for the resources and facilities that it will provide to support developer in-plant and field testing. Resources can include operators to operate the system, other equipment such as aircraft, satellites, or vehicles, or special hardware that might be needed for realistic testing.

- The developer can be required to specify his testing approach in his SDP, including the way he is organized for testing. The developer's Formal Qualification Test plans can be specified in a Software Test Plan, including what will be recorded as environment and resources and the schedule of individual tests.

- As part of the SRS, the developer documents a Requirements Verification Matrix showing what method will be used for the qualification of each requirement, and the level at which qualification will occur (configuration item, system integration, system level). The methods include inspection, analysis, demonstration, and test.

b. Doing

- In the course of the development, the developer produces the Software Test Description describing test cases and test procedures to implement the test approach described in the Software Test Plan.

- Testing is performed by the developer and reviewed by the Government in accordance with plans.

- The developer records test results including problems encountered and SPRs submitted.

c. Generating Actions

- Test results are primarily used by the Government to accept or reject software, or the system itself.

- Test results are used by the developer to make corrections of defects and to generate change requests for requirements.

- Test results can also be analyzed to determine changes in the development process, and in the design of the software, that might improve the results of the tests, and, hence, the quality of the software.

RELATED TECHNIQUES

Complementary

    a. Inspections

    b. Reliability Modeling

    c. SDFs

    d. SPRs.

GLOSSARY

ASD	Aeronautical Systems Division
BCWP	Budgeted Cost of Work Performed
BCWS	Budgeted Cost of Work Scheduled
CALS	Computer-Aided Acquisition and Logistics Support
CASE	Computer-Aided Software Engineering
CCB	Configuration Control Board
CDR	Critical Design Review
CDRL	Contract Data Requirements List
CE	configuration element
CLIN	Contract Line Item Numbers
CM	Configuration Management
COTS	commercial off-the-shelf
CPU	Computer Processing Unit
CR	Clarification Request
CSC	Computer Software Component
CSCI	computer software configuration item
CSU	Computer Software Unit
DID	Data Item Description
DR	Deficiency Report
DT&E	Development Test and Evaluation
ECP	Engineering Change Proposal
ESD	Electronic Systems Division
FCA	functional configuration audit
FQT	Formal Qualification Test
HWCI	Hardware Configuration Item
I/O	input/output
ICD	Interface Control Document
IFPP	Instructions for Proposal Preparation
IOT&E	Initial Operational Test and Evaluation
IRS	Interface Requirements Recommendation
ISO OSI	International Standards Organization Open System Interconnection
IV&V	Independent Verification and Validation
KSLOC	thousand source lines of code
LAN	local area network
MTBF	mean time between failures
NIST	National Institute of Standards and Technology
OOD	Object Oriented Design
OS	operating system

PCA	physical configuration audit
PDR	Preliminary Design Review
PDSS	Post Deployment Software Support
PMR	Program Management Review
PQT	Preliminary Qualification Test
RFP	Request for Proposal
RSQF	Rome Laboratory Software Quality Framework
RTM	Requirements Traceability Matrix
SAIC	
SCE	Software Capability Evaluation
SDCCR	Software Development Capability/Capacity Review
SDD	Software Design Document
SDF	Software Development File
SDP	Software Development Plan
SDR	System Design Review
SEE	Software Engineering Exercise
SEI	Software Engineering Institute
SEP	Software Engineering Prototype
SLOC	source lines of code
SMM	Software Management Metrics
SOW	Statement of Work
SPR	Software Problem Report
SQA	software quality assurance
SRS	Software Requirement Specification
SSDD	System/Segment Design Document
SSR	Software Specification Review
SSS	System/Segment Specification
TRR	Test Readiness Review
USI	user-system interface

PART II

SOFTWARE ERROR ANALYSIS

W.W. Peng
D.R. Wallace
National Institute of Standards and Technology

EXECUTIVE SUMMARY

The main purpose of this document is to provide the software engineering community with current information regarding error analysis for software, which will assist them to do the following:

- Understand how error analysis can aid in improving the software development process;

- Assess the quality of the software, with the aid of error detection techniques;

- Analyze errors for their cause and then fix the errors; and

- Provide guidelines for the evaluation of high-integrity software.

The software industry is currently still young, without sufficient knowledge and adequate standards to guarantee fault-free software. Although research continues to identify better processes for error prevention, with current practices, errors will probably occur during software development and maintenance. Hence, there is the need for error analysis. Error analysis for software includes the activities of detecting errors, collecting and recording error data, analyzing and removing single errors, and analyzing collective error data to remove classes of errors. The collective error data may be used with statistical process control (SPC) techniques to improve the product and the processes used in developing, maintaining, and assuring the quality of software.

This report provides a description of error detection techniques which are cited frequently in technical literature and standards and describes the cost benefits of applying error detection early in the lifecycle. However, error detection alone is not sufficient for removal of an error. Information must be recorded about the error to assist in the analysis of its cause, its removal, and its relationship to the project and to other similar projects. This report provides guidance on data collection, analysis, and removal as well as error detection.

This report describes how several SPC techniques can be used for software quality assurance technique and for process improvement. The report identifies metrics related to software error detection and identifies several software reliability estimation models. Metrics are used to assess the product or process, while SPC techniques are used to monitor a project by observing trends. SPC techniques help to locate major problems in the development process, the assurance processes (e.g., software quality assurance, verification and validation), and the product itself.

The study of software engineering standards reported in [NUREG, NIST204] indicates that standards are beginning to associate requirements for error detection techniques with the quality requirements and problem types of the software project implementing the standard. Further examination of these documents and additional standards and guidelines for high integrity software indicates that these documents vary widely in their recommendations of specific error techniques.   Appendix B provides a summary of the error detection techniques required or recommended by these documents for the assurance of the quality of high integrity software.

This report recommends collection of error data into an organizational database for use by a vendor[1] over several projects, and modified collections of these databases for use by government auditors (e.g., Nuclear Regulatory Commission, Environmental Protection Agency).   Software organizations should consider institutionalizing mechanisms for establishing and maintaining a database of error analysis data within their organization. Over time, it may become apparent that some error analysis techniques are more effective than others with respect to a given type of problem. It may also become apparent that problems in these areas occur most often with certain development practices and less frequently with others.   The database must contain both developmental and operational error data to be effective. In the regulators' environment, auditors may use the information in the database to identify the most error-prone features of specific high integrity systems and may ensure that their audits examine these features carefully. The auditors may use the data to identify acceptance limits on different aspects of a high integrity system.

An organizational database may also play an important role in software reuse within an organization.   In deciding whether or not to reuse a particular software component, one can examine its error history to determine whether it satisfies the level of assurance required by the intended application.   One can evaluate the component by observing its past failure rates and fault densities to ensure that the component is appropriate for reuse. A software component may sometimes be reused to build a system which is of a higher level of assurance than that in which the component was originally used. The database would provide data on the reliability or other quality attributes to help determine how much additional work is needed to increase the quality of the component to the desired level.

---

[1]In this report, the term "vendor" includes software developers.

techniques. Appendix D provides a summary of the error detection techniques required or recommended by these documents for the assurance of the quality of high integrity software.

1. OVERVIEW

This document provides guidance on software error analysis. Error analysis includes the activities of detecting errors, of recording errors singly and across projects, and of analyzing single errors and error data collectively. The purpose of error analysis is to provide assurance of the quality of high integrity software.

The software industry is currently still young, without sufficient knowledge and adequate standards to guarantee fault-free software. Although research continues to identify better processes for error prevention, with current practices, errors will likely be entered into the software some time during development and maintenance. Hence, there is the need for error analysis, to aid in detecting, analyzing, and removing the errors.

The main purpose of this study is to provide the software engineering community with current information regarding error analysis, which will assist them to do the following:

- Understand how error analysis can aid in improving the software development process;

- Assess the quality of software, with the aid of error detection techniques;

- Analyze errors for their cause and then fix the errors; and

- Provide guidelines for the evaluation of high integrity software.

Section 2 discusses how error detection and analysis techniques can be used to improve the quality of software. Section 3 provides a global description of the principal detection techniques used in each software lifecycle phase and cost benefits for selected categories of these techniques. Section 4 provides guidance on collecting individual error data and removing single errors. Section 5 describes techniques for the collection and analysis of sets of error data, including statistical process control techniques and software reliability models. Section 6 provides a summary and recommendations based on this study of error analysis, and Section 7 provides a list of references. Appendix A contains detailed descriptions of common error detection techniques. Appendix B contains the results of a study of standards for high integrity software to determine the extent of coverage of error analysis techniques.

The error detection techniques and statistical techniques described in this report are a representative sampling of the most widely-used techniques and those most frequently referenced in standards, guidelines and technical literature. This report also describes the more common software reliability estimation models, most which are described in the American Institute of Aeronautics and Astronautics (AIAA) draft handbook for software reliability [AIAA]. Inclusion of any technique in this report does not indicate endorsement by the National Institute of Standards and Technology (NIST).

1.1.   Definitions

Definitions of the following key terms used in this report are based on those in [IEEEGLOSS], [JURAN], [FLORAC], [SQE], [SHOOMAN], and [NIST204]. However, this report does not attempt to differentiate between "defect," "error," and "fault," since use of these terms within the software community varies (even among standards addressing these terms). Rather, this report uses those terms in a way which is consistent with the definitions given below, and with other references from which information was extracted.

anomaly. Any condition which departs from the expected. This expectation can come from documentation (e.g., requirements specifications, design documents, user documents) or from perceptions or experiences.
Note: An anomaly is not necessarily a problem in the software, but a deviation from the expected, so that errors, defects, faults, and failures are considered anomalies.

computed measure. A measure that is calculated from primitive measures.

defect. Any state of unfitness for use, or nonconformance to specification.

error. (1) The difference between a computed, observed, or measured value and the true, specified, or theoretically correct value or condition. (2) An incorrect step, process, or data definition. Often called a *bug*. (3) An incorrect result. (4) A human action that produces an incorrect result.
Note: One distinction assigns definition (1) to *error*, definition (2) to *fault*, definition (3) to *failure*, and definition (4) to *mistake*.

error analysis. The use of techniques to detect errors, to estimate/predict the number of errors, and to analyze error data both singly and collectively.

fault. An incorrect step, process, or data definition in a computer program. *See also*: **error**.

failure. Discrepancy between the external results of a program's operation and the software product requirements. A software failure is evidence of the existence of a fault in the software.

high integrity software. Software that must and can be trusted to work dependably in some critical function, and whose failure to do so may have catastrophic results, such as serious injury, loss of life or property, business failure or breach of security. Examples: nuclear safety systems, medical devices, electronic banking, air traffic control, automated manufacturing, and military systems.

primitive measure. A measure obtained by direct observation, often through a simple count (e.g., number of errors in a module).

primitive metric. A metric whose value is directly measurable or countable.

measure. The numerical value obtained by either direct or indirect measurement; may also be the input, output, or value of a metric.

metric. The definition, algorithm or mathematical function used to make a quantitative assessment of product or process.

problem. Often used interchangeably with **anomaly**, although **problem** has a more negative connotation, and implies that an error, fault, failure or defect does exist.

process. Any specific combination of machines, tools, methods, materials and/or people employed to attain specific qualities in a product or service.

reliability (of software). The probability that a given software system operates for some time period, without system failure due to a software fault, on the machine for which it was designed, given that it is used within design limits.

statistical process control. The application of statistical techniques for measuring, analyzing, and controlling the variation in processes.

2. INTRODUCTION TO SOFTWARE ERROR ANALYSIS

Software error analysis includes the techniques used to locate, analyze, and estimate errors and data relating to errors. It includes the use of error detection techniques, analysis of single errors, data collection, metrics, statistical process control techniques, error prediction models, and reliability models.

Error detection techniques are techniques of software development, software quality assurance (SQA), software verification, validation and testing used to locate anomalies in software products. Once an anomaly is detected, analysis is performed to determine if the anomaly is an actual error, and if so, to identify precisely the nature and cause of the error so that it can be properly resolved. Often, emphasis is placed only on resolving the single error. However, the single error could be representative of other similar errors which originated from the same incorrect assumptions, or it could indicate the presence of serious problems in the development process. Correcting only the single error and not addressing underlying problems may cause further complications later in the lifecycle.

Thorough error analysis includes the collection of error data, which enables the use of metrics and statistical process control (SPC) techniques. Metrics are used to assess a product or process directly, while SPC techniques are used to locate major problems in the development process and product by observing trends. Error data can be collected over the entire project and stored in an organizational database, for use with the current project or future projects. As an example, SPC techniques may reveal that a large number of errors are related to design, and after further investigation, it is discovered that many designers are making similar errors. It may then be concluded that the design methodology is inappropriate for the particular application, or that designers have not been adequately trained. Proper adjustments can then be made to the development process, which are beneficial not only to the current project, but to future projects.

The collection of error data also supports the use of reliability models to estimate the probability that a system will operate without failures in a specified environment for a given amount of time. A vendor[2] may use software reliability estimation techniques to make changes in the testing process, and a customer may use these techniques in deciding whether to accept a product.

The error data collected by a vendor may be useful to auditors. Auditors could request that vendors submit error data, but with the understanding that confidentiality will be maintained and that recriminations will not be made. Data collected from vendors could be used by the auditors to establish a database, providing a baseline for comparison when performing evaluations of high integrity software. Data from past projects would provide guidance to auditors on what to look for, by identifying common types of errors, or other features related to errors. For example, it could be determined whether the error rates of the project under evaluation are within acceptable bounds, compared with those of past projects.

---

[2]In this report, the term "vendor" includes software developers.

2.1.   Cost Benefits of Early Error Detection

Ideally, software development processes should be so advanced that no errors will enter a software system during development. Current practices can only help to reduce the number of errors, not prevent *all* errors. However, even if the best practices were available, it would be risky to assume that no errors enter a system, especially if it is a system requiring high integrity.

The use of error analysis allows for early error detection and correction. When an error made early in the lifecycle goes undetected, problems and costs can accrue rapidly. An incorrectly stated requirement may lead to incorrect assumptions in the design, which in turn cause subsequent errors in the code. It may be difficult to catch all errors during testing, since exhaustive testing, which is testing of the software under all circumstances with all possible input sets, is not possible [MYERS]. Therefore, even a critical error may remain undetected and be delivered along with the final product. This undetected error may subsequently cause a system failure, which results in costs not only to fix the error, but also for the system failure itself (e.g., plant shutdown, loss of life).

Sometimes the cost of fixing an error may affect a decision not to fix an error. This is particularly true if the error is found late in the lifecycle. For example, when an error has caused a failure during system test and the location of the error is found to be in the requirements or design, correcting that error can be expensive. Sometimes the error is allowed to remain and the fix deferred until the next version of the software. Persons responsible for these decisions may justify them simply on the basis of cost or on an analysis which shows that the error, even when exposed, will not cause a critical failure. Decision makers must have confidence in the analyses used to identify the impact of the error, especially for software used in high integrity systems.

A strategy for avoiding the high costs of fixing errors late in the lifecycle is to prevent the situation from occurring altogether, by detecting and correcting errors as early as possible. Studies have shown that it is much more expensive to correct software requirements deficiencies late in the development effort than it is to have correct requirements from the beginning [STSC]. In fact, the cost to correct a defect found late in the lifecycle may be more than one hundred times the cost to detect and correct the problem when the defect was born [DEMMY]. In addition to the lower cost of fixing individual errors, another cost benefit of performing error analysis early in development is that the error propagation rate will be lower, resulting in fewer errors to correct in later phases. Thus, while error analysis at all phases is important, there is no better time, in terms of cost benefit, to conduct error analysis than during the software requirements phase.

2.2.   Approach to Selecting Error Analysis Techniques

Planning for error analysis should be part of the process of planning the software system, along with system hazard analysis[3] and software criticality analysis. System hazard analysis is used to identify potential events and circumstances that might lead to problems of varying degrees of severity, from critical failures resulting in loss of life, to less serious malfunctions in the system. Software hazard analysis focuses on the role of the software relative to the hazards. Software criticality analysis may use the results of system and software hazard analyses to identify the software requirements (or design and code elements) whose erroneous implementation would cause the most severe consequences. Criticality analysis may also be used to identify project requirements that are essential to achieving a working software system. Critical software requirements are traced through the development process, so that developers can identify the software elements which are most error-prone, and whose errors would be catastrophic.

The results of hazard analysis and criticality analysis can be used to build an effective error analysis strategy. They aid in choosing the most appropriate techniques to detect errors during the lifecycle (see sec. 3). They also aid in the planning of the error removal process (i.e., the removal of individual errors, as described in sec. 4). Lastly, they aid in the selection of metrics, statistical process control techniques, and software reliability estimation techniques, which are described in section 5. Error analysis efforts and resources can be concentrated in critical program areas. Error analysis techniques should be chosen according to which type of errors they are best at locating. The selection of techniques should take into account the error profile and the characteristics of the development methodology. No project can afford to apply every technique, and no technique guarantees that every error will be caught. Instead, the most appropriate combination of techniques should be chosen to enable detection of as many errors as possible in the earlier phases.

---

[3]In this report, system hazard analysis may also include analysis of threats to security features of the software.

3.   TECHNIQUES FOR DETECTING ERRORS

Software development and maintenance involves many processes resulting in a variety of products collectively essential to the operational software. These products include the statement of the software requirements, software design descriptions, code (source, object), test documentation, user manuals, project plans, documentation of software quality assurance activities, installation manuals, and maintenance manuals. These products will probably contain at least some errors. The techniques described in this section can help to detect these errors. While not all products are necessarily delivered to the customer or provided to a regulatory agency for review, the customer or regulatory agency should have assurance that the products contain no errors, contain no more than an agreed upon level of estimated errors, or contain no errors of a certain type.

This section of the report identifies classes of error detection techniques, provides brief descriptions of these techniques for each phase of the lifecycle, and discusses the benefits for certain categories of these techniques. Detailed descriptions of selected techniques appear in Appendix A. Detailed checklists provided in [NISTIR] identify typical problems that error detection techniques may uncover.

Error detection techniques may be performed by any organization responsible for developing and assuring the quality of the product. In this report, the term "developer" is used to refer to developers, maintainers, software quality assurance personnel, independent software verification and validation personnel, or others who perform error detection techniques.

3.1.   Classes of Error Detection Techniques

Error detection techniques generally fall into three main categories of analytic activities: static analysis, dynamic analysis, and formal analysis. Static analysis is "the analysis of requirements, design, code, or other items either manually or automatically, without executing the subject of the analysis to determine its lexical and syntactic properties as opposed to its behavioral properties" [CLARK]. This type of technique is used to examine items at all phases of development. Examples of static analysis techniques include inspections, reviews, code reading, algorithm analysis, and tracing. Other examples include graphical techniques such as control flow analysis, and finite state machines, which are often used with automated tools. Traditionally, static analysis techniques are applied to the software requirements, design, and code, but they may also be applied to test documentation, particularly test cases, to verify traceability to the software requirements and adequacy with respect to test requirements [WALLACE].

Dynamic analysis techniques involve the execution of a product and analysis of its response to sets of input data to determine its validity and to detect errors. The behavioral properties of the program are also observed. The most common type of dynamic analysis technique is testing. Testing of software is usually conducted on individual components (e.g., subroutines, modules) as they are developed, on software subsystems when they are integrated with one another or with other system components, and on the complete system. Another type of testing is acceptance testing, often conducted at the customer's site, but before the product is accepted by the customer. Other examples of dynamic analyses include simulation, sizing and timing analysis, and prototyping, which may be applied throughout the lifecycle.

Formal methods involve rigorous mathematical techniques to specify or analyze the software requirements specification, design, or code. Formal methods can be used as an error detection technique. One method is to write the software requirements in a formal specification language (e.g., VDM, Z), and then verify the requirements using a formal verification (analysis) technique, such as proof of correctness. Another method is to use a formal requirements specification language and then execute the specification with an automated tool. This animation of the specification provides the opportunity to examine the potential behavior of a system without completely developing a system first.

3.2.   Techniques Used During the Lifecycle

Criteria for selection of techniques for this report include the amount of information available on them, their citation in standards and guidelines, and their recent appearance in research articles and technical conferences. Other techniques exist, but are not included in this report. Tables 3-1a and 3-1b provide a mapping of the error detection techniques described in Appendix A to software lifecycle phases. In these tables, the headings R, D, I, T, IC, and OM represent the requirements, design, implementation, test, installation and checkout, and operation and maintenance phases, respectively. The techniques and metrics described in this report are applicable to the products and processes of these phases, regardless of the lifecycle model actually implemented (e.g., waterfall, spiral). Table B-2 in Appendix B lists which high integrity standards cite these error detection techniques.

Table 3-1a. Error Detection Techniques and Related Techniques (part 1)

TECHNIQUES	R	D	I	T	I C	O M
Algorithm analysis	▪	▪	▪	▪		▪
Back-to-back testing				▪		
Boundary value analysis				▪		
Control flow analysis	▪	▪	▪			▪
Database analysis	▪	▪	▪	▪		▪
Data flow analysis	▪	▪	▪			▪
Data flow diagrams	▪					
Decision tables (truth tables)	▪					

Table 3-1b. Error Detection Techniques and Related Techniques (part 2)

TECHNIQUES	R	D	I	T	I C	O M
Desk checking (code reading)			■			
Error seeding				■		
Finite state machines	■					
Formal methods (formal verification)	■	■				
Information flow analysis			■			
Inspections	■	■	■			
Interface analysis	■	■	■			
Interface testing				■		
Mutation analysis				■		
Performance testing				■		
Prototyping / animation	■	■	■			
Regression analysis and testing	■	■	■	■	■	■
Requirements parsing	■					
Reviews	■	■	■	■	■	■
Sensitivity analysis				■		
Simulation	■	■	■	■	■	■
Sizing and timing analysis		■	■	■		■
Slicing			■			
Software sneak circuit analysis			■			
Stress testing				■		
Symbolic evaluation			■			
Test certification				■	■	■
Tracing (traceability analysis)	■	■	■	■		
Walkthroughs	■	■	■	■	■	■

3.2.1. Requirements

During the requirements phase, static analysis techniques can be used to check adherence to specification conventions, consistency, completeness, and language syntax. Commonly used static analysis techniques during the requirements phase include control flow analysis, data flow analysis, algorithm analysis, traceability analysis, and interface analysis. Control and data flow analysis are most applicable for real time and data driven systems. These flow analyses employ transformation of text describing logic and data requirements into graphic flows which are easier to examine. Examples of control flow diagrams include state transition and transaction diagrams. Algorithm analysis involves rederivation of equations or the evaluation of the suitability of specific numerical techniques. Traceability analysis involves tracing the requirements in the software requirements specification to system requirements. The identified relationships are then analyzed for correctness, consistency, completeness, and accuracy. Interface analysis in this phase involves evaluating the software requirements specification with the hardware, user, operator, and software interface requirements for correctness, consistency, completeness, accuracy, and readability.

Dynamic analysis techniques can be used to examine information flows, functional interrelationships, and performance requirements. Simulation is used to evaluate the interactions of large, complex systems with many hardware, user, and other interfacing software components. Prototyping helps customers and developers to examine the probable results of implementing software requirements. Examination of a prototype may help to identify incomplete or incorrect requirements statements and may also reveal that the software requirements will not result in system behavior the customer wants. Prototyping is usually worthwhile when the functions of the computer system have not previously been used in automated form by the customer. In this case, the customer can change the requirements before costly implementation. Unless the project is small or an automated method can be used to build a prototype quickly, usually only carefully selected functions are studied by prototyping.

One approach for analyzing individual requirements is requirements parsing. This manual technique involves examination to ensure that each requirement is defined unambiguously by a complete set of attributes (e.g., initiator of an action, source of the action, the action, the object of the action, constraints). Because this technique identifies undefined attributes, it may prevent release of incomplete requirements to the designers. In those cases where the requirements are to be represented by a formal language specification, this analysis aids in clarifying a requirement before its transformation.

Languages based on formal methods, i.e., mathematically based languages, may be used to specify system requirements. The act of specifying the software requirements in a formal language forces reasoning about the requirements and becomes an error detection technique. When requirements have been written in a formal language, the task of simulation may be easier. Then, the behavior of the potential system can be observed through use of the simulation. It may be the combination of formal specifications with other error detection techniques (e.g., control flow analysis and data flow analysis) that provides the biggest payoff for using formal methods.

3.2.2. Design

Evaluation of the design provides assurance that the requirements are not misrepresented, omitted, or incompletely implemented, and that unwanted features are not designed into the product by oversight. Design errors can be introduced by implementation constraints relating to timing, data structures, memory space, and accuracy.

Static analysis techniques help to detect inconsistencies, such as those between the inputs and outputs specified for a high level module and the inputs and outputs of the submodules. The most commonly used static analysis techniques during this phase include algorithm analysis, database analysis, (design) interface analysis, and traceability analysis. As in the requirements phase, algorithm analysis examines the correctness of the equations and numerical techniques, but in addition, it examines truncation and rounding effects, numerical precision of word storage and variables (single vs. extended-precision arithmetic), and data typing influences. Database analysis is particularly useful for programs that store program logic in data parameters. Database analysis supports verification of the computer security requirement of confidentiality, by checking carefully the direct and indirect accesses to data. Interface analysis aids in evaluating the software design documentation with hardware, operator, and software interface requirements for correctness, consistency, completeness, and accuracy. Data items should be analyzed at each interface. Traceability analysis involves tracing the software design documentation to the software requirements documentation and vice versa.

Commonly used dynamic analysis techniques for this phase include sizing and timing analysis, prototyping, and simulation. Sizing and timing analysis is useful in analyzing real-time programs with response time requirements and constrained memory and execution space requirements. This type of analysis is especially useful for determining that allocations for hardware and software are made appropriately for the design architecture; it would be quite costly to learn in system test that the performance problems are caused by the basic system design. An automated simulation may be appropriate for larger designs. Prototyping can be used as an aid in examining the design architecture in general or a specific set of functions. For large complicated systems prototyping can prevent inappropriate designs from resulting in costly, wasted implementations.

Formal analysis involves tracing paths through the design specification and formulating a composite function for each, in order to compare these composite functions to that of the previous level. This process ensures that the design continues to specify the same functional solution as is hierarchically elaborated. This process can be applied manually, if the specification is sufficiently formal and exact, but is most feasible only for high level design specifications. However, with automated tools, the functional effects of all levels of the design can be determined, due to the speed and capacity of the tools for manipulating detailed specifications.

3.2.3. Implementation

Use of static analysis techniques helps to ensure that the implementation phase products (e.g., code and related documentation) are of the proper form. Static analysis involves checking that the products adhere to coding and documentation standards or conventions, and that interfaces and data types are correct. This analysis can be performed either manually or with automated tools.

Frequently used static analysis techniques during this phase include code reading, inspections, walkthroughs, reviews, control flow analysis, database analysis, interface analysis, and traceability analysis. Code reading involves the examination by an individual, usually an expert other than the author, for obvious errors. Inspections, walkthroughs, and reviews, which are all used to detect logic and syntax errors, are effective forerunners to testing. As in previous phases, control flow diagrams are used to show the hierarchy of main routines and their subfunctions. Database analysis is performed on programs with significant data storage to ensure that common data and variable regions are used consistently between all calling routines; that data integrity is enforced and no data or variable can be accidentally overwritten by overflowing data tables; and that data typing and use are consistent throughout the program. With interface analysis, source code is evaluated with the hardware, operator, and software interface design documentation, as in the design phase. Traceability analysis involves tracing the source code to corresponding design specifications and vice versa.

One category of static analysis techniques performed on code is complexity analysis. Complexity analysis measures the complexity of code based on specific measurements (e.g., number of parameters passed, number of global parameters, number of operands/operators). Although not an error detection technique, complexity analysis can be used as an aid in identifying where use of error detection techniques should be concentrated and also in locating test paths and other pertinent information to aid in test case generation.

Other static analysis techniques used during implementation which aid in error detection include software sneak circuit analysis and slicing. Software sneak circuit analysis is a rigorous, language-independent technique for the detection of anomalous software (i.e., "sneaks") which may cause system malfunction. The methodology involves creation of a comprehensive "pictorial" database using quasi-electrical symbology which is then analyzed using topological and application "clues" to detect faults in the code [PEYTON]. Slicing is a program decomposition technique used to trace an output variable back through the code to identify all code statements relevant to a computation in the program [LYLE]. This technique may be useful to demonstrate functional diversity.

Dynamic analysis techniques help to determine the functional and computational correctness of the code. Regression analysis is used to reevaluate requirements and design issues whenever any significant code change is made. This analysis ensures awareness of the original system requirements. Sizing and timing analysis is performed during incremental code development and analysis results are compared against predicted values.

A formal method used in the implementation phase is proof of correctness, which is applied to code.

3.2.4. Test

Dynamic analysis in the test phase involves different types of testing and test strategies. Traditionally there are four types of testing: unit, integration, system, and acceptance. Unit testing may be either structural or functional testing performed on software units, modules, or subroutines. Structural testing examines the logic of the units and may be used to support requirements for test coverage, that is, how much of the program has been executed. Functional testing evaluates how software requirements have been implemented. For functional testing, testers usually need no information about the design of the program because test cases are based on the software requirements.

Integration testing is conducted when software units are integrated with other software units or with system components. During integration testing, various strategies can be employed (e.g., top-down testing, bottom-up testing, sandwich testing) but may depend on the overall strategy for constructing the system. Integration testing focuses on software, hardware, and operator interfaces.

Both system testing and acceptance testing execute the complete system. The primary difference is that the developer conducts system testing, usually in the development environment, while the customer conducts acceptance testing (or commissions the developer to conduct the acceptance testing in the presence of the customer). Acceptance testing is supposed to occur in a fully operational customer environment, but in some cases (e.g., nuclear power plants, flight control systems), some parts of the environment may need to be simulated.

For all four types of testing, different strategies may be used, according to . the project's characteristics. Some strategies include stress testing, boundary value testing, and mutation testing. Operational profile testing allows testers to select input data that are of special interest to the customer. For example, input data that causes execution of the most frequently used functions in operation may be the most important profile for testing for some systems. In other cases, it may be more important to choose an input profile that should not occur in reality. For nuclear power plants, this means choosing a profile that causes the software safety system to react;   the system responses can be examined to determine system behavior in adverse circumstances.

A major problem with testing is knowing when to stop. Software reliability estimation techniques, such as those described in section 5 of this report, can be used to estimate the number of errors still present in the system, and to determine how much more testing is needed. Sensitivity analysis, a promising technique emerging from the research community and entering the marketplace, is intended to indicate where to test, and hence to determine how much to test [VOAS]. Because sensitivity analysis is derived from mutation testing which is intended for detecting small changes to a program, this technique depends on code that is already "close to correct" for its effectiveness.

3.2.5. Installation and Checkout

During this phase, it is necessary to validate that the software operates correctly with the operational hardware system and with other software, as specified in the interface specifications. It is also necessary to verify the correctness and adequacy of the installation procedures and certify that the verified and validated software is the same as the executable code approved for installation. There may be several installation sites, each with different parameters. It is necessary to check that the programs have been properly tailored for each site.

The most commonly used dynamic analysis techniques for this phase are regression analysis and test, simulation, and test certification. When any changes to the product are made during this phase, regression analysis is performed to verify that the basic requirements and design assumptions affecting other areas of the program have not been violated. Simulation is used to test operator procedures and to isolate installation problems. Test certification, particularly in critical software systems, is used to verify that the required tests have been executed and that the delivered software product is identical to the product subjected to software verification and validation (V&V).

3.2.6. Operation and Maintenance

During operation of an on-line continuous system, test cases may be constructed that will check periodically if the system is behaving as expected. For any software maintenance activity, error detection techniques should be selected as if the maintenance activity were a new development activity, but considering the impact of new changes to the system. Use of traceability analysis on the software products, including test documentation, is crucial to identifying the extent of use of any selected error detection technique on the total software system. Regression testing must be applied in this phase.

3.3.   Benefits of Classes of Error Detection Techniques

In the early days of computers, static analysis of software involved hours of tedious manual checking of code for structural errors, syntax errors, and other types of errors. Today automation handles the tedious bookkeeping in both design and code activities. In the past, manual reading by an individual not only took longer, but may not always have been thorough. Design tools force consistency to some extent and support other static analyses. Techniques such as control flow analysis were difficult to perform manually, but with modern Computer Aided Software Engineering (CASE) tools, most static analyses can be performed more quickly and efficiently. As the power and ease of use of the tools improve, then static analyses become more effective.

A tool commonly used to perform static analysis is the compiler, which can detect syntactical code errors. The direct costs are the amount of electrical power and resources needed to conduct the compilation. However, not everyone agrees on the usefulness of compilers for producing error-free code. Supporters of Cleanroom engineering, a methodology for developing and assuring the quality of software, argue that the costs of rework and recompile are significant and should not be ignored. They believe that complete reliance on the tools to perform some of the intellectual work may reduce quality, because clean compilations can give a false sense of complete correctness [MILLS]. With Cleanroom engineering, programmers do not compile their code. Instead they spend more time on design, using a "box structure" method, and on analyzing their own work. When the programmers are confident of their work, it is submitted to another group who then compiles and tests the code. The Software Engineering Laboratory (SEL) at the National Aeronautics and Space Administration Goddard Space Flight Center collected sufficient data over 16 years to establish baselines for error and productivity rates. In recent years, two experiments were conducted on the Cleanroom approach [GREEN]. Results of the two Cleanroom experiments compared with SEL baselines show a lower error rate in the finished product and an increase in productivity across the lifecycle.

Software inspection, another static technique, is time consuming because it requires line by line, or graph by graph reading of the software element. Data collected from over 203 software inspections at the Jet Propulsion Laboratory in Pasadena, California, showed a significantly higher density of defects during requirements inspections [KELLY]. However, the defect densities of the products decreased exponentially from the requirements phase to the coding phase, implying that testing and rework will take less time. Code reading is another static analysis technique that has been shown in another SEL study to be quite effective [BASILI]. Researchers found that effectiveness increased with the experience level of the code readers, the reason being that experienced personnel were mentally executing the code. This technique may be difficult to schedule and implement formally; usually it is used when a programmer seeks help from a peer, and is conducted on small sections of code at a time. Also, errors found by code reading may not always be handled with a formal anomaly report.

Inspection and code reading have one drawback in common. The maximum benefits for these techniques are achieved when they are performed on all elements of the design and code, which tends to be time-consuming. Because of the time factor, they are usually conducted on only small portions of a program at a time, usually in three- or four-hour meetings. When the objective is to examine the entire program or many modules for global features, then other techniques with specific objectives (e.g., interface consistency, control flow, logic flow analysis) are more appropriate. Many of the static analysis techniques are intended to be conducted by individual members of a team, perhaps over days, and probably with automated support. There may be interaction among the team, especially to discuss possible anomalies. These types of techniques are effective for examining the integration of design or code modules.

Dynamic analyses tend to use large amounts of computer resources and involve human effort to prepare, execute and analyze tests. Testing can never guarantee that a system is completely correct, but it can demonstrate exactly what will occur under specific circumstances. Testing helps to establish an operational profile under which the system will work correctly. Testing also helps to uncover errors that were previously not discovered. Acceptance testing assures a customer that the software system will behave appropriately under specific circumstances as the customer has requested. Some CASE tools provide test aids (e.g., test case generators, test result capture, documentation). Although the power of modern computers has reduced execution time of test cases, nevertheless, exhaustive testing with all possible inputs under all circumstances is still not possible. In order to obtain maximum benefits from testing, careful planning and development of test goals, and strategies to achieve those goals are required.

While some static and dynamic analyses have become easier to perform with CASE tools, CASE technology has not eliminated all problems of software development and assurance. There are the problems of cost, methodology-dependence, and difficulty in understanding and using them. Two other major problems with CASE include restrictions on using the environments when they are not built on the concept of open systems [NIST187] and when information developed by the tools cannot be readily exchanged among tools of different vendors.

While journal articles and other literature describing usage of formal methods are available, they do not provide sufficient information to draw conclusions about the cost/quality benefits of using formal methods for the assurance of the quality of software. A study of formal methods was funded by NIST, the U.S. Naval Research Laboratory, and the Atomic Energy Control Board of Canada, to determine whether the benefits of using formal methods are significant relative to the costs of using them. The results of this study are published in [NISTGCR]. In the United Kingdom, there is an existing standard for safety critical software used in defense equipment, which requires the use of formal languages for specifications [MOD55].

The cost benefits of using specific error detection techniques or classes of techniques will differ from project to project. A balanced error detection program will depend on many factors, including the consequences of failure caused by an undetected error, the complexity of the software system, the types of errors likely to be committed in developing specific software, the effort needed to apply a technique, the automated support available, and the experience of the development and assurance staff. Another factor to consider is the interplay among techniques (e.g., whether the output of one technique can be used readily by another technique). If a specific error type is likely, then a technique known for finding that type of error should be selected. The application of formal verification techniques is appropriate when failure of the software would be disastrous. For planning a balanced program, an important requirement should be to ensure that analyses are applied to all the software products at all phases of the lifecycle in an orderly manner. The program should be evaluated frequently to ensure that the analyses are being used correctly and are aiding in error detection. The SPC techniques described in section 5 aid in this evaluation.

A final consideration for selecting techniques based on their cost benefit takes into account who will be conducting the analysis, and under what circumstances. For auditors, techniques which examine interfaces across the entire program, control flow, and critical operational paths are more appropriate than those involving detailed line by line analysis (e.g., software code inspection). When an anomaly is found, however, the auditors may choose to examine in greater detail the areas suspected of contributing to the anomaly.

4. REMOVAL OF ERRORS

This section describes the process of analyzing anomalies and removing errors. This is performed after an anomaly has been discovered using any error detection technique, such as those discussed in section 3. Analysis of an anomaly will not only aid in the removal of errors related to the anomaly, but will also help to detect other similar errors which have not yet manifested themselves. In addition, information obtained from this analysis can provide valuable feedback that may improve subsequent efforts and development processes in future projects.

The handling of an anomaly generally follows three steps: identification, investigation, and resolution. However, exact procedures for dealing with an anomaly will depend on many factors. First, it may be that the anomaly is not actually an error.[4] For example, the anomaly may be a result of misinterpreting test results. In these situations, an explanation about why the anomaly is not an error should be recorded, and no further action is required. Second, the procedures will depend on the activity used to detect the anomaly. For example, anomalies discovered during walkthroughs and code reading are often fixed immediately, without having to go through the formal error resolution process. During integration testing, all anomaly reports may be collected and then addressed to locate probable cause and recommend fixes. Third, the severity level of the anomaly will determine how soon the error should be fixed. Generally, the more severe the error, the sooner it needs to be fixed.

The general policy for handling anomalies should include rules/regulations concerning the administration of the entire error removal activity (e.g., who must fill out problem reports, where or to whom this information is distributed, how to close out problem reports, who enters the collected information into the error database). These issues are not addressed in this report, because the policy will be specific to an organization.

General project information which supports the error removal process should be maintained. This information may include, but is not limited to, descriptions of the design methodology, the verification plan used in design, the test plan, the configuration control plan, identification of tools used to design and test software (e.g., CASE tools), and the programming language used.

4.1. Identification

As soon as an anomaly is detected, information about it should be recorded to help identify, analyze, and correct the anomaly. Typically, this information is presented in an anomaly, or problem report. While the formats may differ, reports should include the following types of information.

---

[4]Or, the anomaly may be caused by a problem external to the software under analysis (e.g., the modem used for testing was not configured properly), not by an error in the software. In this case, the information on the anomaly is sent to the responsible party, but is not further addressed by the error removal activity.

Locator. Identify the person(s) who discovered the anomaly including name, address, phone number, email address, fax number, and company identification.

Date and Time. Specify the date and time that the anomaly occurred and/or was discovered. Time can be specified by wall clock time, system time, or CPU time. For distributed systems, specify the time zone.

Activity. Identify the activity taking place at the time the anomaly was discovered. These activities include error detection activities employed during the development and release of a product, including static and dynamic analysis, review, inspection, audit, simulation, timing analysis, testing (unit, integration, system, acceptance), compiling/assembling, and walkthrough.

Phase Encountered. Identify the lifecycle phase in which the anomaly was encountered (e.g., requirements, design, implementation, test, installation and checkout, and operation and maintenance). If possible, specify the activity within the phase (e.g., during preliminary design in the design phase).

Operational Environment. Specify the hardware, software, database, test support software, platform, firmware, monitor/terminal, network, and peripherals being used.

Status of Product. Specify the effect of the problem on the product (e.g., unusable, degraded, affected, unaffected).

Repeatability. Determine if the anomaly is a one-time occurrence, intermittent, recurring, or reproducible.

Symptom. Describe the symptoms, which are indications that a problem exists (e.g., inconsistency between the design and the requirements, violation of a constraint imposed by the requirements, operating system crash, program hang-up, input or output problem, incorrect behavior or result, error message, inconsistent logic or behavior, infinite loop, and unexpected abort).

Location of Symptom. The location of the anomaly can be in the actual product (hardware, software, database, or documentation), the test system, the platform, or in any development phase product (e.g., specification, code, database, manuals and guides, plans and procedures, reports, standards/policies). Identify the documentation that was analyzed, or the code that was executed, the tools and documentation used to support the activity. Identify the specific location(s) where the anomaly is evident in documentation, or the test case in which the anomaly occurred.

Severity. Severity is a measure of the disruption an anomaly gives the user when encountered during operation of the product. Severity can be divided into several levels, with the highest level being catastrophic, and the lowest being at the annoyance level. A severity classification system should be tailored to particular systems or class of systems. The number of levels and the corresponding descriptions of the levels may vary.   An example of a severity classification is given below:

Level 6	Critical.	Major feature not working, system crashes, loss of data
Level 5	Serious.	Impairment of critical system functions, no workaround
Level 4	Major.	Workaround is difficult
Level 3	Moderate.	Workaround is simple
Level 2	Cosmetic.	Tolerable, or fix is deferrable
Level 1	User misunderstanding	
Level 0	No problem (e.g., testing error)	

4.2.   Investigation

Following the identification stage, all errors should be investigated to obtain further information on the nature and cause in order to propose solutions for resolution action or corrective action. Information that should be recorded during this stage include the following:

Phase Introduced. Identify the lifecycle phase in which the error was introduced. If possible, specify the activity within the phase (e.g., during preliminary design in the design phase).

Type. This attribute describes the type of error found, e.g., logic error, computational error, interface/timing error, data handling error, data error, documentation error, document quality error (e.g., out of date, inconsistent, incomplete), and enhancement errors (e.g., errors caused by change in requirements, errors caused by a previous fix).

Location of Error. The location of the error may be the same as the location of the symptom. See *Location of Symptom* in section 4.1.

Cause. Typical causes of an error include human errors (e.g., misunderstanding, omission errors) and inadequate methodology (e.g., incomplete inspection process, inappropriate design methodology).

Units Affected. This attribute identifies the software unit(s) affected by the error and its related fix, e.g., which components, modules, or documents are affected.

Priority. Priority is the degree of importance that is given to the resolution of an error. Based on the priority level, it is determined whether the error should be fixed immediately, eventually, or not at all (e.g., if error becomes obsolete as result of other changes). However, fixes should be performed according to the software configuration management policies of the project. The relationship between the priority scale and the severity scale should be specified by the administrative policy. An example of a priority scale is:

Level 5   Resolve error immediately
Level 4   Error gets high attention
Level 3   Error will be placed in normal queue
Level 2   Use workaround or fix in the interim
Level 1   Will be fixed last
Level 0   Will not be fixed

4.3. Resolution

Error resolution consists of the steps to correct the error. The policy of the project determines if the person who investigates the error will also correct the error. The procedures for distribution and retention of the error information is also identified by the policy. Typically, the recipients of the error information are the project manager, SQA manager, corporate database manager, and the customer. The amount of formalism (e.g., whether the plan needs to be documented) depends on the scope, risk, and size of the project. For small errors in small projects, this scheme may not be necessary.

4.3.1. Resolution Plan

The proposed procedures for resolution action should be documented in a resolution plan.

Item to Fix. Identify the item to be fixed (e.g., name, ID number, revision), the component within the item, text description of the fix.

Estimated Date or Time. Specify the proposed dates for start and completion of the fix.

Personnel. Identify the manager, engineer, or other members responsible for performing the fix and for follow-up.

4.3.2. Resolution Action

The resolution action is the actual fix, i.e., making changes in the product to correct and remove the error. The following information should be provided by the person(s) who perform the resolution action, upon completion.

Date Completed. Specify the date when resolution action (fix) was completed.

Personnel. Identify the person(s) who fixed the error.

Time Length. Specify the number of minutes or hours required for the fix.

Size of Fix. Specify the size of the fix in terms of the number of source lines of code (SLOC) added / modified, or the number of document pages added / modified.

4.3.3. Corrective Action

The corrective action stage is optional, because not all anomalies will require individual corrective actions.

Standards, Policies or Procedures. Identify the standards, policies, or procedures to be revised, created, or reinforced.

Other Action. This includes other revisions to the development process (e.g., implementing training, reallocation of people or resources, and improving or enforcing audit activities).

4.3.4. Follow-up

For all errors, there should be a follow-up to verify that the necessary resolution action or corrective action has been performed correctly.

Personnel. Identify the person or organization that performed follow-up of resolution action and/or corrective action.

Verification of Action. Confirm that the "right fix" has been performed, that the error has actually been removed, and that the fix has not adversely affected other areas of the software.

Disposition. Describe the status of the anomaly, whether it is closed (resolution was implemented and verified, or not within scope of project), deferred, merged with another problem, or referred to another project.

Closeout. Identify procedures for retention of the error data.

4.4.   Use of Individual Error Data

The data that is collected for the purpose of removing a single error can be used for other purposes. This data can aid in removing all errors similar to the original error. In addition to making improvements in the product, data on single errors can be used to improve the current development process. For instance, if many errors are found to be requirements errors, this may prompt a change to the requirements specification process. Data on single errors can also be used in measurement and statistical process control activities such as those discussed in section 5. For example, the data can be used to calculate measures or it can be used as input to control charts. Finally, individual error data can be entered into an error database, in order to maintain an error history of all projects in the organization.

5. TECHNIQUES FOR THE COLLECTION AND ANALYSIS OF ERROR DATA

Techniques for collecting and analyzing sets of error data during the lifecycle aid in understanding, evaluating and improving the development and maintenance process or aid in evaluating or estimating product quality. Software measures provide insights about both process and product. Measures may feed into statistical process control (SPC) techniques; SPC techniques may be used for both process and product evaluation. Software reliability estimation techniques are usually applied only to the product. Most of these techniques operate on error history profiles of error data discovered by error detection techniques.

This section addresses *only* the error aspects of these techniques. Other information may need to be collected when making major decisions to change a policy or development activity (e.g., project information, customer requirements, company policy, methodologies being used, tools being used, number of people using a certain technique). These types of information are not discussed in this report.

5.1. Error History Profile / Database

An error history profile is needed to perform error analysis effectively. An organizational database can be used both to track the status of a project and to track the use of error analysis techniques. Data collected for the purpose of resolving single errors (e.g., source, cause, type, severity), should be placed in the error database to enable the establishment of anomaly histories. Other data collected specifically for the purpose of measurement or statistical process control should also be entered into the database. The database serves as a baseline for validation as well as for improvement. Past mistakes can be avoided from lessons learned. Maintaining a database serves the following purposes:

- To identify which development processes work well (or poorly) for an application domain,

- To support process improvement for the current project as well as for future projects,

- To identify whether the processes are being applied properly (or at all),

- To identify error classes by cause,

- To estimate the error growth rate throughout development, and therefore to be able to adjust plans for assurance activities, and

- To measure the quality of the software at delivery.

Error data collected from an error detection technique in one phase can support process improvement in an earlier lifecycle phase (for future projects), as well as in a later phase. For example, in a presentation at a COMPASS Conference,[5] one panel member explained that analysis of the data collected from code inspections at his organization revealed that a high percentage of the code errors were the result of errors in the software requirements specification. In response to this finding, the organization began investigating the use of formal languages for specifying software requirements. This example demonstrates the necessity of collecting and analyzing data for both error removal and process improvement.

Data histories can help managers to recognize when there is a significant deviation from project plans during development. Past error data can be used to estimate the number of expected errors at different times in the development cycle. For instance, if the reported error count for a particular product was smaller than was expected, compared with similar past projects, this may suggest that the development team generated an unusually low number of errors. However, further investigation may reveal that the project was behind schedule, and to save time, planned inspections were not held. Thus, many existing errors remained undetected, so that the low error count did not reflect the true quality of the product. This example illustrates how a history profile enables an organization to recognize and correct a process problem to avoid delivering a product with residual errors.

5.2.   Data Collection Process

This section describes the process of collecting error data for a specific purpose (e.g., to use with control charts). Some of the error data may include data previously collected during error detection. This data can be retrieved from the organizational database, or can be collected directly upon discovery or during resolution of an error. Data must be collected properly in order for any error analysis technique to be effective. The recommended steps of the data collection process are listed below [AIAA]:

1.   Establish the objectives.

2.   Prepare a data collection plan. The plan may include the following recommended elements:

Data definition and type. Specify/define the data to be collected and the type (i.e., attribute or variable data). An attribute is a characteristic that an item may or may not possess. It is obtained by noting the presence or absence of a characteristic and counting occurrences of the characteristic with a specified unit. For example: a module may or may not contain a defect. This type of data takes on only discrete (integer) values. Variable data is obtained by recording a numerical value for each item observed. Variable data can be either continuous or discrete. Examples: cost of fixing an error (continuous), lines of code (discrete).

---

[5]Dr. John Kelly, of the Jet Propulsion Laboratory, was a member of the "Formal Methods in Industry" panel at the 1992 COMPASS Conference, held at NIST in Gaithersburg, Maryland on June 15-18, 1992. The panel discussion was not documented in the conference proceedings.

Analysis technique. Identify the technique requiring the data. Each technique has unique data requirements, so the technique to be used should be specified prior to data collection.

Measurement method. Measurements can be taken by equipment, observation, or selecting data from existing records. The reliability, determined by accuracy and precision, of the measurement method must be established prior to data collection.

Sampling Procedure. The data collection interval, amount of data to be collected, and the sampling method should be specified (e.g., random sampling using a random number table). When determining the data collection interval, issues such as process volume, process stability, and cost should be considered.

Personnel. Identify persons responsible for specific data collection tasks.

Forms for data reporting (e.g., electronic spreadsheet, paper forms, etc.).

Recording and processing of data. One method for processing data is *blocking*, the separating of data into potential comparison categories during the recording of data. Blocking can be accomplished by recording each category separately, or through labeling information that enables future sorting.

Monitoring. Describe how the data collection process is to be monitored.

3.   Apply tools. Automated tools should be considered whenever possible, in order to minimize impact on the project's schedule. Factors to consider include the following: availability of the tool, reliability of the tool, cost of purchasing or developing the tool, and whether it can handle any necessary adjustments.

4.   Provide training. Once tools and plans are in place, training should be provided to ensure that data collectors understand the purpose of the measurements and know explicitly what data is to be collected.

5.   Perform trial run. A trial run of the data collection plan should be made to resolve any problems or misconceptions about the plan. This can save vast amounts of time and effort.

6.   Implement the plan. Collect the data and review them promptly, so that problems can be resolved before the disappearance of information required to resolve them (e.g., if test results on a screen are not saved).

7.   Monitor data collection. Monitor the process to ensure that objectives are met and that procedures are implemented according to the data collection plan.

8.   Use the data. Use the data as soon as possible to achieve maximum benefit.

9.   Provide feedback to all involved. Those involved need to know what impact their efforts had, and the end result. This will enable them to understand the purpose of their efforts and agree to undertake similar tasks in the future.

Additional recommendations for the data collection process are listed below [ROOK]:

- Data collection should be integrated into the development process (e.g., as part of the quality management system).

- Data collection should be automated whenever possible.

- Time-scales between data collection and data analysis should be minimized.

- Data should be treated as a company resource and facilities should be available to keep historical records of projects as well as to monitor current projects.

- The problem of motivating personnel to keep accurate records should not be underestimated. Proper training and quick analysis facilities are essential, but are not sufficient.

5.3.   Metrics

Within the software engineering community, there is much confusion and inconsistency over the use of the terms metric and measure. In this report, a metric is defined to be the mathematical definition, algorithm, or function used to obtain a quantitative assessment of a product or process. The actual numerical value produced by a metric is a measure. Thus, for example, cyclomatic complexity is a metric, but the value of this metric is the cyclomatic complexity measure.

Data on individual errors (see sec. 4) can be used to calculate metrics values. Two general classes of metrics include the following:

management metrics, which assist in the control or management of the development process; and
quality metrics, which are predictors or indicators of the product qualities

Management metrics can be used for controlling any industrial production or manufacturing activity. They are used to assess resources, cost, and task completion. Examples of resource-related metrics include elapsed calendar time, effort, and machine usage. Typical metrics for software estimate task completion include percentage of modules coded, or percentage of statements tested. Other management metrics used in project control include defect-related metrics. Information on the nature and origin of defects are used to estimate costs associated with defect discovery and removal. Defect rates for the current project can be compared to that of past projects to ensure that the current project is behaving as expected.

Quality metrics are used to estimate characteristics or qualities of a software product. Examples of these metrics include complexity metrics, and readability indexes for software documents. The use of these metrics for quality assessment is based on the assumptions that the metric measures some inherent property of the software, and that the inherent property itself influences the behavioral characteristics of the final product.

Some metrics may be both management metrics and quality metrics, i.e., they can be used for both project control and quality assessment. These metrics include simple size metrics (e.g., lines of code, number of function points) and primitive problem, fault, or error metrics. For example, size is used to predict project effort and time scales, but it can also be used as a quality predictor, since larger projects may be more complex and difficult to understand, and thus more error-prone.

A disadvantage of some metrics is that they do not have an interpretation scale which allows for consistent interpretation, as with measuring temperature (in degrees Celsius) or length (in meters). This is particularly true of metrics for software quality characteristics (e.g., maintainability, reliability, usability). Measures must be interpreted relatively, through comparison with plans and expectations, comparison with similar past projects, or comparison with similar components within the current project. While some metrics are mathematically-based, most, including reliability models, have not been proven.

Since there is virtually an infinite number of possible metrics, users must have some criteria for choosing which metrics to apply to their particular projects. Ideally, a metric should possess all of the following characteristics:

- Simple - definition and use of the metric is simple
- Objective - different people will give identical values; allows for consistency, and prevents individual bias
- Easily collected - the cost and effort to obtain the measure is reasonable
- Robust - metric is insensitive to irrelevant changes; allows for useful comparison
- Valid - metric measures what it is supposed to; this promotes trustworthiness of the measure

Within the software engineering community, two philosophies on measurement are embodied by two major standards organizations. A draft standard on software quality metrics sponsored by the Institute for Electrical and Electronics Engineers Software Engineering Standards Subcommittee supports the single value concept. This concept is that a single numerical value can be computed to indicate the quality of the software; the number is computed by measuring and combining the measures for attributes related to several quality characteristics. The international community, represented by the ISO/IEC organization through its Joint Technical Committee, Subcommittee 7 for software engineering appears to be adopting the view that a range of values, rather than a single number, for representing overall quality is more appropriate.

5.3.1. Metrics Throughout the Lifecycle

Metrics enable the estimation of work required in each phase, in terms of the budget and schedule. They also allow for the percentage of work completed to be assessed at any point during the phase, and establish criteria for determining the completion of the phase.

The general approach to using metrics, which is applicable to each lifecycle phase, is as follows: [ROOK]

• Select the appropriate metrics to be used to assess activities and outputs in each phase of the lifecycle.

• Determine the goals or expected values of the metrics.

• Determine or compute the measures, or actual values.

• Compare the actual values with the expected values or goals.

• Devise a plan to correct any observed deviations from the expected values.

Some complications may be involved when applying this approach to software. First, there will often be many possible causes for deviations from expectations and for each cause there may be several different types of corrective actions. Therefore, it must be determined which of the possible causes is the actual cause before the appropriate corrective action can be taken. In addition, the expected values themselves may be inappropriate, when there are no very accurate models available to estimate them.

In addition to monitoring using expected values derived from other projects, metrics can also identify anomalous components that are unusual with respect to other components values in the same project. In this case, project monitoring is based on internally generated project norms, rather than estimates from other projects.

The metrics described in the following subsections are defined in [ROOK], [IEEE982.2] and [AIRFORCE], [SQE], and [ZAGE] and comprise a representative sample of management and quality metrics that can be used in the lifecycle phases to support error analysis. This section does not evaluate or compare metrics, but provides definitions to help readers decide which metrics may be useful for a particular application.

5.3.1.1. Metrics Used in All Phases

Primitive metrics such as those listed below can be collected throughout the lifecycle. These metrics can be plotted using bar graphs, histograms, and Pareto charts as part of statistical process control. The plots can be analyzed by management to identify the phases that are most error prone, to suggest steps to prevent the recurrence of similar errors, to suggest procedures for earlier detection of faults, and to make general improvements to the development process.

Problem Metrics

Primitive problem metrics.

Number of problem reports per phase, priority, category, or cause
Number of reported problems per time period
Number of open real problems per time period
Number of closed real problems per time period
Number of unevaluated problem reports
Age of open real problem reports
Age of unevaluated problem reports
Age of real closed problem reports
Time when errors are discovered
Rate of error discovery

Cost and Effort Metrics

Primitive cost and effort metrics.
Time spent
Elapsed time
Staff hours
Staff months
Staff years

Change Metrics

Primitive change metrics.

Number of revisions, additions, deletions, or modifications
Number of requests to change the requirements specification and/or design during lifecycle phases after the requirements phase

Fault Metrics

Primitive fault metrics.   Assesses the efficiency and effectiveness of fault resolution/removal activities, and check that sufficient effort is available for fault resolution/removal.

Number of unresolved faults at planned end of phase
Number of faults that, although fully diagnosed, have not been corrected, and number of outstanding change requests

Number of requirements and design faults detected during reviews and walkthroughs

5.3.1.2. Requirements Metrics

The main reasons to measure requirements specifications is to provide early warnings of quality problems, to enable more accurate project predictions, and to help improve the specifications.

Primitive size metrics. These metrics involve a simple count. Large components are assumed to have a larger number of residual errors, and are more difficult to understand than small components; as a result, their reliability and extendibility may be affected.

Number of pages or words
Number of requirements
Number of functions

Requirements traceability. This metric is used to assess the degree of traceability by measuring the percentage of requirements that has been implemented in the design. It is also used to identify requirements that are either missing from, or in addition to the original requirements. The measure is computed using the equation: RT = R1/R2 x 100%, where R1 is the number of requirements met by the architecture (design), and R2 is the number of original requirements. [IEEE982.2]

Completeness (CM). Used to determine the completeness of the software specification during requirements phase. This metric uses eighteen *primitives* (e.g., number of functions not satisfactorily defined, number of functions, number of defined functions, number of defined functions not used, number of referenced functions, and number of decision points). It then uses ten *derivatives* (e.g., functions satisfactorily defined, data references having an origin, defined functions used, reference functions defined), which are derived from the primitives. The metric is the weighted sum of the ten derivatives expressed as $CM = \sum w_i D_i$, where the summation is from i=1 to i=10, each weight w_i has a value between 0 and 1, the sum of the weights is 1, and each D_i is a derivative with a value between 1 and 0. The values of the primitives also can be used to identify problem areas within the requirements specification. [IEEE982.2]

Fault-days number. Specifies the number of days that faults spend in the software product from its creation to their removal. This measure uses two primitives: the phase, date, or time that the fault was introduced, and the phase, date, or time that the fault was removed. The fault days for the ith fault, (FD_i), is the number of days from the creation of the fault to its removal. The measure is calculated as follows: $FD = \sum FD_i$.

This measure is an indicator of the quality of the software design and development process. A high value may be indicative of untimely removal of faults and/or existence of many faults, due to an ineffective development process. [IEEE982.2]

Function points. This measure was originated by Allan Albrecht at IBM in the late 1970's, and was further developed by Charles Symons. It uses a weighted sum of the number of inputs, outputs, master files and inquiries in a product to predict development size [ALBRECHT]. To count function points, the first step is to classify each component by using standard guides to rate each component as having low, average, or high complexity. The second basic step is to tabulate function component counts. This is done by entering the appropriate counts in the Function Counting Form, multiplying by the weights on the form, and summing up the totals for each component type to obtain the Unadjusted Function Point Count. The third step is to rate each application characteristic from 0 to 5 using a rating guide, and then adding all the ratings together to obtain the Characteristic Influence Rating. Finally, the number of function points is calculated using the equation

$$\text{Function pts.} = \text{Unadjusted function} * (.65 + .01 * \text{Character Influence Rating})$$
$$\text{point count} \hspace{4cm} \text{[SQE]}$$

5.3.1.3. Design Metrics

The main reasons for computing metrics during the design phase are the following: gives early indication of project status; enables selection of alternative designs; identifies potential problems early in the lifecycle; limits complexity; and helps in deciding how to modularize so the resulting modules are both testable and maintainable. In general, good design practices involve high cohesion of modules, low coupling of modules, and effective modularity. [ZAGE]

Size Metrics

Primitive size metrics. These metrics are used to estimate the size of the design or design documents.

> Number of pages or words
> DLOC (lines of PDL)
> Number of modules
> Number of functions
> Number of inputs and outputs
> Number of interfaces

(Estimated) number of modules (NM). Provides measure of product size, against which the completeness of subsequent module based activities can be assessed. The estimate for the number of modules is given by, NM = S/M, where S is the estimated size in LOC, M is the median module size found in similar projects. The estimate NM can be compared to the median number of modules for other projects. [ROOK]

Fault Metrics

Primitive fault metrics. These metrics identify potentially fault-prone modules as early as possible. [ROOK]

> Number of faults associated with each module
> Number of requirements faults and structural design faults detected during detailed design

Complexity Metrics

Primitive complexity metrics. Identifies early in development modules which are potentially complex or hard to test. [ROOK]

> Number of parameters per module
> Number of states or data partitions per parameter
> Number of branches in each module

Coupling. Coupling is the manner and degree of interdependence between software modules [IEEE982.2]. Module coupling is rated based on the type of coupling, using a standard rating chart, which can be found in [SQE]. According to the chart, *data coupling* is the best type of coupling, and *content coupling* is the worst. The better the coupling, the lower the rating. [SQE], [ZAGE]

Cohesion. Cohesion is the degree to which the tasks performed within a single software module are related to the module's purpose. The module cohesion value for a module is assigned using a standard rating chart, which can be found in [SQE]. According to the chart, the best cohesion level is *functional*, and the worst is *coincidental*, with the better levels having lower values. Case studies have shown that fault rate correlates highly with cohesion strength. [SQE], [ZAGE]

(Structural) fan-in / fan-out. Fan-in/fan-out represents the number of modules that *call/are called by* a given module. Identifies whether the system decomposition is adequate (e.g., no modules which cause bottlenecks, no missing levels in the hierarchical decomposition, no unused modules ("dead" code), identification of critical modules). May be useful to compute maximum, average, and total fan-in/fan-out. [ROOK], [IEEE982.2]

Information flow metric (C). Represents the total number of combinations of an input source to an output destination, given by, $C = C_i \times (\text{fan-in} \times \text{fan-out})^2$, where C_i is a code metric, which may be omitted. The product inside the parentheses represents the total number of paths through a module. [ZAGE]

Design Inspection Metrics

Staff hours per major defect detected. Used to evaluate the efficiency of the design inspection processes. The following primitives are used: time expended in preparation for inspection meeting (T1), time expended in conduct of inspection meeting (T2), number of major defects detected during the ith inspection (S_i), and total number of inspections to date (I). The staff hours per major defect detected is given below, with the summations being from i=1 to i=I.

$$M = \frac{\sum (T1 + T2)_i}{\sum S_i}$$

This measure is applied to new code, and should fall between three and five. If there is significant deviation from this range, then the matter should be investigated. (May be adapted for code inspections). [IEEE982.2]

Defect Density (DD). Used after design inspections of new development or large block modifications in order to assess the inspection process. The following primitives are used: total number of unique defects detected during the ith inspection or ith lifecycle phase (D_i), total number of inspections to date (I), and number of source lines of design statements in thousands (KSLOD). The measure is calculated by the ratio
$$DD = \frac{\sum D_i}{KSLOD}$$ where the sum is from i=1 to i=I.

This measure can also be used in the implementation phase, in which case the number of source lines of executable code in thousands (KSLOC) should be substituted for KSLOD. [IEEE982.2]

Test Related Metrics.

Test related primitives. Checks that each module will be / has been adequately tested, or assesses the effectiveness of early testing activities. [ROOK]

> Number of integration test cases planned/executed involving each module
> Number of black box test cases planned/executed per module
> Number of requirements faults detected during testing (also re-assesses quality of requirements specification)

5.3.1.4. Implementation Metrics

Metrics used during the implementation phase can be grouped into four basic types: size metrics, control structure metrics, data structure metrics, and other code metrics.

Size Metrics

Lines of Code (LOC). Although lines of code is one of the most popular metrics, it has no standard definition.[6] The predominant definition for line of code is "any line of a program text that is not a comment or blank line, regardless of the number of statements or fragments of statements on the line." [SQE] It is an indication of size, which allows for estimation of effort, timescale, and total number of faults. For the same application, the length of a program partly depends on the language the code is written in, thus making comparison using LOC difficult. However, LOC can be a useful measure if the projects being compared are consistent in their development methods (e.g., use the same language, coding style). Because of its disadvantages, the use of LOC as a management metric (e.g., for project sizing beginning from the requirements phase) is controversial, but there are uses for this metric in error analysis, such as to estimate the values of other metrics. The advantages of this metric are that it is conceptually simple, easily automated, and inexpensive. [SQE]

Halstead software science metrics. This set of metrics was developed by Maurice Halstead, who claimed they could be used to evaluate the mental effort and time required to create a program, and how compactly a program is expressed. These metrics are based on four primitives listed below:

n_1 = number of unique operators
n_2 = number of unique operands
N_1 = total occurrences of operators
N_2 = total occurrences of operands

The program length measure, N, is the sum of N_1 and N_2. Other software science metrics are listed below. [SQE]

Vocabulary: $n = n_1 + n_2$
Predicted length: $N^\wedge = (n_1 * \log_2 n_1) + (n_2 * \log_2 n_2)$
Program volume: $V = N * \log_2 n$
Effort: $E = (n_1 N_2 N \log_2 n)/(2 n_2)$
Time: $T = E/ß$; Halstead $ß=18$
Predicted number of bugs: $B = V/3000$

Control Structure Metrics

Number of entries/exits per module. Used to assess the complexity of a software architecture, by counting the number of entry and exit points for each module. The equation to determine the measure for the ith module is simply $m_i = e_i + x_i$, where e_i is

---

[6]The SEI has made an effort to provide a complete definition for LOC. See [PARK].

the number of entry points for the ith module, and x_i is the number of exit points for the ith module. [IEEE982.2]

Cyclomatic complexity (C). Used to determine the structural complexity of a coded module in order to limit its complexity, thus promoting understandability. In general, high complexity leads to a high number of defects and maintenance costs. Also used to identify minimum number of test paths to assure test coverage. The primitives for this measure include the number of nodes (N), and the number of edges (E), which can be determined from the graph representing the module. The measure can then be computed with the formula, $C = E - N + 1$. [IEEE982.2], [SQE]

Data Structure Metrics

Amount of data. This measure can be determined by primitive metrics such as Halstead's n_2 and N_2, number of inputs/outputs, or the number of variables. These primitive metrics can be obtained from a compiler cross reference. [SQE]

Live variables. For each line in a section of code, determine the number of live variables (i.e., variables whose values could change during execution of that section of code). The average number of live variables per line of code is the sum of the number of live variables for each line, divided by the number of lines of code. [SQE]

Variable scope. The variable scope is the number of source statements between the first and last reference of the variable. For example, if variable A is first referenced on line 10, and last referenced on line 20, then the variable scope for A is 9. To determine the average variable scope for variables in a particular section of code, first determine the variable scope for each variable, sum up these values, and divide by the number of variables [SQE]. With large scopes, the understandability and readability of the code is reduced.

Variable spans. The variable span is the number of source statements between successive references of the variable. For each variable, the average span can be computed. For example, if the variable X is referenced on lines 13, 18, 20, 21, and 23, the average span would be the sum of all the spans divided by the number of spans, i.e., $(4+1+0+1)/4 = 1.5$. With large spans, it is more likely that a far back reference will be forgotten. [SQE]

5.3.1.5. Test Metrics

Test metrics may be of two types: metrics related to test results or the quality of the product being tested; and metrics used to assess the effectiveness of the testing process.

PRODUCT METRICS
Defect/Error/Fault Metrics

Primitive defect/error/fault metrics. These metrics can be effectively used with SPC techniques, such as bar charts, and Pareto diagrams. These metrics can also be used to form percentages (e.g., percentage of logic errors = number of logic errors ÷ total number of errors).

> Number of faults detected in each module
> Number of requirements, design, and coding faults found during unit and integration testing
> Number of errors by type (e.g., number of logic errors, number of computational errors, number of interface errors, number of documentation errors)
> Number of errors by cause or origin
> Number of errors by severity (e.g., number of critical errors, number of major errors, number of cosmetic errors)

Fault density (FD). This measure is computed by dividing the number of faults by the size (usually in KLOC, thousands of lines of code). It may be weighted by severity using the equation

$$FD_w = (W_1 \, S/N + W_2 \, A/N + W_3 \, M/N) \,/\, Size$$

where N = total number of faults
           S = number of severe faults
           A = number of average severity faults
           M = number of minor faults
           W_i = weighting factors (defaults are 10, 3, and 1)

FD can be used to perform the following: predict remaining faults by comparison with expected fault density; determine if sufficient testing has been completed based on predetermined goals; establish standard fault densities for comparison and prediction. [IEEE982.2], [SQE]

Defect age. Defect age is the time between when a defect is introduced to when it is detected or fixed. Assign the numbers 1 through 6 to each of the lifecycle phases from requirements to operation and maintenance. The defect age is then the difference of the numbers corresponding to the phase introduced and phase detected. The average defect age = $\dfrac{\Sigma \text{ (phase detected - phase introduced)}}{\text{number of defects}}$, the sum being over all the defects. [SQE]

Defect response time. This measure is the time between when a defect is detected to when it is fixed or closed. [SQE]

Defect cost. The cost of a defect may be a sum of the cost to analyze the defect, the cost to fix it, and the cost of failures already incurred due to the defect. [SQE]

Defect removal efficiency (DRE). The DRE is the percentage of defects that have been removed during a process, computed with the equation:

$$DRE = \frac{\text{Number of defects removed}}{\text{Number of defects at start of process}} \times 100\%$$

The DRE can also be computed for each lifecycle phase and plotted on a bar graph to show the relative defect removal efficiencies for each phase. Or, the DRE may be computed for a specific process (e.g., design inspection, code walkthrough, unit test, six-month operation, etc.). [SQE]

PROCESS METRICS
Test case metrics

Primitive test case metrics.

Total number of planned white/black box test cases run to completion
Number of planned integration tests run to completion
Number of unplanned test cases required during test phase

Coverage metrics[7]

Statement coverage. Measures the percentage of statements executed (to assure that each statement has been tested at least once). [SQE]

Branch coverage. Measures the percentage of branches executed. [SQE]

Path coverage. Measures the percentage of program paths executed. It is generally impractical and inefficient to test all the paths in a program. The count of the number of paths may be reduced by treating all possible loop iterations as one path. [SQE] Path coverage may be used to ensure 100 percent coverage of critical (safety or security related) paths.

Data flow coverage. Measures the definition and use of variables and data structures. [SQE]

---

[7]Commercial tools are available for statement coverage, branch coverage, and path coverage, but only private tools exist for data flow coverage. [BEIZER] Coverage tools report the percentage of items covered and lists what is not covered. [SQE]

Test coverage. Measures the completeness of the testing process. Test coverage is the percentage of requirements implemented (in the form of defined test cases or functional capabilities) multiplied by the percentage of the software structure (in units, segments, statements, branches, or path test results) tested. [AIRFORCE]

Failure metrics

Mean time to failure (MTTF). Gives an estimate of the mean time to the next failure, by accurately recording failure times t_i, the elapsed time between the ith and the (i-1)st failures, and computing the average of all the failure times. This metric is the basic parameter required by most software reliability models. High values imply good reliability. [IEEE982.2]

Failure rate. Used to indicate the growth in the software reliability as a function of test time and is usually used with reliability models. This metric requires two primitives: t_i, the observed time between failures for a given severity level i, and f_i, the number of failures of a given severity level in the ith time interval. The failure rate $\lambda(t)$ can be estimated from the reliability function R(t), which is obtained from the cumulative probability distribution F(t) of the time until the next failure, using a software reliability estimation model, such as the non-homogeneous Poisson process (NHPP) or Bayesian type model. The failure rate is $\lambda(t) = -1/R(t) \left[\dfrac{dR(t)}{dt}\right]$ where R(t) = 1 - F(t). [IEEE982.2]

Cumulative failure profile. Uses a graphical technique to predict reliability, to estimate additional testing time needed to reach an acceptable reliability level, and to identify modules and subsystems that require additional testing. This metric requires one primitive, f_i, the total number of failures of a given severity level i in a given time interval. Cumulative failures are plotted on a time scale. The shape of the curve is used to project when testing will be complete, and to assess reliability. It can provide an indication of clustering of faults in modules, suggesting further testing for these modules. A non-asymptotic curve also indicates the need for continued testing. [IEEE982.2]

5.3.1.6. Installation and Checkout Metrics

Most of the metrics used during the test phase are also applicable during installation and checkout. The specific metrics used will depend on the type of testing performed. If acceptance testing is conducted, a requirements trace may be performed to determine what percentage of the requirements are satisfied in the product (i.e., number of requirements fulfilled divided by the total number of requirements).

5.3.1.7. Operation and Maintenance Metrics

Every metric that can be applied during software development may also be applied during maintenance. The purposes may differ somewhat. For example, requirements traceability may be used to ensure that maintenance requirements are related to predecessor requirements, and that the test process covers the same test areas as for the development. Metrics that were used during development may be used again during maintenance for comparison purposes (e.g., measuring the complexity of a module before and after modification). Elements of support, such as customer perceptions, training, hotlines, documentation, and user manuals, can also be measured.

Change Metrics

Primitive change metrics.

Number of changes
Cost/effort of changes
Time required for each change
LOC added, deleted, or modified
Number of fixes, or enhancements

Customer Related Metrics

Customer ratings. These metrics are based on results of customer surveys, which ask customers to provide a rating or a satisfaction score (e.g., on a scale of one to ten) of a vendor's product or customer services (e.g., hotlines, fixes, user manual). Ratings and scores can be tabulated and plotted in bar graphs.

Customer service metrics.

Number of hotline calls received
Number of fixes for each type of product
Number of hours required for fixes
Number of hours for training (for each type of product)

5.4.   Statistical Process Control Techniques

Statistical process control is the application of statistical methods to provide the information necessary to continuously control or improve processes throughout the entire lifecycle of a product [OPMC]. SPC techniques help to locate trends, cycles, and irregularities within the development process and provide clues about how well the process meets specifications or requirements. They are tools for measuring and understanding process variation and distinguishing between random inherent variations and significant deviations so that correct decisions can be made about whether to make changes to the process or product.

To fully understand a process, it is necessary to determine how the process changes over time. To do this, one can plot error data (e.g., total number of errors, counts of specific types of errors) over a period of time (e.g., days, weeks, lifecycle phases) and then interpret the resulting pattern. If, for instance, a large number of errors are found in a particular phase, an investigation of the activities in that phase or preceding ones may reveal that necessary development activities were omitted (e.g., code reviews were not conducted during the implementation phase). A plot of the sources of errors may show that a particular group is the most frequent source of errors. Further investigation may confirm that members of the group do not have sufficient experience and training. A plot of the number of specific types of errors may show that many errors are related to incorrect or unclear requirements specifications (e.g., requirements are written in a way that consistently causes misinterpretations, or they fail to list enough conditions and restrictions). This would indicate that the process of requirements specification needs to be modified.

There are several advantages to using SPC techniques. First, errors may be detected earlier or prevented altogether. By monitoring the development process, the cause of the error (e.g., inadequate standards, insufficient training, incompatible hardware) may be detected before additional errors are created. Second, using SPC techniques is cost-effective, because less effort may be required to ensure that processes are operating correctly than is required to perform detailed checks on all the outputs of that process. Thus, higher quality may be achieved at a lower development expense. Finally, use of SPC techniques provides quantitative measures of progress and of problems so less guesswork is required [DEMMY].

Despite the advantages, there are also several potential disadvantages. To be successful, SPC requires discipline, planning, continuous commitment to the timely solution of process problems, and frequent access to information from the software lifecycle process [DEMMY].

5.4.1. Control Chart

The primary statistical technique used to assess process variation is the control chart. The control chart displays sequential process measurements relative to the overall process average and control limits. The upper and lower control limits establish the boundaries of normal variation for the process being measured. Variation within control limits is attributable to random or chance causes, while variation beyond control limits indicates a process change due to causes other than chance -- a condition that may require investigation. [OPMC] The upper control limit (UCL) and lower control limit (LCL) give the boundaries within which observed fluctuations are typical and acceptable. They are usually set, respectively, at three standard deviations above and below the mean of all observations. There are many different types of control charts, pn, p, c, etc., which are described in Table 5-1. This section is based on [OPMC], [SMITH], [CAPRIO], and [JURAN].

Table 5-1. Types of Control Charts

TYPE	DESCRIPTION	IMPLEMENTATION
np	number of nonconforming units (e.g., number of defective units)	The number of units in each sample with the selected characteristic is plotted; sample size is constant.
p	fraction of nonconforming units (e.g., fraction of defective units)	For each sample, the fraction nonconforming, obtained by dividing the number nonconforming by the total number of units observed, is plotted; sample size can change.
c	number of nonconformities (e.g.; number of errors)	For each sample, the number of occurrences of the characteristic in a group is plotted; sample size is constant.
u	number of nonconformities per unit (e.g., number of errors per unit)	For each sample, the number of nonconformities per unit, obtained by dividing the number of nonconformities by the number of units observed, is plotted; sample size can change.
X	single observed value	The value for each sample of size 1 is plotted.
XB	X-Bar	For each sample, the mean of 2 to 10 observations (4 or 5 are optimal) is plotted.
R	range	The difference between the largest and smallest values in each sample is plotted.
XM	median	The median of each sample is plotted.
MR	moving range	The difference between adjacent measurements in each sample is plotted.

Implementation

1. Identify the purpose and the characteristics of the process to be monitored.
2. Select the appropriate type of control chart based on the type of characteristic measured, the data available, and the purpose of the application.
3. Determine the sampling method (e.g., number of samples (n), size of samples, time frame).
4. Collect the data.
5. Calculate the sample statistics: average, standard deviation, upper and lower control limits.
6. Construct the control chart based on sample statistics.
7. Monitor the process by observing pattern of the data points and whether they fall within control limits.

Interpretation

The existence of *outliers*, or data points beyond control limits, indicates that non-typical circumstances exist. A *run*, or consecutive points on one side of the average line (8 in a row, or 11 of 12, etc.) indicates a shift in process average. A *sawtooth* pattern, which is a successive up and down trend with no data points near the average line, indicates overadjustment or the existence of two processes. A *trend*, or steady inclining or declining progression of data points represents gradual change in the process. A *hug*, in which all data points fall near the average line, may indicate unreliable data. A *cycle*, or a series of data points which is repeated to form a pattern, indicates a cycling process.

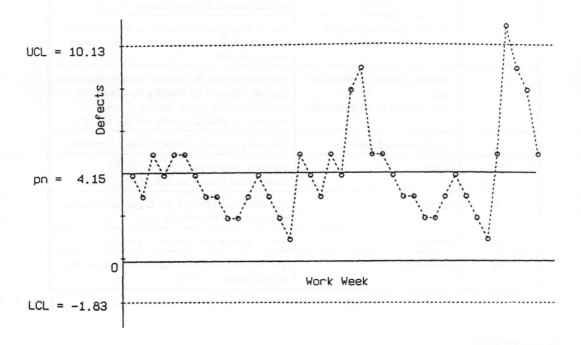

Figure 5-1. Example np Control Chart - Number of Defects Per Work Week.

Application Examples

Control charts are applicable to almost any measurable activity. Some examples for software include the following: number of defects/errors, training efforts, execution time, and number of problem reports per time period. An example of a np control with hypothetical data is shown in Figure 5-1. In this example, the number of samples (n) is 100. Each data point represents the number of defects found in the software product in a work week.

5.4.2. Run Chart

A run chart is a simplified control chart, in which the upper and lower control limits are omitted. The purpose of the run chart is more to determine trends in a process, rather than its variation. Although very simple, run charts can be used effectively to monitor a process, e.g., to detect sudden changes and to assess the effects of corrective actions. Run charts provide the input for establishing control charts after a process has matured or stabilized in time. Limitations of this technique are that it analyzes only one characteristic over time, and it does not indicate if a single data point is an outlier. This section is based on [OPMC] and [CAPRIO].

Implementation

1.   Decide which outputs of a process to measure.
2.   Collect the data.
3.   Compute and draw the average line.
4.   Plot the individual measurements chronologically.
5.   Connect data points for ease of interpretation.

Interpretation

See Interpretation for Control Charts.

Application Examples

Run charts are applicable to almost any measurable activity. Some examples for software include the following: number of defects/errors, number of failures, execution time, and downtime.

5.4.3. Bar Graph

A bar graph is a frequency distribution diagram in which each bar represents a characteristic/ attribute, and the height of the bar represents the frequency of that characteristic. The horizontal axis may represent a continuous numerical scale (e.g., hours), or a discrete non-numerical scale (e.g., Module A, Module B or Requirements Phase, Design Phase). Generally, numerical-scale bar charts in which the bars have equal widths are more useful for comparison purposes; numerical-scale bar charts with unequal intervals can be misleading because the characteristics with the largest bars (in terms of area) do not necessarily have the highest frequency. This section is based on [SMITH].

Implementation

1.   Define the subject and purpose.
2.   Collect the data. Check that the sample size is sufficient.
3.   Sort the data by frequency (or other measure) of characteristics.

4.   For numerical-scale bar charts, determine the number of bars and the width of the bars (class width), by trying series of class widths, avoiding too fine or too coarse a granularity. The class widths in a chart may be all the same, or they may vary (as in fig. 5-2b), depending on how one wants to show the distribution of the data.

5.   Construct the chart and draw the bars. The height of a bar represents the frequency of the corresponding characteristic.

Interpretation

In a simple bar graph in which the characteristics being measured are discrete and non-numerical (e.g., in fig. 5-2a) or if each bar has the same width, the measures for each characteristic can be compared simply by comparing the heights of the bars. For numerical-scale graphs with unequal widths, one can still compare the heights of the bars, but should remember not to interpret large bars as necessarily meaning that a large proportion of the entire population falls in that range.

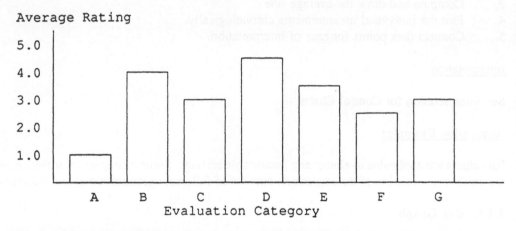

Figure 5-2a. Example Bar Chart - Customer Ratings (5 is best, 1 is worst).

Application Examples

Bar graphs are useful for analyzing and displaying many different types of data. It is mostly used to compare the frequencies of different attributes. For example, in Figure 5-2a, it is used to plot the average customer rating for each evaluation category (e.g., customer service, hotlines, overall satisfaction). The graph shows clearly that Category D has the highest rating. Figure 5-2b illustrates how numerical-scale bar charts can be used for software analysis. Based on hypothetical data, it shows the percentage of modules falling in each defect range. For instance, the graph shows that 30% of all modules contain 10-20 defects and 5% contain 20-25 defects. Other examples of characteristics that may be plotted include: number or percentage of errors by lifecycle phase, by type, or by cause, and number or percentage of problem reports by phase or by type. See also section 5.3.1.1 on primitive problem metrics for additional examples.

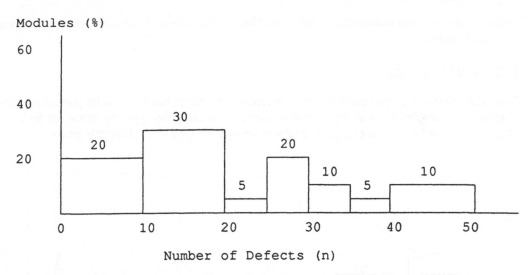

Figure 5-2b. Example Bar Chart - Number of Modules with *n* Defects.

5.4.4. Pareto Diagram

A Pareto diagram is a special use of the bar graph in which the bars are arranged in descending order of magnitude. The purpose of Pareto analysis, using Pareto diagrams, is to identify the major problems in a product or process, or more generally, to identify the most significant causes for a given effect. This allows a developer to prioritize problems and decide which problem area to work on first. This section is based on [OPMC] and [CAPRIO].

<u>Implementation</u>

1.   Follow the steps for constructing a bar graph, except that the bars should be in descending order of magnitude (height).
2.   Determine the "vital few" causes by drawing a cumulative percent line and applying the 20/80 rule.
3.   Compare and identify the major causes. Repeat process until root cause of the problem is revealed.

<u>Interpretation</u>

Pareto analysis is based on the 20/80 rule, which states that approximately 20% of the causes (the "vital few") account for 80% of the effects (problems). The "vital few" can be determined by drawing a cumulative percent line and noting which bars are to the left of the point marking 80% of the total count. The vital few are usually indicated by significantly higher bars and/or a relatively steep slope of the cumulative percent line. In Figure 5-2, the vital few are logic, computational, and interface errors since 80% of the errors are found in these modules. By knowing the primary causes of a problem or effect, the developer can decide where efforts should be concentrated.

Application Examples

Most data that can be plotted on a non-numerical scale bar graph can also be plotted on a Pareto diagram. Examples include: number or percentage of errors by type, by cause, or by lifecycle phase, and number or percentage of problem reports by type or by lifecycle phase.

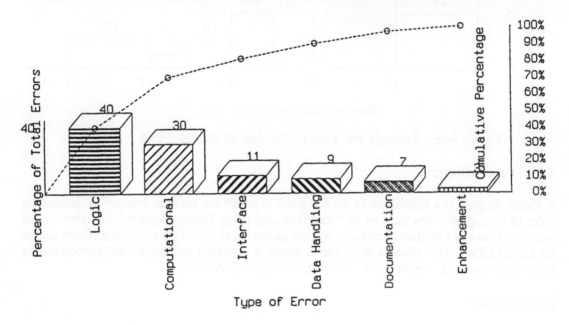

Figure 5-3. Example Pareto Chart - Percentage of Defects by Type.

5.4.4. Histogram

A histogram is a frequency distribution diagram in which the frequencies of occurrences of the different variables being plotted are represented by bars. The purpose is to determine the shape of the graph relative to the normal distribution (or other distributions). It is often confused with a bar graph, in which the frequency of a variable is indicated by the height of the bars. In a histogram, the frequency is indicated by the *area* of the bar. Histograms can only be used with variable data, which require measurements on a continuous scale. Only one characteristic can be shown per histogram, and at least 30 observations representing homogenous conditions are needed. This section is based on [OPMC], [CAPRIO], and [FREEDMAN].

Implementation

1.   Define the subject and purpose.
2.   Collect the data and organize from smallest to largest values. Check that sample size is sufficient.
3.   Calculate the range (r), i.e. the difference between the largest and smallest values.
4.   Decide arbitrarily on the number of bars (k), usually between 7 and 13.
5.   To make bars of equal width, use the equation, w = r/k to calculate the interval or width (w) of the bars.
6.   Sort the data into the appropriate intervals and count the number of data points that fall in each interval.
7.   Calculate the frequencies (actual counts or percent) for each interval.
8.   Draw the bars. The height of the bar is calculated by dividing the frequency by w, the width of the bar (in horizontal units).

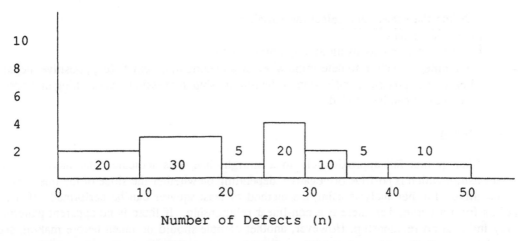

Figure 5-4. Example Histogram - Number of Modules with n Defects.

Interpretation

A histogram is a frequency distribution, in which the area of each bar is always proportional to the actual percentage of the total falling in a given range. For example, Figure 5-4 shows that 30% of all modules contain 10-20 defects, indicated by the largest bar. Both Figure 5-4 and Figure 5-2a are plotted with the same data. Note the difference in the relative size of the bars. If the bars are of equal width, then the histogram is equivalent to a bar graph, in which the relative size of the bars depends only on their heights. A histogram can be compared to the normal distribution (or other distribution). For example, if the graph is off-center or skewed, this may indicate that a process requires adjustment.

Application Examples

Histograms are essentially used for the same applications as bar graphs, except that the horizontal scale in a histogram must be numerical, usually representing a continuous random variable. See Application Examples for Bar Graphs.

5.4.5. Scatter Diagram

A scatter diagram is a plot of the values of one variable against those of another variable to determine the relationship between them. This technique was popularized by Walter Shewhart at Bell Laboratories. Scatter diagrams are used during analysis to understand the cause and effect relationship between two variables. They are also called correlation diagrams. This section is based on [KITCHENHAM], [OPMC], and [CAPRIO].

Implementation

1.   Define the subject and select the variables.
2.   Collect the data.
3.   Plot the data points using an appropriate scale.
4.   Examine the pattern to determine whether any correlation exists (e.g., positive, negative). For a more precise specification of the relationship, regression, curve fitting or smoothing techniques can be applied.

Interpretation

If the data points fall approximately in a straight line, this indicates that there is a linear relationship, which is positive or negative, depending on whether the slope of the line is positive or negative. Further analysis using the method of least squares can be performed. If the data points form a curve, then there is a non-linear relationship. If there is no apparent pattern, this may indicate no relationship. However, another sample should be taken before making such a conclusion.

Application Examples

The following are examples of pairs of variables that might be plotted:

*   Complexity vs. defect density (example shown in fig. 5-5)
*   Effort vs. duration (of an activity)
*   Failures vs. time
*   Failures vs. size
*   Cost vs. time

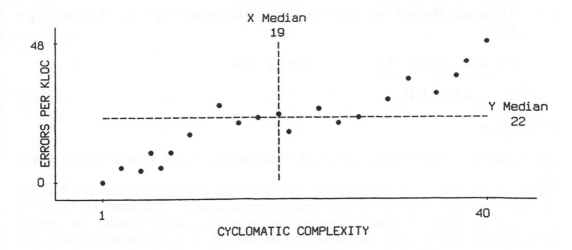

Figure 5-5. Scatter Diagram With Hypothetical Data - Complexity vs. Defect Density.

5.4.6. Method of Least Squares (Regression Technique)

This technique can be used in conjunction with scatter diagrams to obtain a more precise relationship between variables. It is used to determine the equation of the regression line, i.e., the line that "best fits" the data points. With this equation, one can approximate values of one variable when given values of the other. The equation of the line is $Y = a + bX$, where a and b are constants which minimize S, the sum of squares of the deviations of all data points from the regression line. For any sample value x_i of X, the expected Y value is $a + bx_i$. This section is based on [OPMC], [CAPRIO], and [SMITH].

<u>Implementation</u>

1. Collect n data values for each of the 2 variables, X and Y, denoted by $x_1, x_2, ..., x_n$ and $y_1, y_2, ..., y_n$.
2. Minimize $S = \Sigma (y_i - a - bx_i)^2$ by first taking the partial derivative of S with respect to a and then with respect to b, setting these derivatives to zero, and then solving for a and b.

3.   The results obtained from steps should be the following,[8] where $X_B = \Sigma x_i/n$ and $Y_B = \Sigma y_i/n$:

$$b = \frac{\Sigma (X_i - X_B)(Y_i - Y_B)}{\Sigma (X_i - X_B)^2} \qquad a = Y_B - bX_B$$

Interpretation

The constant a represents the intercept of the regression line, i.e., the value of Y when X is 0, and
b represents the slope of the regression line. The idea of this technique is to minimize S, so that all data points will be as close to the regression line as possible. The reason for taking the squares of the deviations, rather than simply the deviations, is so that positive and negative deviations will not cancel each other when they are summed. It would also be possible to sum the absolute values of the deviations, but absolute values are generally harder to work with than squares.

Application Examples

See Application Examples for Scatter Diagrams.

5.5.   Software Reliability Estimation Models

"Reliability" is used in a general sense to express a degree of confidence that a part or system will successfully function in a certain environment during a specified time period [JURAN]. Software reliability estimation models can predict the future behavior of a software product, based on its past behavior, usually in terms of failure rates. Since 1972, more than 40 software reliability estimation models have been developed, with each based on a certain set of assumptions characterizing the environment generating the data. However, in spite of much research effort, there is no universally applicable software reliability estimation model which can be trusted to give accurate predictions of reliability in all circumstances [BROCKLEHURST].

It is usually possible to obtain accurate reliability predictions for software, and to have confidence in their accuracy, if appropriate data is used [ROOK]. Also, the use of reliability estimation models is still under active research, so improvements to model capability are likely. Recent work by Littlewood (1989), for example, involves the use of techniques for improving the accuracy of predictions by learning from the analysis of past errors [ROOK], and recalibration [BROCKLEHURST].

---

[8]Another form of the equation for b, which is often easier to compute is

$$b = \frac{\Sigma X_i Y_i - nX_B Y_B}{\Sigma X_i^2 - n(X_B)^2}$$

Some problems have been encountered by those who have tried to apply reliability estimation models in practice. The algorithms used to estimate the model parameters may fail to converge. When they do, the estimates can vary widely as more data is entered [DACS]. There is also the difficulty of choosing which reliability model to use, especially since one can not know a priori which of the many models is most suitable in a particular context [BROCKLEHURST]. In general, the use of these models is only suitable for situations in which fairly modest reliability levels are required [ROOK].

There are three general classes of software reliability estimation models: nonhomogeneous Poisson process (NHPP) models, exponential renewal NHPP models, and Bayesian models. Some of the more common reliability estimation models are described below [DUNN], [LYU].

• Jelinski-Moranda (JM). One of the earliest models, it assumes the debugging process is purely deterministic, that is, that each defect in the program is equally likely to produce failure (but at random times), and that each fix is perfect, i.e., introduces no new defects. It also assumes that the failure rate is proportional to the number of remaining defects and remains constant between failures. This model tends to be too optimistic and to underestimate the number of remaining faults; this effect has been observed in several actual data sets.

• Goel-Okumoto (GO). This model is similar to JM, except it assumes the failure rate (number of failure occurrences per unit of time) improves continuously in time.

• Yamada Delayed S-Shape. This model is similar to GO, except it accounts for the learning period that testers go through as they become familiar with the software at the start of testing.

• Musa-Okumoto (MO). This NHPP model is similar to GO, except it assumes that later fixes have a smaller effect on a program's reliability than earlier ones. Failures are assumed to be independent of each other.

• Geometric. This model is a variation of JM, which does not assume a fixed, finite number of program errors, nor does it assume that errors are equally likely to occur.

• Schneidewind. Similar to JM, this model assumes that as testing proceeds with time, the error detection process changes, and that recent error counts are usually more useful than earlier counts in predicting future counts.

• Bayesian Jelinski-Moranda (BJM) Model. This model is similar to JM, except that it uses a Bayesian inference scheme, rather than maximum likelihood. Although BJM does not drastically underestimate the number of remaining errors, it does not offer significant improvement over JM. Actual reliability predictions of the two models are usually very close.

- Littlewood. This model attempts to answer the criticisms of JM and BJM by assuming that different faults have different sizes, i.e., they contribute unequally to the unreliability of the software. This assumption represents the uncertainty about the effect of a fix.

- Littlewood-Verrall (LV). This model takes into account the uncertainty of fault size and efficacy of a fix (i.e., a fix is of uncertain magnitude and may make a program less reliable), by letting the size of the improvement in the failure rate at a fix vary randomly.

- Brooks and Motley (BM). The BM binomial and Poisson models attempt to consider that not all of a program is tested equally during a testing period and that only some portions of the program may be available for testing during its development.

- Duane. This model assumes that the failure rate changes continuously in time, i.e., it follows a nonhomogeneous Poisson process. The cumulative failure rate when plotted against the total testing time on a ln-ln graph follows a straight line. The two parameters for the equation of the line can be derived using the method of least squares.

Implementation

The following is a generic procedure for estimating software reliability [AIAA]. It can be tailored to a specific project or lifecycle phase; thus some steps may not be used in some applications.

1. Identify the application. The description of the application should include, at a minimum, the identification of the application, the characteristics of the application domain that may affect reliability, and details of the intended operation of the application system.

2. Specify the requirement. The reliability requirement should be specific enough to serve as a goal (e.g., failure rate of 10^{-9} per hour).

3. Allocate the requirement. The reliability requirement may be distributed over several components, which should be identified.

4. Define failure. A specific failure definition is usually agreed upon by testers, developers, and users prior to the beginning of testing. The definition should be consistent over the life of the project. Classification of failures (e.g., by severity) is continuously negotiated.

5. Characterize the operational environment. The operational environment should be described in terms of the system configuration (arrangement of the system's components), system evolution and system operational profile (how system will be used).

6. Select tests. The test team selects the most appropriate tests for exposing faults. Two approaches to testing can be taken: testing duplicates actual operational environments as

closely as possible; or testing is conducted under more severe conditions than expected in normal operational environments, so that failures can occur in less time.

7. Select the models. The user should compare the models prior to selection based on the following criteria: predictive validity, ease of parameter measurement, quality of the model's assumptions, capability, applicability, simplicity, insensitivity to noise, and sensitivity to parameter variations.

8. Collect data. See section 5.2.

9. Determine the parameters. There are three common methods of estimating the parameters from the data: method of moments, least squares, and maximum likelihood. Each of these methods has useful attributes, but maximum likelihood estimation is the most commonly used approach. However, for some models, the maximum likelihood method does not yield equations for the parameters in closed form, so instead numerical methods (e.g., Newton's method) must be used [ROME]. As stated previously, some datasets may cause the numerical methods not to converge. There exist automated software reliability engineering tools, which are capable of performing parameter estimation.

10. Validate the model. The model should be continuously checked to verify that it fits the data, by using a predictive validity criteria or a traditional statistical goodness-of-fit test (e.g., Chi-square).

11. Perform analysis. The results of software reliability estimation may be used for several purposes, including, but not limited to, estimating current reliability, forecasting achievement of a reliability goal, establishing conformance with acceptance criteria, managing entry of new software features or new technology into an existing system, or supporting safety certification.

Interpretation

A disadvantage of these models is that they rely on testing and hence are used rather late in the development life cycle. The models are usually time based, that is, the probability is based on time to failure. Research is needed to identify how to use more valuable parameters with these models. See [ROOK]

Application Examples

Applicability of the models should be examined through various sizes, structures, functions and application domains. An advantage of a reliability model is its usability in different development and operational environments, and in different lifecycle phases. Software reliability models should be used when dealing with the following situations:

- Evolving software (i.e., software that is incrementally integrated during testing)
- Classification of failure severity
- Incomplete failure data
- Hardware execution rate differences
- Multiple installations of the same software
- Project environments departing from model assumptions

6.   SUMMARY

Error analysis for software consists of many activities to assure the quality of delivered software. The activities include error detection, analysis, resolution on an individual level and also on a collective level. In the latter case, the collective data may be used to locate common errors within a product, to identify areas for improvement in software development and maintenance, and to identify areas for improvement in error analysis.

Many activities of error analysis may be conducted during the early phases of the software development lifecycle to prevent error propagation and to reduce costs of fixing the errors at a later time in the lifecycle. Finding the root cause of an error discovered in system test may require analysis of code, design specifications, software requirements documentation, and perhaps analysis and test documentation. Correction of the error results in additional verification and testing activities through the lifecycle products. The time spent initially in preparing correctly stated software requirements will pay off in reduced time needed for rework in the later phases.

The error detection techniques described in this report are a representative sampling of the most widely-used error detection techniques and those most frequently referenced in standards, guidelines and technical literature. The report also describes some techniques which represent new approaches and are not yet widespread. The techniques include those that examine software products without executing the software, those that execute (or simulate the execution of) the software, and those that are based on mathematical analysis and proof of correctness techniques. Evidence of the effectiveness of any of these techniques may be hard to find. Journal articles report success of some techniques, but most often anecdotal evidence is provided through conference presentations and discussions among colleagues.

With many techniques to choose from, appropriate selection for a specific project depends on the characteristics of the project, such as the types of problems most likely to occur. Other selection criteria, which are outside the scope of this report, include parameters like development processes, skill of the technical staff, project resources, and quality requirements of the project.

The study of standards for high integrity software reported in [NUREG, NIST204] indicated that these standards are beginning to require techniques of all kinds with some guidelines attempting to base the requirement on the quality requirements and problem types of the software project. An examination of approximately 50 standards, draft standards, and guidelines indicates that these documents vary widely in their recommendations for error analysis.

Error detection is only one activity of error analysis. Information about the detected error must be reported and delivered to any persons responsible for correcting the error, managing the project, analyzing the data for process improvement and identifying similar problems in the product. Individual problem reports may be collected and analyzed using statistical process control techniques, to determine and monitor the efficiency and adequacy of the development process. Findings which result from using SPC techniques should be used as feedback to improve the development process for the current, as well as future, products. Data on single errors is also used in estimating software reliability and in predicting the number of errors (at later stages in the lifecycle).

Vendors should use error analysis to collect error data and to build corporate memory databases for use across projects. They may use the error information to identify appropriate techniques for similar projects and to better understand how to produce quality software systems.

Regulatory agencies should also consider establishing and maintaining a database of error analysis data for software systems. Willingness of vendors to participate must include mechanisms to assure confidentiality of proprietary information and that vendor data will not be used in a recriminatory sense. The database must contain both developmental and operational error data for effective use. Vendors, auditors, regulators, and the software engineering community may all benefit from use of error databases.

Auditors may use the information in the database to identify the most error-prone features of specific high integrity systems and may ensure that their audits examine these features carefully. The auditors may use the data to identify acceptance limits on different aspects of the high integrity software safety system.

Regulators may use the information from a database in several ways. First, over time, it may become apparent that some error analysis techniques are more effective than others with respect to a given type of problem. It may also become apparent that problems in these areas occur most often with certain development practices or occur less frequently with other development practices. This knowledge may influence recommendations in regulatory documents.

Finally, careful analysis of the information in the database may enable the software engineering community in general to identify research needs for software development practices to prevent specific problems from occurring and error analysis techniques to locate problems as soon as possible in the software lifecycle.

7.   REFERENCES

[AIAA]
R-013-1992, "Recommended Practice for Software Reliability," American Institute of Aeronautics and Astronautics, Space-Based Observation Systems Committee on Standards, Software Reliability Working Group, 1992, c/o Jim French, AIAA Headquarters, 370 L'Enfant Promenade, SW, Washington, DC 20024-2518W.

[AIRFORCE]
AFSCP 800-14, Air Force Systems Command, Software Quality Indicators, "Management Quality Insight," Department of the Air Force, January 20, 1987.

[ALBRECHT]
Albrecht, Allan J. and John E. Gaffney, Jr., "Software Function, Source Lines of Code, and Development Effort Prediction: A Software Science Validation," IEEE Transactions on Software Engineering, Vol. SE-9, No. 6, November, 1983.

[ANS104]
ANSI/ANS-10.4-1987, "Guidelines for the Verification and Validation of Scientific and Engineering Computer Programs for the Nuclear Industry," American Nuclear Society, May 13, 1987.

[ASMENQA2]
ASME NQA-2a-1990 Part 2.7, "Quality Assurance Requirements for Nuclear Facility Applications," The American Society of Mechanical Engineers, November 1990.

[BASILI]
Basili, V.R. and R.W. Selby, "Comparing the Effectiveness of Software Testing Strategies," IEEE Transactions on Software Engineering, IEEE Computer Society, Volume SE-13, Number 12, December 1987, pp. 1278-1296.

[BEIZER]
Beizer, Boris, Software Testing Techniques, Van Nostrand Reinhold Company, New York, 1983.

[BROCKLEHURST]
Brocklehurst, S., P. Y. Chan, Bev Littlewood, and John Snell, "Recalibrating Software Reliability Models," IEEE Transactions on Software Engineering, Vol. 16, No. 4, 1990.

[CAPRIO]
Caprio, William H., "The Tools for Quality," Total Quality Management Conference, Ft. Belvoir, Virginia, July 13-15, 1992.

[CLARK]
   Clark, Peter, and Bard S. Crawford, Evaluation and Validation (E&V) Reference Manual, TASC No. TR-5234-3, Version 3.0, February 14, 1991.

[DACS]
   "Software Reliability Models," DACS Newsletter, Data & Analysis Center for Software, Volume X, Number 2, Summer, 1992.

[DEMILLO]
   DeMillo, Richard A. et al. Software Testing and Evaluation, The Benjamin/Cummings Publishing Company, Inc., Menlo Park, CA, 1987.

[DEMMY]
   Demmy, W. Steven and Arthur B. Petrini, "Statistical Process Control in Software Quality Assurance," Proceedings of the 1989 National Aerospace and Electronics Conference, NAECON, May 22-26, 1989, Dayton, OH, IEEE, Inc., Piscataway, NJ, p. 1585-1590.

[DUNN]
   Dunn, Robert. Software Defect Removal, McGraw-Hill, Inc., 1984.

[EWICS3]
   Bishop, P. G. (ed.), Dependability of Critical Computer Systems 3 - Techniques Directory, The European Workshop on Industrial Computer Systems Technical Committee 7 (EWICS TC7), Elsevier Science Publishers Ltd, 1990.

[FAGAN]
   Fagan, M. E., "Design and Code Inspections to Reduce Errors in Program Development," IBM Systems Journal, Volume 15, Number 3, 1976.

[FLORAC]
   CMU/SEI-92-TR-ZZZ, "Software Quality Measurement: A Framework for Counting Problems, Failures, and Faults," William Florac, The Quality Subgroup of the Software Metrics Definition Working Group and the Software Process Measurement Project Team, Software Engineering Institute, Carnegie Mellon University, Pittsburgh, PA, Draft, 1992.

[FREEDMAN]
   Freedman, David, Robert Pisani, and Roger Purves, "Statistics," W.W. Norton & Company, Inc., New York, 1978.

[GRADY]
   Grady, Robert B. and Caswell, Deborah, Software Metrics: Establishing a Company-Wide Program, Prentice-Hall, Inc., Englewood Cliffs, New Jersey, 1987.

[GREEN]
   Green, Scott E. and Rose Pajerski, "Cleanroom Process Evolution in the SEL," Proceedings of the Sixteenth Annual Software Engineering Workshop, National Aeronautics and Space Administration, Goddard Space Flight Center, Greenbelt, MD 20771, December 1991.

[IEC65A94]
   IEC 65A(Secretariat)94, "Draft British Standard 0000: Software for Computers in the Application of Industrial Safety-Related Systems," WG9, December 6, 1989.

[IEC65A122]
   IEC 65A(Secretariat)122, "Software for Computers in the Application of Industrial Safety-Related Systems," WG9, Version 1.0, September 26, 1991.

[IEEEGLOSS]
   ANSI/IEEE Std 610.12, "IEEE Standard Glossary of Software Engineering Terminology," The Institute of Electrical and Electronics Engineers, February, 1991.

[IEEEP1044]
   IEEE P1044, "Draft Standard of: A Standard Classification for Software Errors, Faults, and Failures," The Institute of Electrical and Electronics Engineers, August 1991.

[IEEE982.2]
   ANSI/IEEE Std 982.2-1988, "Guide for the Use of IEEE Standard Dictionary of Measures to Produce Reliable Software," The Institute of Electrical and Electronics Engineers, June, 1989.

[IEEE1012]
   ANSI/IEEE Std 1012-1986, "IEEE Standard for Software Verification and Validation Plans," The Institute of Electrical and Electronics Engineers, Inc., November 14, 1986.

[JURAN]
   Juran, J. M. (ed.), Juran's Quality Control Handbook, 4th ed., McGraw-Hill, Inc., New York, 1988.

[KELLY]
   Kelly, John C., Joseph S. Sherif, and Jonathan Hops, "An Analysis of Defect Densities Found During Software Inspections," Proceedings of the Fifteenth Annual Software Engineering Workshop, National Aeronautics and Space Administration, Goddard Space Flight Center, Greenbelt, MD 20771, November, 1990.

[KITCHENHAM]
   Kitchenham, B. A. and B. Littlewood, Measurement for Software Control and Assurance, Elsevier Science Publishers Ltd, London and New York, 1989.

[LYLE]
Lyle, Jim, "Program Slicing," to be published in Encyclopedia of Software Engineering, John Wiley Publishing Co., New York, New York.

[LYU]
Lyu, Michael and Allen Nikora, "Applying Reliability Models More Effectively," IEEE Software, Vol. 9., No. 4, July, 1992.

[MAKOWSKY]
Makowsky, Lawrence C., Technical Report, USA-BRDEC-TR//2516, "A Guide to Independent Verification and Validation of Computer Software," United States Army, Belvoir Research, Development and Engineering Center, June 1992.

[MILLER]
Miller, Keith W., et al, "Estimating the Probability of Failure When Testing Reveals No Failures," IEEE Transactions on Software Engineering, Vol.18, No.1, January 1992.

[MILLS]
Mills, H. D., M. Dyer, and R. C. Linger, "Cleanroom Software Engineering," IEEE Software, September, 1987, pp. 19-25.

[MOD55]
Interim Defence Standard 00-55, "The Procurement of Safety Critical Software in Defence Equipment," Parts 1 and 2, Ministry of Defence, UK, April 5, 1991.

[MYERS]
Myers, Glenford J., The Art of Software Testing, John Wiley & Sons, New York, 1979.

[NBS93]
Powell, Patricia B., NBS Special Publication 500-93, "Software Validation, Verification, and Testing Technique and Tool Reference Guide," U.S. Department of Commerce/National Bureau of Standards (U.S.), September 1982.

[NIST187]
NIST SPEC PUB 500-187, "Application Portability Profile (APP) The U.S. Government's Open System Environment Profile OSE/1 Version 1.0," U.S. Department of Commerce/National Institute of Standards and Technology, April 1991.

[NIST204]
Wallace, D.R., L.M. Ippolito, D.R. Kuhn, NIST SPEC PUB 500-204, "High Integrity Software Standards and Guidelines," U.S. Department of Commerce/National Institute of Standards and Technology, September, 1992.

[NISTGCR]
Craigen, Dan, Susan Gerhart, Ted Ralston, NISTGCR 93/626, "An International Survey of Industrial Applications of Formal Methods," Volumes 1 and 2, U.S. Department of Commerce/National Institute of Standards and Technology, March, 1993.

[NISTIR]
Wallace, D.R., W.W. Peng, L.M. Ippolito, NISTIR 4909,"Software Quality Assurance: Documentation and Reviews," U.S. Department of Commerce/National Institute of Standards and Technology, 1992.

[NUREG]
Wallace, D.R., L.M. Ippolito, D.R. Kuhn, NUREG/CR-5930, "High Integrity Software Standards and Guidelines," U.S. Nuclear Regulatory Commission, September, 1992.

[OPMC]
The Organizational Process Management Cycle Programmed Workbook, Interaction Research Institute, Inc., Fairfax, Virginia.

[PARK]
Park, Robert, CMU/SEI-92-TR-20, ESC-TR-92-20, "Software Size Measurement: A Framework for Counting Source Statements," Software Engineering Institute, Carnegie Mellon University, September, 1992.

[PEYTON]
Peyton and Hess, "Software Sneak Analysis," IEEE Seventh Annual Conference of the Engineering in Medicine and Biology Society, The Institute of Electrical and Electronics Engineers, 1985.

[PUTNAM]
Putnam, Lawrence H. and Ware Myers, Measures for Excellence, Reliable Software On Time, Within Budget, Prentice-Hall, Inc., Englewood Cliffs, NJ, 1992.

[RIFKIN]
Rifkin, Stan and Charles Cox, "Measurement in Practice," Technical Report, CMU/SEI-91-TR-16, ESD-TR-91-16, Carnegie Mellon University, 1991.

[ROME]
Iuorno, Rocco and Robert Vienneau, "Software Measurement Models," Draft, Prepared for Rome Air Development Center, Griffiss Air Force Base, NY, July 1987.

[ROOK]
Rook, Paul, Software Reliability Handbook, Elsevier Science Publishers Ltd, Crown House, London and New York, 1990.

[SCHULMEYER]
Schulmeyer, G. Gordon. Zero Defect Software, McGraw-Hill, Inc., 1990.

[SHOOMAN]
Shooman, Martin L., "A Class of Exponential Software Reliability Models," Workshop on Software Reliability, IEEE Computer Society Technical Committee on Software Reliability Engineering, Washington, DC, April 13, 1990.

[SQE]
"Software Measurement," Seminar Notebook, Version 1.2, Software Quality Engineering, 1991.

[SMITH]
Smith, Gary, Statistical Reasoning, Allyn and Bacon, Boston, MA, 1991.

[STSC]
MAC010/STSC, "Software Management Guide," Software Technology Center, Hill AFB, UT 84-56, October, 1990.

[ROME]
Proceedings of the 3rd Annual Software Quality Workshop; Alexandria Bay, New York; August 11-15, 1991, Rome Laboratory, Griffiss AFB, New York.

[VOAS]
Voas, Jeffrey M. and Keith W. Miller," A Model for Improving the Testing of Reusable Software Components," 10th Pacific Northwest Software Quality Conference, October 19-21, 1992, Portland, Oregon.

[WALLACE]
Wallace, Dolores R. "Software Verification and Validation," to be published in Encyclopedia of Software Engineering, John Wiley Publishing Co., New York, NY.

[WALLACEFUJII]
Wallace, Dolores R. and Roger U. Fujii, "Verification and Validation: Techniques to Assure Reliability," IEEE Software, May 1989.

[ZAGE]
Zage, Wayne M. "Code Metrics and Design Metrics; An ACM Professional Development Seminar," November 19, 1991.

APPENDIX A. ERROR DETECTION TECHNIQUES

A.1. Algorithm Analysis

Description:

The purpose is to determine the correctness of an algorithm with respect to its intended use, to determine its operational characteristics, or to understand it more fully in order to modify, simplify, or improve. The analysis involves rederiving equations or evaluating the suitability of specific numerical techniques. Algorithms are analyzed for correctness, efficiency (in terms of time and space needed), simplicity, optimality, and accuracy. Algorithm analysis also examines truncation and round-off effects, numerical precision of word storage and variables (e.g., single- vs. extended-precision arithmetic), and data typing influences.

Advantages:
*   Effective and useful in general

Disadvantages:
*   A particular analysis depends on the particular model of computation (e.g, Turing machine, random access machine). If the assumptions of the model are inappropriate, then the analysis will be inaccurate.

Type of Errors Detected:
*   Incorrect, inappropriate, or unstable algorithms
*   Program does not terminate
*   Inability to operate on the full range of data - e.g., trigonometric routine only works in the first quadrant
*   Incorrect analysis of computational error (effect of round-off and truncation errors)
*   Incompatible data representations - e.g., input in lbs., program processes kilograms
*   Incompatibility with hardware or software resources

References: [IEEE1012], [DUNN], [WALLACE], [NBS93]

A.2. Back-to-Back Testing

Description:

This technique is used to detect test failures by comparing the output of two or more programs implemented to the same specification. The same input data is applied to two or more program versions and their outputs are compared to detect anomalies. Any test data selection strategy can be used for this type of testing, although random testing is well suited to this approach. Also known as comparison testing.

Advantages:
*   Permits a large number of tests to be made with little effort

- Rapid fault detection

Disadvantages:
- Requires the construction of at least one secondary program, although this may be available as part of the overall development
- Discrepancies must be analyzed manually to determine which program is at fault (it is not sufficient to assume that majority is always correct)

Types of Errors Detected:
- Does not detect specific errors, only anomalies or discrepancies between programs

References: [EWICS3]

A.3. Boundary Value Analysis

Description:
The purpose is to detect and remove errors occurring at parameter limits or boundaries. The input domain of the program is divided into a number of input classes. The tests should cover the boundaries and extremes of the classes. The tests check that the boundaries of the input domain of the specification coincide with those in the program. The value zero, whether used directly or indirectly, should be used with special attention (e.g., division by zero, null matrix, zero table entry). Usually, boundary values of the input produce boundary values for the output. Test cases should also be designed to force the output to its extreme values. If possible, a test case which causes output to exceed the specification boundary values should be specified. If output is a sequence of data, special attention should be given to the first and last elements and to lists containing zero, one, and two elements.

Advantages:
- Verifies that program will behave correctly for any permissible input or output

Disadvantages:
- No significant disadvantages in itself but for programs with many types of input cannot test all combinations of input and therefore cannot identify problems resulting from unexpected relationships between input types

Types of Errors Detected
- Algorithm errors
- Array size
- Specification errors

References: [MYERS]

A.4. Control Flow Analysis/Diagrams

Description:
This technique is most applicable to real time and data driven systems. Logic and data requirements are transformed from text into graphic flows, which are easier to analyze. Examples of control flow diagrams include PERT, state transition, and transaction diagrams. For large projects, control flow analysis using control flow diagrams that show the hierarchy of main routines and subfunctions are useful to understand the flow of program control. Purpose is to detect poor and potentially incorrect program structures. The program is represented by a directed graph, which is analyzed for the errors below.

Advantages:
•   Simple to apply
•   Readily automated

Disadvantages:
•   Results require some interpretation. Identified anomalies may not be faults.
•   Sometimes difficult to deal with "aliasing" where different variables are associated with the same locations in memory

Types of Errors Detected:
•   Inaccessible/unreachable code
•   Knotted code - If code is well-structured the directed graph can be reduced to a single node. If code is poorly structured, it can only be reduced to a "knot" composed of several nodes.

References: [IEEE1012], [EWICS3]

A.5. Database Analysis

Description:
Database analysis is performed on programs with significant data storage to ensure that common data and variable regions are used consistently between all call routines; data integrity is enforced and no data or variable can be accidentally overwritten by overflowing data tables; data access through indirect access is checked; and data typing and use are consistent throughout all program elements. Useful for programs that store program logic in data parameters. The purpose is to ensure that the database structure and access methods are compatible with the logical design. Diagrams are useful for understanding user privileges.

Advantages:
•   Supports interface analysis

Disadvantages:
* May require manual examination of diagrams for access problems

Types of Errors Detected:
* Inconsistent use of data types
* Incorrect access protections

References: [IEEE1012]

A.6. Data Flow Analysis

Description:
The purpose is to detect poor and potentially incorrect program structures. Data flow analysis combines the information obtained from the control flow analysis with information about which variables are read or written in different portions of code. May also be used in the design and implementation phases.

Advantages:
* Readily automated
* Easy to apply

Disadvantages:
* Requires some interpretation
* Some anomalies may not be faults

Types of Errors Detected:
* Undefined input/output data or format
* Incorrect data flow
* Variables that are read before they are written (likely to be an error, and is bad programming practice)
* Omitted code - indicated by variables that are written more than once without being read
* Redundant code - indicated by variables that are written but never read

References: [EWICS3], [IEEE1012]

A.7. Data Flow Diagrams

Description:
Data flow diagrams are used to describe the data flow through a program in a diagrammatic form. They show how data input is transformed to output, with each stage representing a distinct transformation. The diagrams use three types of components:

1. Annotated bubbles - bubbles represent transformation centers and the annotation specifies the transformation
2. Annotated arrows - arrows represent the data flow in and out of the transformation centers, annotations specify what the data is
3. Operators (AND, XOR) - used to link the annotated arrows

Data flow diagrams only describe data, and should not include control or sequencing information. Each bubble can be considered a black box which, as soon as its inputs are available, transforms them to outputs. Each should represent a distinct transformation, whose output is somehow different from its input. There are no rules regarding the overall structure of the diagram.

Advantages:
- They show transformations without making assumptions about how the transformations are implemented.

Disadvantages:
- Inability to provide information about the transformation process

Type of Errors Detected:
- Incorrect data input/output
- Inconsistencies in data usage

References: [IEC65A94]

A.8. Decision Tables (Truth Tables)

Description:
The purpose is to provide a clear and coherent analysis of complex logical combinations and relationships. This method uses two-dimensional tables to concisely describe logical relationships between boolean program variables.

Advantages:
- Their conciseness and tabular nature enable the analysis of complex logical combinations expressed in code.
- Potentially executable if used as specifications

Disadvantages:
- Tedious effort required

Types of Errors Detected:
- Logic

References: [IEC65A122]

A.9. Desk Checking (Code Reading)

Description:
Code is read by an expert, other than the author of the code, who performs any of the following: looking over the code for obvious defects, checking for correct procedure interfaces, reading the comments to develop a sense of what the code does and then comparing it to its external specifications, comparing comments to design documentation, comparing comments to design documentation, stepping through with input conditions contrived to "exercise" all paths including those not directly related to the external specifications, checking for compliance with programming standards and conventions, any combination of the above.

Advantages:
- Inexpensive
- Capable of catching 30% of all errors, if performed meticulously
- Can be more effective than functional testing or structural testing (NASA Goddard Space Flight Center experiment, see [BASILI])

Disadvantages:
- Requires enormous amount of discipline
- Few people are able to use this technique effectively
- Usually less effective than walkthroughs or inspections

Types of errors detected:
  LOGIC AND CONTROL
- unreachable code
- improper nesting of loops and branches
- inverted predicates
- incomplete predicates
- improper sequencing of processes
- infinite loops
- instruction modification
- failure to save or restore registers
- unauthorized recursion
- missing labels or code
- unreferenced labels

  COMPUTATIONAL
- missing validity tests
- incorrect access of array components
- mismatched parameter lists
- initialization faults
- anachronistic data
- undefined variables
- undeclared variables

- misuse of variables (locally and globally)
- data fields unconstrained by natural or defined data boundaries
- inefficient data transport

OTHER
- calls to subprograms that do not exist
- improper program linkages
- input-output faults
- prodigal programming
- failure to implement the design

References: [WALLACE], [DUNN], [BEIZER], [BASILI]

A.10. Error Seeding

Description:
The purpose of this technique is to determine whether a set of test cases is adequate. Some known error types are inserted into the program, and the program is executed with the test cases under test conditions. If only some of the seeded errors are found, the test case set is not adequate. The ratio of found seeded errors to the total number of seeded errors is approximate equal to the ratio of found real errors to total number of errors, or

$$\frac{\text{Number of seeded errors found}}{\text{Total number of seeded errors}} = \frac{\text{Number of real errors found}}{\text{Total number of real errors}}$$

In the equation, one can solve for the total number of real errors, since the values of the other three are known. Then, one can estimate the number of errors remaining by subtracting the number of real errors found from the total number of real errors. The remaining test effort can then be estimated. If all the seeded errors are found, this indicates that either the test case set is adequate, or that the seeded errors were too easy to find.

Advantages:
- Provides indication that test cases are structured adequately to locate errors.

Disadvantages:
- For this method to be valid and useful, the error types and the seeding positions must reflect the statistical distribution of real errors.

Types of Errors Detected:
- Does not detect errors, but determines adequacy of test set

References: [IEC65A122]

A.11. Finite State Machines

Description:

The purpose is to define or implement the control structure of a system. Many systems can be defined in terms of their states, inputs, and actions. For example, a system is in state S_1, receives an input I, then carries out action A, and moves to state S_2. By defining a system's actions for every input in every state we can completely define a system. The resulting model of the system is a finite state machine (FSM). It is often drawn as a state transition diagram, which shows how the system moves from one state to another, or as a matrix in which the dimensions are state and input. Each matrix entry is identified by a state and input, and it specifies the action and new state resulting from receipt of the input in the given state.

Advantages:
*   Allows important properties to be checked mechanically and reliably.
*   Simple to work with

Disadvantages:
*   None that are major

Types of Errors Detected:
*   Incomplete requirements specification - check that there is an action and new state for every input in every state
*   Inconsistent requirements - check that only one state change is defined for each state and input pair

References: [EWICS3]

A.12. Formal Methods (Formal Verification, Proof of Correctness, Formal Proof of Program)

Description:

The purpose is to check whether software fulfills its intended function. Involves the use of theoretical and mathematical models to prove the correctness of a program without executing it. The requirements should be written in a formal specification language (e.g., VDM, Z) so that these requirements can then be verified using a proof of correctness. Using this method, the program is represented by a theorem and is proved with first-order predicate calculus. A number of assertions are stated at various locations in the program, and are used as pre and post conditions to various paths in the program. The proof consists of showing that the program transfers the preconditions into the postconditions according to a set of logical rules, and that the program terminates.

Advantages:
*   Allows for rigorous statement concerning correctness

- Possibly the only way of showing the correctness of general WHILE loops

Disadvantages:
- Time consuming to do manually
- Requires enormous amount of intellectual effort
- Must be checked mechanically for human errors
- Difficult to apply to large software systems
- If formal specifications are not used in the design, then formal verification (proof of correctness after implementation tends to be extremely difficult
- Only applicable to sequential programs, not concurrent program interactions

References: [IEC65A122], [ROOK]

A.13. Information Flow Analysis

Description:
An extension of data flow analysis, in which the actual data flows (both within and between procedures) are compared with the design intent. Normally implemented with an automated tool where the intended data flows are defined using a structured comment that can be read by the tool.

Advantages:
- Simple to apply
- Readily automated

Disadvantages:
- Results require some interpretation
- Some anomalies may not be faults

Types of Errors Detected:
- Undefined input / output data or format
- Incorrect flow of information

References: [EWICS3]

A.14. (Fagan) Inspections

Description:
An inspection is an evaluation technique in which software requirements, design, code, or other products are examined by a person or group other than the author to detect faults, violations of development standards, and other problems. An inspection begins with the distribution of the item to be inspected (e.g., a specification, some code, test data). Each participant is required to analyze the item on his own. During the inspection, which is the meeting of all the participants,

the item is jointly analyzed to find as many errors as possible. All errors found are recorded, but no attempt is made to correct the errors at that time. However, at some point in the future, it must be verified that the errors found have actually been corrected. Inspections may also be performed in the design and implementation phases.

Advantages:
- Provides comprehensive statistics on classes of errors
- Studies have shown that inspections are an effective method of increasing product quality (e.g., reliability, usability, maintainability)
- Effective for projects of all sizes
- Qualitative benefits: less complex programs, subprograms written in a consistent style, highly visible system development, more reliable estimating and scheduling, increased user satisfaction, improved documentation, less dependence on key personnel for critical skills

Disadvantages:
- Inspectors must be independent of programmers
- Programmers may feel inspection is a personal attack on their work
- Time consuming, involving several staff (2 or 3 pages of not-difficult code may take 3 h to inspect)

Type of Errors Detected:
- Weak modularity
- Failure to handle exceptions
- Inexpansible control structure
- Nonexisting or inadequate error traps
- Incomplete requirements
- Infeasible requirements
- Conflicting requirements
- Incorrect specification of resources

References: [DUNN], [FAGAN], [IEC65A94], [MYERS], [NBS93]

A.15. Interface Analysis

Description:
This technique is used to demonstrate that the interfaces of subprograms do not contain any errors or any errors that lead to failures in a particular application of the software or to detect all errors that may be relevant. Interface analysis is especially important if interfaces do not contain assertions that detect incorrect parameter values. It is also important after new configurations of pre-existing subprograms have been generated. The types of interfaces that are analyzed include external, internal, hardware/hardware, software/software, software/hardware, and software/database. Interface analysis may include the following:

- Analysis of all interface variables at their extreme positions
- Analysis of interface variables individually at their extreme values with other interface variables at normal values
- Analysis of all values of the domain of each interface variable with other interface variables at normal values

Advantages:
- Can locate problems that would prevent system from functioning due to improper interfaces
- Especially useful for software requirements verification and design verification
- When used with prototyping or simulation, can find many critical errors that would be costly to correct in the delivered system
- Software design tools exist for analysis of interfaces, during design phase

Disadvantages:
- Manual effort may be time-consuming

Types of Errors detected:
- Input / output description errors (e.g., values of input variables altered)
- Actual and formal parameters mismatch (precision, type, units, and number)
- Incorrect functions used or incorrect subroutine called
- Inconsistency of attributes of global variables (common, etc.)
- Incorrect assumptions about static and dynamic storage of values (i.e., whether local variables are saved between subroutine calls)
- Inconsistencies between subroutine usage list and called subroutine

References: [WALLACE], [MAKOWSKY]

A.16. Interface Testing

Description:
Similar to interface analysis, except test cases are built with data that tests all interfaces. Interface testing may include the following:

- Testing all interface variables at their extreme positions
- Testing interface variables individually at their extreme values with other interface variables at normal values
- Testing all values of the domain of each interface variable with other interface variables at normal values
- Testing all values of all variables in combination (may be feasible only for small interfaces).

Advantages:
*   Locates errors that may prevent system from operating at all or locates errors in timing of interface responses (e.g., slow system response to users was a factor in the failure of the THERAC medical system)

Disadvantages:
*   Without automation of design, or code modules, manual searching for interface parameters in all design or code modules can be time consuming

Types of Errors Detected:
*   Input / output description errors
*   Inconsistent interface parameters

References: [IEC65A122]

A.17. Mutation Analysis

Description:
The purpose is to determine the thoroughness with which a program has been tested, and in the process, detect errors. This procedure involves producing a large set of versions or "mutations" of the original program, each derived by altering a single element of the program (e.g., changing an operator, variable, or constant). Each mutant is then tested with a given collection of test data sets. Since each mutant is essentially different from the original, the testing should demonstrate that each is in fact different. If each of the outputs produced by the mutants differ from the output produced by the original program and from each other, then the program is considered adequately tested and correct.

Advantages:
*   Applicable to any algorithmic solution specification
*   Results are good predictors of operational reliability

Disadvantages:
*   Likely to require significant amounts of human analyst time and good insight
*   Requires good automated tools to be effective
*   Reliable only if all possible mutation errors are examined
*   Cannot assure the absence of errors which cannot be modeled as mutations

Type of Errors Detected:
*   Any errors that can be found by test

References: [ANS104], [NBS93], [DEMILLO]

A.18. Performance Testing

Description:
The purpose is to measure how well the software system executes according to its required response times, cpu usage, and other quantified features in operation. These measurements may be simple to make (e.g., measuring process time relative to volumes of input data) or more complicated (e.g., instrumenting the code to measure time per function execution).

Advantages:
*   Useful for checking timing synchronization of functions, memory locations, memory requirements and other performance features.

Disadvantages:
*   Caution required in instrumenting code to ensure the instrumentation itself does not interfere with processing of functions or with locations of bytes under examination

Types of Errors Detected:
*   Timing, synchronization, and memory allocation

References: [ROOK]

A.19. Prototyping / Animation

Description:
Purpose is to check the feasibility of implementing a system against the given constraints and to communicate the specifier's interpretation of the system to the customer, in order to locate misunderstandings. A subset of system functions, constraints, and performance requirements are selected. A prototype is built using high level tools, is evaluated against the customer's criteria, and the system requirements may be modified as a result of this evaluation.

Advantages:
*   Better communication with customer
*   Early detection of problems
*   Check feasibility of new ideas or techniques

Disadvantages:
*   Unnecessary and expensive if problem is well understood
*   Tools are needed for quick implementation

Types of Errors Detected:
*   User related
*   Interface related
*   Omitted functions

- Undesired functions
- Poorly defined functionality (e.g., specifications that do not cover all expected cases)
- Errors in the specification that lead to inconsistent states, failure conditions, erroneous results
- Contradictions in requirements
- Impossibility, infeasibility of requirements

A.20. Regression Analysis and Testing

Description:
Regression analysis is used to reevaluate requirements and design issues whenever any significant code change is made. It involves retesting of a software product to detect faults made during modification, to verify that modification has not caused unintended side effects, and to verify that the modified software still meets its specified requirements. Any changes made during installation and test are reviewed using regression analysis and test to verify that the basic requirements and design assumptions, which affect other areas of the program, have not been violated.

Advantages:
- Effectiveness depends on the quality of the data used. If tests based on the functional requirements are used to create the test data, technique is highly effective

Disadvantages:
- Expense can appear to be prohibitive, especially for small changes. However, it can often be determined which functions may be affected by a given change, so that the amount of testing can be reduced in these cases

Types of Errors Detected:
- Errors caused by system modifications or corrections

References: [ANS104], [WALLACE], [IEEE1012], [NBS93]

A.21. Requirements Parsing

Description:
This technique involves the examination of individual requirements statements to ensure that each statement is complete, readable, accurate, and consistent with other requirements. The manual technique requires analysis of the attributes of a statement: initiator of action, the action, the object of the action, conditions (e.g., when positive state reached), constraints (limits), source of action, destination (e.g., printer, screen, plotter), mechanism, reason for the action. When the data from a set of requirements is examined collectively, the results of the analysis may aid in identifying trends.

Advantages:
- Promotes clarity, correctness, completeness, testability, and accuracy
- Can help to establish an English base from which to write a formal specification

Disadvantages:
- Very narrow look at each requirement. Could detract from analysis of more global examination of how the requirements fit together.

Types of errors detected:
- Inconsistency in requirements
- Incomplete requirement
- Untestable requirement

A.22. Reviews

Description:
A review is a meeting at which the requirements, design, code, or other products of a software development project are presented to the user, sponsor, or other interested parties for comment and approval, often as a prerequisite for concluding a given phase of the software development process. Usually held at end of a phase, but may be called when problems arise. Often referred to as "Formal Review" versus desktop review of materials.

Advantages:
- Provides opportunity to change course of a project before start of next phase.
- Because scope of review is usually broad, gives opportunity to recognize global problems

Disadvantages:
- If participants do not have materials ahead of time and spend time preparing, review will accomplish little or nothing.
- Attention focus on major issues

References: [ANS104], [IEEE1028]

A.23. Sensitivity Analysis

Description:
Sensitivity analysis is a new method of quantifying ultra-reliable software during the implementation phase. It is based on the fault-failure model of software and attempts to approximate this model. There are three necessary conditions:

1. The fault must be executed.
2. The fault must affect the computational data state directly after the fault location.
3. The affected data state must propagate to an output variable.

Sensitivity analysis is based on the premise that software testability can predict the probability that failure will occur when a fault exists given a particular input distribution. A sensitive location is one in which faults cannot hide during testing. The approach expects reasonably "close to correct" code; results are tied to selected input distribution. The internal states are perturbed to determine sensitivity. Researchers of this technique have developed a tool that performs several analyses on source code to estimate the testability and sensitivity of the code. These analyses require instrumentation of the code and produce a count of the total executions through an operation (execution analysis), an infection rate estimate, and a propagation analysis.

Advantages:
*   While software testing provides some quantification of reliability, sensitivity analysis provides quantification of software testing.
*   Presents a different approach to software reliability assessment, which usually is based on an exponential distribution of remaining faults over time.
*   Promising research that those needing ultra-reliable software should continue to follow.

Disadvantages:
*   Intended to operate on code that has already been formally verified
*   Still new, so that effectiveness of this technique is not yet known and use is not yet widespread
*   Developed and currently promoted by only one company
*   Tool is not sold, but rather the service of operating the tool on a client's code is sold

Types of Errors Detected:
*   None, but is an aid to error detection techniques

References: [MILLER], [VOAS]

A.24. Simulation

Description:
Simulation is used to test the functions of a software system, together with its interface to the real environment, without modifying the environment in any way. The simulation may be software only or a combination of hardware and software. Simulation is used to evaluate the interactions of large, complex systems with many hardware, user, and other interfaces. A model of the system to be controlled by the actual system under test is created. This model mimics the behavior of the controlled system, and is for testing purposes only. It must provide all inputs of the system under test which will exist when that system is installed; respond to outputs from the system in a way which accurately represents the controlled system; have provision for operator inputs to provide any perturbations with which the system under test is required to cope. When software is being tested, the simulation may be a simulation of the target hardware with its inputs and outputs. In the installation phase, it is used to test operator procedures and to help isolate installation problems.

Advantages:
- Enables simulation of critical aspects of the software that would not be practical to analyze manually.
- Provides means of performing functional tests of the system's behavior in the event of catastrophes which could not otherwise not be tested
- Can provide a means of achieving "long term" test in a short period
- Can provide a means of investigating behavior at critical points by slowing the timescale or single stepping

Disadvantages:
- Difficult to achieve independently of the software being tested
- May require considerable resource both to create the simulation and to operate it
- Dependent on a model of the system which itself could contain safety related flaws

Types of Errors Detected:
- Interface errors
- Logical errors
- Errors in performance

References: [IEEE1012], [WALLACE], [IEC65A122], [IEC65A94]

A.25. Sizing and Timing Analysis

Description:
Sizing/timing analysis is performed during incremental code development by obtaining program sizing and execution timing values to determine if the program will satisfy processor size and performance requirements allocated to the software. Significant deviations between actual and predicted values is a possible indication of problems or the need for additional examination. This technique is most applicable to real-time programs having response time requirements and constrained memory execution space requirements.

Advantages:
- Opportunity to study sequence of operations, especially interfaces between humans and response to user commands
- Indicator of whether integrated system will perform appropriately

Disadvantages:
- Time consuming when conducted by poring over control flow or data flow diagrams
- When timing results are collected by executing code, must be careful that test code does not alter timing as it would be without the test code

Types of Error Detected:
- Unacceptable processor load
- Control structure ignores processing priorities

References: [WALLACE], [DUNN], [IEEE1012]

A.26. Slicing

Description:
Slicing is a program decomposition technique that is based on extracting statements relevant to a specific computation from a program. It produces a smaller program that is a subset of the original program. Without intervening irrelevant statements, it is easier for a programmer interested in a subset of the program's behavior to understand the corresponding slice rather than to deal with the entire program. This technique can be applied to program debugging, testing, parallel program execution and software maintenance. Several variations of this technique have been developed, including program dicing, dynamic slicing and decomposition slicing.

Advantages:
* Readily automated
* Reduces time needed for debugging and testing

Disadvantages:
* Resource consuming tool/ method

Types of Errors Detected:
* Aids in finding root of errors during debugging and testing, by narrowing the focus of investigation

References: [LYLE]

A.27. Software Sneak Circuit Analysis

Description:
This technique is used to detect an unexpected path or logic flow which causes undesired program functions or inhibits desired functions. Sneak circuit paths are latent conditions inadvertently designed or coded into a system, which can cause it to malfunction under certain conditions.

To perform sneak circuit analysis, source code is first converted, usually by computer, into an input language description file into topological network trees. Then the trees are examined to identify which of the six basic topological patterns appear in the trees. Analysis takes place using checklists of questions about the use and relationships between the basic topological components.

Advantages:
* Effective in finding errors not usually detected by desk checking or standard V&V techniques

- Applicable to programs written in any language
- Applicable to hardware, software, and the combined system

Disadvantages:
- Labor intensive
- Likely to be performed late in the development cycle, so changes will be costly

Types of Error Detected:
- Unintended functions/outputs

References: [PEYTON], [EWICS3]

A.28. Stress Testing

Description:
Involves testing the response of the system to extreme conditions (e.g., with an exceptionally high workload over a short span of time) to identify vulnerable points within the software and to show that the system can withstand normal workloads. Examples of testing conditions that can be applied include the following:

- If the size of the database plays an important role, then increase it beyond normal conditions.
- Increase the input changes or demands per time unit beyond normal conditions.
- Tune influential factors to their maximum or minimal speed.
- For the most extreme case, put all influential factors to the boundary conditions at the same time.

Under these test conditions, the time behavior can be evaluated and the influence of load changes observed. The correct dimension of internal buffers or dynamic variables, stacks, etc. can be checked.

Advantages:
- Often the only method to determine that certain kinds of systems will be robust when maximum numbers of users are using the system, at fastest rate possible (e.g., transaction processing) and to identify that contingency actions planned when more than maximum allowable numbers of users attempt to use system, when volume is greater than allowable amount, etc.

Disadvantages:
- Requires large resources

Types of Errors Detected:
- Design errors related to full-service requirements of system and errors in planning defaults when system is over-stressed

References: [MYERS]

A.29. Symbolic Execution

Description:
This is an evaluation technique in which program execution is simulated using symbols rather than actual values for input data, and program output is expressed as logical or mathematical expressions involving these symbols.

Advantages:
- No input data values are needed
- Results can be used in program proving
- Useful for discovering a variety of errors

Disadvantages:
- Result will consist of algebraic expressions which easily get very bulky and difficult to interpret
- Difficult to analyze loops with variable length
- For most programs, the number of possible symbolic expressions is excessively large
- Unlikely to detect missing paths
- Studies have shown that in general, it is not more effective than the combined use of other methods such as static and dynamic analyses

Types of Errors Detected:
- None, but is an aid for detecting errors. A person must verify the correctness of the output generated by symbolic execution in the same way that output is verified when generated by executing a program over actual values.

References: [ANS104], [EWICS3], [NBS93]

A.30. Test Certification

Description:
The purpose is to ensure that reported test results are the actual finding of the tests. Test related tools, media, and documentation shall be certified to ensure maintainability and repeatability of tests. This technique is also used to show that the delivered software product is identical to the software product that was subjected to V&V.

Advantages:
- Assurance that the test results are accurately presented
- Assurance that the corrected version of product is in compliance with test findings

Disadvantages:

- Often mistaken as a certification of system quality

Type of Errors Detected:
- Incorrect test results reported
- Tests reported that never occurred
- Incorrect version of product shipped

References: [IEEE1012]

A.31. Traceability Analysis (Tracing)

Description:
There are several types of traceability analysis, including requirements trace, design trace, code trace, and test trace. Traceability analysis is the process of verifying that each specified requirement has been implemented in the design / code, that all aspects of the design / code have their basis in the specified requirements, and that testing produces results compatible with the specified requirements.

Advantages:
- Highly effective for detecting errors during design and implementation phases
- Valuable aid in verifying completeness, consistency, and testability of software
- Aids in retesting software when a system requirement has been changed

Disadvantages:
- No significant disadvantages

Types of Errors Detected:

REQUIREMENTS:
- Omitted functions
- Higher-order requirement improperly translated
- Software specification incompatible with other system specifications

DESIGN:
- Omission or misinterpretation of specified requirements
- Detailed design does not conform to top-level design
- Failure to conform to standards

CODE:
- Omission or misinterpretation of specified requirements
- Code does not conform to detailed design
- Failure to conform to standards

TEST:

- Software does not perform functions and produce outputs in conformance with the requirements specification

References: [DUNN], [ANS104], [NBS93]

A.32. Walkthroughs

Description:
A walkthrough is an evaluation technique in which a designer or programmer leads one or more other members of the development team through a segment of design or code, while the other members ask questions and make comments about technique, style, and identify possible errors, violations of development standards, and other problems. Walkthroughs are similar to reviews, but are less formal. Other essential differences include the following:

- Participants are fellow programmers rather than representatives of other functions
- Frequently no preparation
- Scope - standards usually ignored. Successful static analysis results generally not confirmed
- Checklists are rarely used
- Follow-up is often ignored

Advantages:
- Less intimidating than formal reviews
- Identifies the most error-prone sections of the program, so more attention can be paid to these sections during testing
- Very effective in finding logic design and coding errors

Disadvantages:
- Designers or programmers may feel walkthrough is an attack on their character or work

Types of Errors Detected:

- Interface
- Logic
- Data
- Syntax

References: [ANS104], [DUNN], [IEC65A94]

APPENDIX B. ERROR ANALYSIS TECHNIQUES CITED IN SOFTWARE STANDARDS

For [NUREG, NIST204], NIST conducted a survey of software engineering standards and guidelines used in the assurance of the quality of high integrity systems. Many of those documents require or recommend use of software quality assurance and software verification and validation techniques to locate errors in all phases of the software lifecycle. However, these techniques may not be sufficient to detect all errors. NIST extended that study to include other standards and guidelines in order to determine the extent of recommendations, requirements, and guidance for error analysis techniques. The results of this study are presented here.

This study included the examination of approximately 50 documents, which include software standards, draft standards, and guidelines, all selected from a bibliographic search. These documents pertain to high integrity systems, such as safety systems for nuclear power plants, message transmitting devices, medical devices, and other safety-critical software. The list of documents that were reviewed, with the full document titles and corresponding identifiers, are shown in Table B-1.

One objective of this study of standards was to determine whether there is readily available supporting literature on techniques that are required by the standards. The study showed that in most cases, there is not adequate information available in the standards on how to use the techniques, and that a developer would have to rely on library searches (e.g., books, journal articles) or information collected from previous projects. Another objective of this study was to look for consensus in the standards to determine which techniques are generally agreed upon by experts for use.

Results showed that the standards varied in coverage of techniques. Some address techniques in detail, while others only mention them. The study also found that some commonly used techniques like complexity analysis were cited infrequently. Yet, technical literature and availability of complexity metrics tools indicate that complexity analysis is often used to support error detection.

The specific findings are presented in Table B-2 below. For each technique, the table specifies the type, the standards which cite the technique, and the depth of discussion, e.g., whether the technique is mentioned, recommended, defined, or required. Although all of the selected documents were reviewed, information on them does not appear in the table unless they address error analysis in some way.

Only a few techniques are explicitly required. These techniques may be required only under certain circumstances (e.g., reviews are required only during the design phase). Many standards only mention techniques, and do not define, recommend, or require their use. Techniques that are "mentioned" may be examples of appropriate techniques that satisfy certain criteria. A few standards provide extensive information on several techniques, such as IEC65A(Secretariat)122 and AFISC SSH 1-1.

Several documents have appendices which are not part of the standard, but are included with the standard for information purposes. These include ANSI/IEEE-ANS-7-4.3.2-19XX Draft 2, ANSI/ANS-10.4-1987, and ANSI/IEEE Std 1012-1986. The appendices provide short definitions of the selected techniques.

FIPS 101 recommends techniques that can be used in each lifecycle phase. ANSI/IEEE Std 1012-1986 provides similar information in a chart containing optional and required techniques and specifies the lifecycle phases in which they can be used.

Table B-1. List of Reviewed Documents

IDENTIFIER	NUMBER AND TITLE
AFISC SSH 1-1	AFISC SSH 1-1, "Software System Safety," Headquarters Air Force Inspection and Safety Center, 5 September 1985.
ANSI X9.9-1986	ANSI X9.9-1986, "Financial Institution Message Authentication (Wholesale)," X9 Secretariat, American Bankers Association, August 15, 1986.
ANSI X9.17-1985	ANSI X9.17-1985, "Financial Institution Key Management (Wholesale)," X9 Secretariat, American Bankers Association, April 4, 1985.
ANSI/ANS-10.4-1987	ANSI/ANS-10.4-1987, "Guidelines for the Verification and Validation of Scientific and Engineering Computer Programs for the Nuclear Industry," American Nuclear Society, May 13, 1987.
ANSI/ASQC A3-1987	ANSI/ASQC A3-1987, "Quality Systems Terminology," American Society or Quality Control, 1987.
ANSI/IEEE Std 730.1-1989	ANSI/IEEE Std 730.1-1989, "IEEE Standard for Software Quality Assurance Plans," Institute of Electrical and Electronics Engineers, Inc., October 10, 1989.
ANSI/IEEE Std 1012-1986	ANSI/IEEE Std 1012-1986, "IEEE Standard for Software Verification and Validation Plans," The Institute of Electrical and Electronics Engineers, Inc., November 14, 1986.
ANSI/IEEE-ANS-7-4.3.2-19XX	ANSI/IEEE-ANS-7-4.3.2-1982, "Application Criteria for Programmable Digital Computer Systems in Safety Systems of Nuclear Power Generating Stations," American Nuclear Society, 1982. AND ANSI/IEEE-ANS-7-4.3.2-19XX, Draft 2, as of November, 1991.
AQAP-13	AQAP-13, "NATO Software Quality Control System Requirements," NATO, August 1991.
ASME NQA-1-1989 Supplement 17S-1	Supplement 17S-1, ASME NQA-1-1989, "Supplementary Requirements for Quality Assurance Records," The American Society of Mechanical Engineers.
ASME NQA-2a-1990	ASME NQA-2a-1990, "Quality Assurance Requirements for Nuclear Facility Applications," The American Society of Mechanical Engineers, November 1990.
ASME NQA-3-1989	ASME NQA-3-1989, "Quality Assurance Program Requirements for the Collection of Scientific and Technical Information for Site Characterization of High-Level Nuclear Waste Repositories," The American Society of Mechanical Engineers, March 23, 1990.
CAN/CSA-Q396.1.2-89	CAN/CSA-Q396.1.2-89, "Quality Assurance Program for Previous Developed Software Used in Critical Applications," Canadian Standards Association, January 1989.

IDENTIFIER	NUMBER AND TITLE
CSC-STD-003-85	CSC-STD-003-85, "Computer Security Requirements--Guidance for Applying the Department of Defense Trusted Computer System Evaluation Criteria in Specific Environments," Department of Defense, 25 June 1985.
DLP880	DLP880, "(DRAFT) Proposed Standard for Software for Computers in the Safety Systems of Nuclear Power Stations (based on IEC Standard 880)," David L. Parnas, Queen's University, Kingston, Ontario, March, 1991.
DOD 5200.28-STD	DOD 5200.28-STD, "Department of Defense Trusted Computer System Evaluation Criteria," Department of Defense, December 1985.
E.F.T. Message Authentication Guidelines	Criteria and Procedures for Testing, Evaluating, and Certifying Message Authentication Devices for Federal E.F.T. Use," United States Department of the Treasury, September 1, 1986.
FDA/HIMA (DRAFT)	FDA/HIMA, "(DRAFT) Reviewer Guidance for Computer-Controlled Devices," Medical Device Industry Computer Software Committee, January 1989.
FIPS 74	FIPS 74, "Guidelines for Implementing and Using the NBS Data Encryption Standard," U.S. Department of Commerce/National Bureau of Standards, 1981 April 1.
FIPS 81	FIPS 81, "DES Modes of Operation," U.S. Department of Commerce/ National Bureau of Standards, 1980 December 2.
FIPS 46-1	FIPS 46-1, "Data Encryption Standard," U.S. Department of Commerce/National Bureau of Standards, 1988 January 22.
FIPS 101	FIPS 101, "Guideline for Lifecycle Validation, Verification, and Testing of Computer Software," U.S. Department of Commerce/National Bureau of Standards, 1983 June 6.
FIPS 132	FIPS 132, "Guideline for Software Verification and Validation Plans," U.S. Department of Commerce/National Bureau of Standards, 1987 November 19.
FIPS 140 FS 1027	FIPS 140 FS 1027, "General Security Requirements for Equipment Using the Data Encryption Standard," General Services Administration, April 14, 1982.
FIPS 140-1	FIPS 140-1, "Security Requirements for Cryptographic Modules," U.S. Department of Commerce/National Institute of Standards and Technology, 1990 May 2.
Guide to the Assessment of Reliability	"89/97714-Guide to the Assessment of Reliability of Systems Containing Software," British Standards Institution, 12 September 1989.
Guideline for the Categorization of Software	"Guideline for the Categorization of Software in Ontario Hydro's Nuclear Facilities with Respect to Nuclear Safety," Revision 0, Nuclear Safety Department, June 1991.

IDENTIFIER	NUMBER AND TITLE
Guidelines for Assuring Testability (DRAFT)	"(DRAFT) Guidelines for Assuring Testability," The Institution of Electrical Engineers, May 1987.
IEC 880	IEC 880, "Software for Computers in the Safety Systems of Nuclear Power Stations," International Electrotechnical Commission, 1986.
IEC 880 Supplement	45A/WG-A3(Secretary)42, "(DRAFT) Software for Computers Important to Safety for Nuclear Power Plants as a Supplement to IEC Publication 880," International Electrotechnical Commission Technical Committee: Nuclear Instrumentation, Sub-Committee 45A: Reactor Instrumentation, Working Group A3: Data Transmission and Processing Systems, May 1991.
IEC65A(Secretariat)122	IEC/TC65A WG9, "89/33006 DC - (DRAFT) Software for Computers in the Application of Industrial Safety-Related Systems," British Standards Institution, 6 December 1989.
IEC65A(Secretariat)123	IEC/TC65A WG10, "89/33005 DC - (DRAFT) Functional Safety of Electrical/Electronic/Programmable Electronic Safety-Related Systems: Generic Aspects, Part 1: General Requirements," British Standards Institution, January 1992.
IFIP WG 10.4	IFIP WG 10.4, "Dependability: Basic Concepts and Terminology," IFIP Working Group on Dependable Computing and Fault Tolerance, October 1990.
Interim Defence Std 00-55	Interim Defence Standard 00-55, "The Procurement of Safety Critical Software in Defence Equipment," Parts 1 and 2, Ministry of Defence, 5 April 1991.
Interim Defence Std 00-56	Interim Defence Standard 00-56, "Hazard Analysis and Safety Classification of the Computer and Programmable Electronic System Elements of Defence Equipment," Ministry of Defence, 5 April 1991.
ISO 9000	ISO 9000, "International Standards for Quality Management," May 1990.
ITSEC 1.1989	ITSEC 1.1989, "Criteria for the Evaluation of Trustworthiness of Information Technology (IT) Systems," GISA - German Information Security Agency, 1989.
ITSEC 1.2 1991	ITSEC 1.2 1990, "Information Technology Security Evaluation Criteria (ITSEC)," Provisional Harmonised Criteria, June 28, 1990.
Management Plan Documentation Standard	"Management Plan Documentation Standard and Data Item Descriptions (DID)," NASA, 2/28/89.
MIL-HDBK-347	MIL-HDBK-347, "Mission-Critical Computer Resources Software Support," Department of Defense, 22 May 90.
MIL-STD-882B	MIL-STD-882B, "System Safety Program Requirements," Department of Defense, 30 March 1984.

IDENTIFIER	NUMBER AND TITLE
NCSC-TG-005	NCSC-TG-005, "Trusted Network Interpretation of the Trusted Computer System Evaluation Criteria," National Computer Security Center, 31 July 1987.
NCSC-TG-021	NCSC-TG-021, "Trusted Database Management System Interpretation of the Trusted Computer System Evaluation Criteria," National Computer Security Center, April 1991.
NPR-STD-6300	NPR-STD-6300, "Management of Scientific, Engineering and Plant Software," Office of New Production Reactors, U.S. Department of Energy, March 1991.
NSA Spec. 86-16	NSA Spec. 86-16, "Security Guidelines for COMSEC Software Development," National Security Agency, 10 July 1986.
NSWC TR 89-33	NSWC TR 89-33, "Software Systems Safety Design Guidelines and Recommendations," Naval Surface Warfare Center, March 1989.
Ontario Hydro Standard	"Standard for Software Engineering of Safety Critical Software," Rev. 0, Ontario Hydro, December 1990.
P1228 (DRAFT)	P1228, "(DRAFT) Standard for Software Safety Plans," The Institute of Electrical and Electronics Engineers, Inc, July 19, 1991.
Product Specification Documentation	"Product Specification Documentation Standard and Data Item Descriptions (DID)," NASA, 2/28/89.
Programmable Electronic Systems	"Programmable Electronic Systems in Safety Related Applications," Parts 1 and 2, Health and Safety Executive, 1987.
RTCA/DO-178A	RTCA/DO-178A, "Software Considerations in Airborne Systems and Equipment Certification," Radio Technical Commission for Aeronautics, March, 1985.
SafeIT	"SafeIT," Volumes 1 and 2, Interdepartmental Committee on Software Engineering, June 1990.
UL 1998	UL 1998, "The Proposed First Edition of the Standard for Safety-Related Software," Underwater Laboratories, August 17, 1990.

Table B-2. Error Analysis Techniques Cited in Reviewed Documents

TECHNIQUE	DESCRIPTION	STANDARDS	STATUS
acceptance sampling	statistical technique for quality control	ANSI/ASQC A3-1987	Recommended during installation, defined in glossary
acceptance testing	formal testing to determine if system satisfies acceptance criteria and to enable customer to decide whether or not to accept the product	FIPS 101; Guidelines for Assuring Testability (DRAFT); ISO 9000 (9004); FDA/HIMA (DRAFT); ANSI/IEEE Std 1012-1986	Recommended, defined in glossary Defined briefly Mentioned Mentioned Defined briefly
algorithm analysis	check that algorithms are correct, appropriate, stable, and meet all accuracy, timing, and sizing requirements	ANSI/ANS-10.4-1987; ANSI/IEEE Std 1012-1986	Defined in appendix only Optional, in appendix
analysis of variance	statistical technique for comparing the means of two or more groups to see if the means differ significantly as a result of some factor/treatment	ISO 9000 (9004)	Mentioned
boundary value analysis (boundary checking)	input test data is selected to create on or around range limits of input or output variable ranges in order to remove errors occurring at parameter limits or boundaries	Guide to the Assessment of Reliability; FDA/HIMA (DRAFT); NSWC TR 89-33; IEC65A(Secretariat)122; SafeIT	Defined briefly Recommended (p. 17) Required Recommended and defined Recommended
cause-effect graphing	method of designing test cases by translating a requirements specification into a Boolean graph that links input conditions (causes) with output conditions (effect), analyzing graph to find all combinations of causes that will result in each effect, and identifying test cases that exercise each cause-effect relationship	ANSI/ANS-10.4-1987	Defined in appendix only

TECHNIQUE	DESCRIPTION	STANDARDS	STATUS
code inspection	an inspection of the code *See inspection*	E.F.T. Message Authentication Guidelines; IFIP WG 10.4; FDA/HIMA (DRAFT)	Gives checklist to be used during code inspection Mentioned Mentioned
compiler checks	static analysis	IFIP WG 10.4	Mentioned
complexity analysis software complexity metrics	static analysis of the complexity of the code using code metrics (e.g. McCabe's, cyclomatic complexity, number of entries/exits per module)	IFIP WG 10.4	Mentioned
constraint analysis	used to ensure that the program operates within the constraints imposed by the requirements, design, and target computer	P1228 (DRAFT)	Defined briefly
control charts	statistical technique used to assess, monitor, and maintain the stability of a process by plotting characteristics of the process on a chart over time and determining whether the variance is within statistical bounds	ANSI/ASQC A3-1987	Mentioned
control flow analysis	check that the proposed control flow is free of problems, e.g., unreachable or incorrect design or code elements	Guidelines for Assuring Testability (DRAFT); ANSI/IEEE Std 1012-1986; Interim Defence Std 00-55 (Part 2); FDA/HIMA (DRAFT)	Described briefly Optional, in appendix Defined briefly Mentioned
criticality analysis	identifies all software requirements that have safety implications; a criticality level is assigned to each safety-critical requirement	P1228 (DRAFT)	Defined briefly
cusum techniques/quality control charts	statistical technique involving	ISO 9000 (9004)	Mentioned

TECHNIQUE	DESCRIPTION	STANDARDS	STATUS
data (use) analysis	used to evaluate the data structure and usage in the code; to ensure that data items are defined and used properly; usually performed in conjunction with logic analysis	Guidelines for Assuring Testability; P1228 (DRAFT); Interim Defence Std 00-55 (part 2); UL 1998	Described briefly Defined briefly Defined briefly Required
database analysis	check that the database structure and access methods are compatible with the logical design	ANSI/IEEE Std 1012-1986	Optional, in appendix
data flow / corruption analysis	graphical analysis technique to trace behavior of program variables as they are initialized, modified, or referenced when the program executes	IFIP WG 10.4; FIPS 101; FDA/HIMA (DRAFT); RTCA/DO-178A; ANSI/IEEE Std 1012-1986	Mentioned Recommended during design phase Mentioned Recommended Optional, in appendix
data flow diagrams	a graphical technique that shows how data inputs are transformed to outputs, without detailing the implementation of the transformations	IEC65A(Secretariat)122; SafeIT	Recommended and defined Recommended
desk checking (code reading)	the reviewing of code by an individual to check for defects and to verify the correctness of the program logic flow, data flow, and output	ANSI/IEEE-ANS-7-4.3.2-19XX, Draft 1; Guidelines for Assuring Testability; AFISC SSH 1-1	Defn. briefly in appendix only Mentioned Defined
error guessing	use of experience and intuition combined with knowledge and curiosity to add uncategorized test cases to the designed test case set in order to detect and remove common programming errors	IEC65A(Secretariat)122; SafeIT	Recommended and defined Recommended
error seeding	used to ascertain whether a test case set is adequate by inserting known error types into the program, and examining the ability of the program to detect the seeded errors	IEC65A(Secretariat)122; SafeIT	Recommended and defined Recommended

TECHNIQUE	DESCRIPTION	STANDARDS	STATUS
execution flow and timing analysis	See data flow analysis and sizing and timing analysis	RTCA/DO-178A	Recommended
factorial analysis	statistical technique	ISO 9000 (9004)	Mentioned
Fagan inspections	a formal audit on quality assurance documents aimed at finding errors and omissions	IEC65A(Secretariat)122; SafeIT	Recommended and defined Recommended
failure data models	statistical / probabilistic technique for assessing software reliability	Guide to the Assessment of Reliability	Defined
finite state automata/ finite state machines/ state transition diagram	modelling technique that defines the control structure of a system and is used to perform static analysis of system behavior	IFIP WG 10.4; FIPS 140-1; IEC65A(Secretariat)122; SafeIT	Mentioned Required Recommended and defined Recommended
(formal) mathematical modelling	modelling technique, static analysis	ANSI/ASQC A3-1987; IEC65A(Secretariat)122; SafeIT; Management Plan Documentation Standard	Mentioned Recommended and defined Recommended Mentioned
formal analysis (formal proofs, formal verification, formal testing)	use of rigorous mathematical techniques to analyze the algorithms of a solution for numerical properties, efficiency, and/or correctness formal verification - proving mathematically that a program satisfies its specifications	ITSEC 1991 ANSI/ANS-10.4-1987; ANSI/IEEE-ANS-7-4.3.2-19XX, Draft 2; Guide to the Assessment of Reliability; Guidelines for Assuring Testability (DRAFT); SafeIT; P1228 (DRAFT); IEC65A(Secretariat)122; NCSC-TG-005	Defined, required p. 98 Defined in appendix only Defn. briefly in appendix only Defined briefly Defined Recommended Mentioned Recommended and defined Defined
frequency distribution	a graph that displays the frequency of a variable as a bar, whose area represents the frequency	ANSI/ASQC A3-1987	Mentioned

TECHNIQUE	DESCRIPTION	STANDARDS	STATUS
functional testing	application of test data derived from the specified functional requirements without regard to the final program structure	ANSI/IEEE-ANS-7-4.3.2-19XX, Draft 2; IFIP WG 10.4; Guide to the Assessment of Reliability; FIPS 101; ANSI/ANS-10.4-1987; IEC65A(Secretariat)122; SafeIT; NCSC-TG-005; FDA/HIMA (DRAFT)	Defined in appendix only Mentioned Defined briefly Defined in glossary Defined in appendix only Recommended and defined Recommended Mentioned, defined Mentioned
global roundoff analysis of algebraic processes (algorithmic analysis)	determines how rounding errors propagate in a numerical method for permissible sets of input data; one type of algorithm analysis	ANSI/ANS-10.4-1987	Defined, in appendix only
information flow analysis	extension of data flow analysis	Guidelines for Assuring Testability; Interim Defence Std 00-55 (part 2)	Described briefly Defined briefly
inspection	software requirements, design, code, or other products are examined by a person or group other than the author to detect faults, violations of standards, and other problems	IFIP WG 10.4; Guide to the Assessment of Reliability; FIPS 101; ANSI/ANS-10.4-1987; ANSI/ASQC A3-1987; FDA/HIMA (DRAFT)	Mentioned Defined briefly Defined in glossary, recommended for design phase Defined in appendix only Defined briefly Defined in glossary
integrated critical path analysis		MIL-STD-882B	Mentioned

TECHNIQUE	DESCRIPTION	STANDARDS	STATUS
integration testing	orderly progression of testing in which software elements, hardware elements, or both, are combined and tested until all intermodule communication links have been integrated	FIPS 101; FDA/HIMA (DRAFT)	Defined in glossary Mentioned
interface analysis (testing)	checking that intermodule communication links are performed correctly; ensures compatibility of program modules with each other and with external hardware and software	IEEE Std 1012-1986; FIPS 101; MIL-HDBK-347; NSWC TR 89-33; P1228 (DRAFT)	Required Recommended during design phase, defined in glossary Required Required Defined briefly
logic analysis	evaluates the sequence of operations represented by the coded program and detects programming errors that might create a hazard	P1228 (DRAFT)	Defined briefly
Markov models	graphical technique used to model a system with regard to its failure states in order to evaluate the reliability, safety or availability of the system	Interim Defence Standard 00-56 IEC65A(Secretariat)122	Mentioned Recommended and defined
measure of central tendency and dispersion	statistical technique for quality control	ANSI/ASQC A3-1987	Mentioned
module functional analysis	verifies the relevance of software modules to safety-critical requirements, assuring that each requirement is adequately covered and that a criticality level is assigned to each module	P1228 (DRAFT)	Defined briefly
mutation analysis (testing)	process of producing a large set of program versions, each derived from a trivial alteration to the original program, and evaluating the ability of the program test data to detect each alteration	IFIP WG 10.4; ANSI/ANS-10.4-1987	Mentioned In appendix only
NO-GO (path) testing	type of failure testing	UL 1998; NSWC TR 89-33	Required Required

TECHNIQUE	DESCRIPTION	STANDARDS	STATUS
peer review	software requirements, design, code, or other products are examined by persons whose rank, responsibility, experience, and skill are comparable to that of the author	ANSI/ANS-10.4-1987	Defined in appendix only
performance modelling	modelling of the system to ensure that it meets throughput and response requirements for specific functions, perhaps combined with constraints on use of toal system resources	IEC65A(Secretariat)122; SafeIT	Recommended and defined Recommended
periodic testing	security testing	NCSC-TG-005	Mentioned, defined
penetration testing	security testing in which the penetrators attempt to circumvent the security features of a system	NCSC-TG-005	Mentioned, defined in glossary
Petri nets	graphical technique used to model relevant aspects of the system behavior and to assess and improve safety and operational requirements through analysis and re-design	IFIP WG 10.4; AFISC SSH 1-1; MIL-STD-882B; P1228 (DRAFT); IEC65A(Secretariat)122	Mentioned Defined Mentioned Mentioned Recommended and defined
proof of correctness	use of techniques of mathematical logic to infer that a relation between program variables assumed true at program entry implies that another relation between them holds at program exit	IFIP WG 10.4; FIPS 101; Guidelines for Assuring Testability; IEC65A(Secretariat)122; AFISC SSH 1-1	Mentioned Defined in glossary Defined briefly Recommended Defined
protocol testing	security testing	NCSC-TG-005	Mentioned and defined
prototyping/animation	check the feasibility of implementing a system against the given constraints by building and evaluating a prototype with respect to the customer's criteria; dynamic test of code through execution	Interim Defence Std 00-55 (Part 2); Guide to the Assessment of Reliability; Management Plan Documentation Standard; IEC65A(Secretariat)122; SafeIT	Defined Defined briefly Defined briefly in glossary Recommended and defined Recommended

TECHNIQUE	DESCRIPTION	STANDARDS	STATUS
regression technique	statistical technique for determining from actual data the functional relationship between 2 or more correlated variables	ISO 9000 (9004); ANSI/ASQC A3-1987	Mentioned Recommended
regression analysis / testing	selective retesting of a product to detect faults introduced during modification, to verify that modification had no unintended side effects and that the modified software still meets specified requirements	Guide to the Assessment of Reliability; FIPS 101; ANSI/ANS-10.4-1987; MIL-HDBK-347; P1228 (DRAFT); ANSI/IEEE Std 1012-1986; NSWC TR 89-33	Defined briefly Defined in glossary Defined in appendix only Required Mentioned Optional, in appendix Required
reliability block diagram	technique for modelling the set of events that must take place and conditions which must be fulfilled for a successful operation of a system or task	Guide to the Assessment of Reliability (part 6 of BS 5760); Interim Defence Std 00-56; IEC65A(Secretariat)122	Mentioned Recommended and defined
reliability growth models	a statistical model used to predict the current software failure rate and hence the operational reliability	Guide to the Assessment of Reliability	Mentioned
requirements analysis (review)	involves translation of informal prose requirements into formal representation in order to identify aspects of the requirements needing clarification or further definition	ASME NQA-2a-1990; FDA/HIMA (DRAFT); FIPS 101	Required Mentioned Defined in Appendix B

TECHNIQUE	DESCRIPTION	STANDARDS	STATUS
reviews and audits Includes: formal review, software requirements review, (preliminary) design review, critical design review, managerial review, contract review, functional audit, physical audit, in-process audit, SCM plan review, etc.	meeting at which software requirements, design, code or other product is presented to the user, sponsor, or other interested parties for comment and approval, often as a prerequisite for concluding a given phase of the software lifecycle	ANSI/IEEE Std 1012-1986; ISO 9000 (9000-3); ISO 9000 (9001); E.F.T. Message Authentication Guidelines; Guide to the Assessment of Reliability; FIPS 101; Guidelines for Assuring Testability; ANSI/ANS-10.4-1987; Management Plan Documentation Standard; CAN/CSA-Q396.1.2-89; ASME NQA-2a-1990; ANSI/ASQC A3-1987; FDA/HIMA (DRAFT); IEC65A(Secretariat)122; SafeIT; ANSI/IEEE 730.1-1989	Mgmt. review defined, req'd Recommended for design Mgmt., contract review req'd Mentioned Defined briefly Recommended during reqmts. Mentioned Defined in appendix only Defined briefly in glossary Defined briefly Required Defined briefly Defined in glossary Recommended and defined Recommended Described briefly, gives documentation requirements
safety evaluation/risk analysis	statistical analysis	ISO 9000 (9004)	Mentioned
simulation (simulation analysis)	simulate critical aspects of the software environment to analyze logical or performance characteristics that would not be practical to analyze manually use of an executable model to examine the behavior of the software	ANSI/IEEE Std 1012-1986; FIPS 101; Guidelines for Assuring Testability (DRAFT); IEC65A(Secretariat)122; SafeIT; ANSI/IEEE Std 1012-1986	Optional, in glossary Defined in glossary Described briefly Recommended and defined Recommended Optional, in appendix
sizing and timing analysis	determine whether the program will satisfy processor size and performance requirements allocated to software	P1228 (DRAFT); ANSI/IEEE Std 1012-1986	Defined Optional, in appendix

TECHNIQUE	DESCRIPTION	STANDARDS	STATUS
specification analysis	evaluates each safety-critical requirement with respect to quality attributes (e.g., testability)	P1228 (DRAFT); FDA/HIMA (DRAFT)	Defined briefly Mentioned
sneak circuit analysis	graphical technique which relies on the recognition of basic topological patterns in the software structure, used to detect an unexpected path or logic flow which, under certain conditions, initiates an undesired function or inhibits a desired function	AFISC SSH 1-1; MIL-STD-882B; IEC65A(Secretariat)122; SafeIT; P1228 (DRAFT)	Defined Mentioned Recommended and defined Recommended Mentioned
standards audit	check to ensure that applicable standards are used properly	FIPS 101	Recommended during code phase, defined in glossary
statistical sampling inspection	method for evaluating a product by testing random samples	ISO 9000 (9004)	Mentioned
statistical testing	type of testing where the test patterns are selected according to a defined probability distribution on the input domain	IFIP WG 10.4	Mentioned, defined in glossary
stress testing	testing a product using exceptionally high workload in order to show that it would stand normal workloads easily	NCSC-TG-005; IEC65A(Secretariat)122; FDA/HIMA (DRAFT)	Mentioned, defined Defined Mentioned
structural analysis (testing)	uses automated tool that seeks and records errors in the structural makeup of a program	ANSI/IEEE-ANS-7-4.3.2-19XX, Draft 2; IFIP WG 10.4; Guide to the Assessment of Reliability; AFISC SSH 1-1	Defined in appendix only Mentioned, defined in glossary Defined briefly Defined
structure diagrams	a notation complementing data flow diagrams, shows hierarchy of system as a tree; shows relationships between program units without including information about the order of execution of these units	IEC65A(Secretariat)122; SafeIT	Recommended and defined Recommended

TECHNIQUE	DESCRIPTION	STANDARDS	STATUS
symbolic evaluation (execution)	program execution is simulated using symbols rather than actual numerical values for input data, and output is expressed as logical or mathematical expressions involving these symbols	IFIP WG 10.4; Guide to the Assessment of Reliability; FIPS 101; ANSI/ANS-10.4-1987	Mentioned, defined in glossary Defined briefly Recommended for code, defined in glossary Defined in appendix only
system test	testing an integrated hardware and software system to verify that the system meets it specified requirements	FIPS 101; FDA/HIMA (DRAFT)	Defined in glossary Mentioned
test certification	check that reported test results are the actual findings of the tests. Test-related tools, media, and documentation should be certified to ensure maintainability and repeatability of tests	ANSI/IEEE Std 1012-1986	Optional, in appendix
tests of significance	statistical technique	ISO 9000 (9004); ANSI/ASQC A3-1987	Mentioned Mentioned
tracing (traceability analysis)	cross-checking between software products (e.g. design and code) of different lifecycle phases for consistency, correctness, and completeness	ANSI/ANS-10.4-1987; ANSI/IEEE Std 1012-1986	Defined in appendix only Required
unit testing (module testing)	testing of a module for typographic, syntactic, and logical errors, for correct implementation of its design, and satisfaction of its requirements	FIPS 101 FDA/HIMA (DRAFT)	Defined in glossary, in appd. Mentioned

TECHNIQUE	DESCRIPTION	STANDARDS	STATUS
walkthroughs	evaluation technique in which a designer or programmer leads one or more other members of the development team through a segment of design or code, while the other members ask questions and comment about technique, style, and identify possible errors, violations of standards, and other problems evaluation technique in which development personnel lead others through a structured examination of a product	ANSI/IEEE-ANS-7-4.3.2-19XX, Draft 2 IFIP WG 10.4; Guide to the Assessment of Reliability; FIPS 101; ANSI/ANS-10.4-1987; FDA/HIMA (DRAFT); RTCA/DO-178A; MIL-STD-882B; IEC65A(Secretariat)122; SafeIT; AFISC SSH 1-1; ANSI/IEEE Std 1012-1986	Defn. briefly in appendix only Mentioned Defined briefly Defined in glossary Defined in appendix only Mentioned Recommended Mentioned Recommended and defined Recommended Defined Optional, in appendix

PART III

INCREASING SOFTWARE CONFIDENCE: WHERE WE'RE HEADED IN SOFTWARE TESTING TECHNOLOGY

Deborah A. Cerino
Roger J. Dziegiel, Jr.
Rome Laboratory

1.0 INTRODUCTION

In the past decade, many specialized software testing philosophies and testing techniques have evolved. Some of these testing philosophies are time-consuming and impractical while others are practical but only for small programs. Automating the testing process is a goal that needs to be attained for testing to be cost-effective and practical for any size or type of software program. Two testing techniques have been explored under Rome Laboratory (C3CB) R&D programs. These programs developed automated testing tools which support these techniques. One testing technique is mutation analysis and the other technique is decision-to-decision path analysis. A comparison of these testing techniques via two test tools was performed. This technical report describes the testing process and the results of this comparison.

2.0 BACKGROUND

Testing is that phase in the software life cycle where a program is symbolically or physically executed with the intent of gaining confidence in its correctness.[1] The basic problem, therefore, is finding a test selection criterion, a rule to select sets of test cases that will constitute a reliable test. Early in the 1970's, as part of software testing's theoretical foundations, J. B. Goodenough and S. L. Gerhart defined the concept of a reliable test which they believed was sufficient for verifying any program's correctness. As it turned out their ambitious theory was not practical in the real world.

Real world software testers began implementing test strategies which work on particular classes of programs or particular classes of errors. There are two classes of testing strategies: non-traditional and traditional. The most widely used testing strategies are traditional (also called manual) test strategies which include deskchecking, code walkthroughs, and inspections. Non-traditional test strategies are more extensive. TABLE 1 shows the non-traditional strategies in a matrix format. Non-traditional strategies include structure dependent and structure independent test strategies, both of which may be categorized as either deterministic or random strategies.

---

[1] A. Goel, Syracuse University Publication, September 1987.

344

Structure dependent testing is based on the structural properties of the program code.   Structure independent testing is based on the specifications (requirements) of the program, and is not concerned with the design or code structure.   Deterministic testing is performed by taking into account the structure and/or specifications of the program during test case selection.   Random testing assumes that all test input is created equal.   It assumes that any input is as good, for testing purposes, as any other input.

	Structure Dependent (White Box)	Structure Independent (Black Box)
Deterministic	Statement Testing Branch Testing Path Testing Structured Testing Symbolic Testing Domain Testing Mutation Testing	Equivalence Partitioning Boundary Value Analysis Cause-Effect Graphing Design-Based Functional Testing
Random	Randomized Partition Testing	SIAD Tree Testing

**NON-TRADITIONAL
TESTING STRATEGIES**

TABLE 1

Since it is virtually impossible to test a program with all possible inputs to see if it produces the correct outputs, current research efforts have concentrated on testing strategies which are more practical than such brute force methods. Test strategies must be reasonable in effort, in order to be cost effective. For these reasons, testing strategies which select only a small subset of the entire   possible   input   domain   are   being   pursued.   While   these testing techniques cannot guarantee program correctness, they provide the tester with a higher level of confidence in the program. Thus, as stated by E. W. Dijkstra and generally accepted as a maxim, "testing can only be used to detect the presence of errors, never their absence."

The two testing strategies examined here are structure dependent strategies.

3.0 TESTING STRATEGIES

3.1 MUTATION TESTING

Mutation testing is based on the "competent programmer hypothesis", it assumes the program under test has been written by a skilled (i.e., competent) programmer.[1] It then follows that the program would be almost correct, and differ from a truly correct program by only a few small errors. Mutation testing allows a tester to gauge whether a set of test data is adequate to detect those errors. This strategy makes a series of minor changes to a program being tested, creating a series of programs known as mutant programs. Each program is the same as the original program except for a single syntactic change. This minor change can be in the form of constant replacement, arithmetic, relational, logical or logical operator replacement, statement deletion, and statement addition (i. e., Return, Continue, or a Trap statement).[2]

The process consists of determining the expected output for each test case of the original program, generating a set of mutant programs, determining the mutant output for each test case, and comparing the mutant output with the expected output for each test case and mutant. If the mutant's output is different from the expected output for a test case, then that mutant is said to be discovered and "killed" by that test case and the mutant is said to be "dead." Otherwise, it remains "alive" but may still be killed by a subsequent test case. Live mutants provide important test information. A mutant may remain alive for one of three reasons:

---

1   R. A. DeMillo, et al., Purdue University/University of Florida, Software Engineering Research Center, "An Overview of the Mothra Software Testing Environment," SERC-TR-3-P.

2   R. A. DeMillo, et al., Purdue University/University of Florida, Software Engineering Research Center, "The Mothra Software Testing Environment," User's Manual, SERC-TR-4-P.

a.   The test data is inadequate.   This means that the test data may not have covered (i.e., exercised) that portion of the program.

> Example: In the test program (ref, page 14) the input test data "(3,3,5)" and "(5,3,3)" each exercise different parts of the program.   If one is not included in the test data, part of the program will not be exercised.

b.   The mutant program is equivalent to the original program. If the mutant program and the original program always produce the same output, there is no way for the test data to distinguish between the original program and the mutant program.   It may mean that the programs are essentially the same.

> Example: Consider a program that first checks all input variables to make sure they are greater than zero, and exits if the inputs are negative.   One mutant type is the "absolute value insertion" (ref, Table 2).   This mutant operator replaces each variable in a program by the absolute value of the variable.   However, since the original program is designed such that that particular variable is always positive, this mutant will always produce the same output as the original program, and is therefore equivalent.

c.   There exists an error in the program.   If the output of the original program and the mutant program is the same and the test data has   exercised that portion of code, and the mutant program is not equivalent to the original program, then an error is uncovered.

> Example: See Figures 10, 11, 14, and 17 for mutants remaining which remain after test case execution and are not equivalent   to the original program.

3.2 DECISION TO DECISION PATH (DD-PATH) TESTING - BRANCH TESTING

DD-PATH analysis uses a very simple structure dependent   test criteria strategy;   i.e., cover all the edges (branches) of the program's directed flow graph (ref FIGURE 1).   This insures that not only every branch of the program will be executed at least once, but that every statement will also be executed.   DD-PATH testing is frequently called Branch testing.   DD-PATH testing insures the execution   of every loop and control flow at least once.   It involves inserting statements or routines into the program to be tested to record properties of the executing program.   It does not affect the functional behavior of the program.   A decision point is either the entry point of a module, or a place where more than one possible path, or decision occurs. The path that is followed from one decision point to the next is called a decision-to-decision path[1] (ref FIGURE 2).

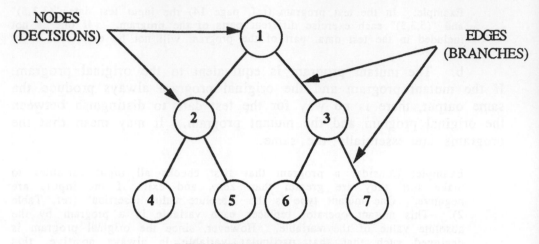

NODES
(DECISIONS)

EDGES
(BRANCHES)

DIRECTED FLOW GRAPH
FIGURE 1

Path testing is a more stringent test criterion than DD-PATH testing. Path testing covers all the edge-to-edge transitions in the directed flow graph. This means that path testing covers all possible ways to traverse from the start of the program to its ending statement. Most times it is impossible to test all the paths or combinations of branches in a large program. Programs with many loops may have an infinite number of paths. However, it is possible to test all DD-PATHs. Analytic information consists of a listing of the DD-PATHs of the program undergoing analysis and the number of times each DD-PATH is executed when the program is executed. For more effective testing, all DD-PATHs and as many paths or branch combinations as possible should be tested. The goal is to increase the amount of code tested.

---

1   General Research Corporation, "RXVP80, The Verification and Validation System for Fortran," User's Manual, 1985, 5-9.

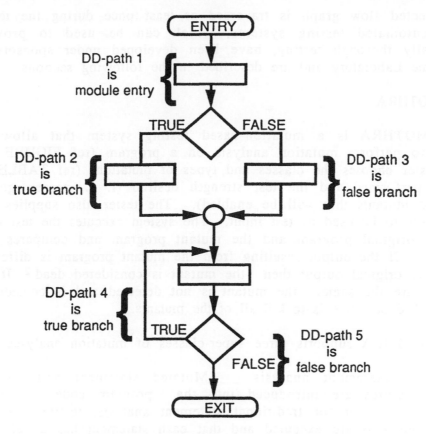

DECISION-TO-DECISION PATH EXAMPLE

FIGURE 2

4.0 AUTOMATED TESTING TOOLS

Manually testing software can be a very tiresome, time consuming, costly, and error-prone task. Since a great deal of manhours are traditionally expended in program testing, automated testing tools are gaining acceptance, especially in space and military applications. According to E. Miller in "Structurally Based Automatic Program Testing,"[1] most application programs written in FORTRAN can be tested minimally thorough with a relatively small number of test cases. A test is minimally thorough if each and every branch in

---

1   Miller, E. F., et al., "Structurally Based Automatic Program Testing," EASCON-74, Washington D.C., October 1974.

its directed flow graph is traversed at least once during the test.[1] Two automated testing systems, which can be used to provide minimally thorough testing, have been developed under sponsorship of Rome Laboratory and are described in the following sections.

4.1 MOTHRA

MOTHRA is a mutation-based testing system that allows a tester to perform mutation analysis on a program (ref FIGURE 3). The tester chooses the classes and types of mutations (ref TABLE 2) to be performed and the test strength desired (i. e., percentage of selected mutants that will be enabled). The tester also supplies the test cases to be used as test input. The system executes the test data on the original program and the mutant program and compares the output.   If the output resulting from the mutant program is different from the original output then the mutant is considered dead.[2] If the outputs are the same, the mutant is not detected and is considered alive. The objective is to kill all of the mutants.

MOTHRA supports three super-classes of mutation analyses:

a.   Statement analysis.   Mutated statement and control structures are introduced into the program code.   These mutants test for traditional statement analysis, testing that all statements are executed and that each statement has an effect.

b.   Predicate and domain analysis.   Mutated expressions, arithmetic operators, and constants are introduced into the program code.   These mutants test predicate boundaries and data domains.

c.   Coincidental correctness.   Scalar variables, array references, and constants are replaced with other values.   These mutated programs detect errors that are undetected by other testing strategies when, due to the nature of the test data, the program just happens to (coincidentally) produce the correct output results.

---

[1]   Huang, J. C., "An Approach to Program Testing," ACM Computing Surveys, September 1975, 113-128.

[2]   R. A. DeMillo, et al., Purdue University/University of Florida, Software Engineering Research Center, "An Overview of the Mothra Software Testing Environment," SERC-TR-3-P, 1-3.

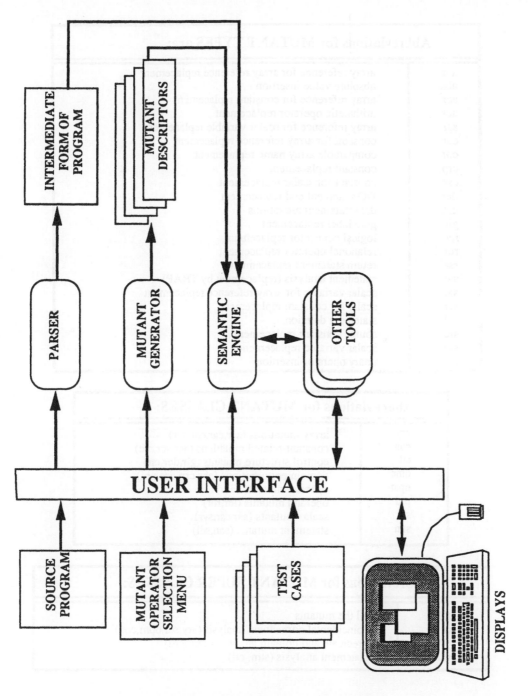

THE MUTATION PROCESS

FIGURE 3

Abbreviations for MUTANT TYPES are:

aar	array reference for array reference replacement
abs	absolute value insertion
acr	array reference for constant replacement
aor	arithmetic operator replacement
asr	array reference for scalar variable replacement
car	constant for array reference replacement
cnr	comparable array name replacement
crp	constant replacement
csr	constant for scalar replacement
der	DO statement end replacement
dsa	data statement alterations
glr	goto label replacement
lcr	logical connector replacement
ror	relational operator replacement
rsr	return statement replacement
san	statement analysis (replacement by TRAP)
sar	scalar variable for array reference replacement
scr	scalar for constant replacement
sdl	statement deletion
src	source constant replacement
svr	scalar variable replacement
uoi	unary operator insertion

Abbreviations for MUTANT CLASSES:

ary	array mutations (aar,car,cnr,sar)
con	constant-related mutations (acr,scr,src)
ctl	control structure mutants (glr,der,rsr)
dmn	domain perturbations (abs,crp,dsa,uoi)
opm	operator mutants (aor)
prd	operand mutants (lcr,ror)
scl	scalar mutants (asr,csr,svr)
stm	statement mutants (san,sdl)

Abbreviations for MUTANT SUPER CLASSES:

all	all the mutants
cca	coincidental correctness analysis (ary,scl,opm,con)
pda	predicate and domain analysis (dmn,prd)
sal	statement analysis (stm, ctl)

MOTHRA MUTANT OPERATORS

TABLE 2

MOTHRA has evolved from previous work in mutation systems. The first was PIMS in 1979, a FORTRAN subset prototype, EXPER an experimental vehicle in 1980, CMS.1 a COBOL system in 1981 and FMS.3 an enhancement of EXPER in 1983. MOTHRA is designed to allow the testing of software at all test stages in the development process. It can accommodate units ranging from 10 to 100,000,000 lines of code. It currently supports FORTRAN 77, and follow-on work is planned to support the Ada programming language. An attractive feature of mutation analysis is that it includes statement and branch coverage, as it performs mutation analysis. In addition, the mutation score of a particular program (i. e., dead mutants/total # of mutants) indicates the adequacy of the data used to test the program, and is also a potential predictor of operational reliability. A potential problem of mutation analysis systems is the amount of disk storage and manpower required for the testing of the programs. However, MOTHRA allows the user to choose a subset of mutants that is very manageable and still adequate for testing purposes.

MOTHRA was developed by Georgia Institute of Technology (with a subcontract to Purdue University), under the sponsorship of Rome Laboratory contract F30602-85-C-0255. MOTHRA currently runs under 4.3BSD UNIX[1], System V UNIX, and Ultrix-32 V3.0[2].

4.2 RXVP80[3]

Research EXportable Verification Program for the 80's (RXVP80) is a software testing tool used to test and verify FORTRAN programs. RXVP80 can analyze FORTRAN 66, FORTRAN 77 and most FORTRAN extensions to the standards.

RXVP80 performs static as well as dynamic analysis of programs. Static analyses are those which do not require execution of the user's program, but which collect information on the structure of the program. Static analyses provides information on control structure, symbol usage, calling hierarchy, as well as unreachable code.

Dynamic analyses require execution of the user's program and provides run-time execution coverage information. As part of execution coverage analysis (ref FIGURE 4), the user's source code is

---

[1]   UNIX is a trademark of Bell Laboratories.

[2]   Ultrix and Ultrix-32 are trademarks of Digital Equipment Corporation.

[3]   RXVP80 is a trademark of General Research Corporation, Santa Barbara, CA.

instrumented (i.e., software probes are inserted) with statements that trace the execution of the program. The execution of this instrumented program produces a set of data that trace the DD-PATHs and/or statements executed during the test run. A number of reports that show the extent of program testing is then produced from the data. The information provided indicates the thoroughness of the tests, including which DD-PATHs are taken, which DD-PATHs are not taken, and how often each DD-PATH is traversed. RXVP80 provides the capability to test for 100% branch and statement coverage of a program.

The dynamic analysis portion of the RXVP80 was used in analysis of the test program and its performance was matched against both MOTHRA's statement and predicate & domain analyses capabilities as these strategies were similar in their proposed detection of errors.

RXVP80 is a commercial product from General Research Corporation (Santa Barbara, CA) that resulted from a Rome Laboratory (C3CB) effort entitled "FORTRAN Automated Verification System" (FAVS), contract F30602-76-C-0436.

5.0 THE TEST PROGRAM

The test program used for automated testing by MOTHRA and RXVP80 determines the type of triangle (scalene, isosceles, or equilateral) from the data that is entered. The program user must provide the length of the three sides of the triangle as integer inputs. The program checks for negative integers or zero in the input and, if found, it determines the input to be "not a valid triangle." A triangle program was chosen because of its popularity in the software testing literature. The triangle classification program in "Theories of Program Testing & the Application of Revealing Subdomains" by Weyuker and Ostrand is widely used to validate software testing techniques. The test program used in this experiment is somewhat different. In this program, the input does not have to be in ascending or descending order. For example, the input can be entered as, (3,3,5), (5,3,3), or (3,5,3). Because this program allows any order, to test this program you must test all combinations of input! Even if the tester does not immediately see this at first glance, by using these tools it becomes apparent that, for example, (3,3,5) does not exercise the same statements as (5,3,3). Thus, test

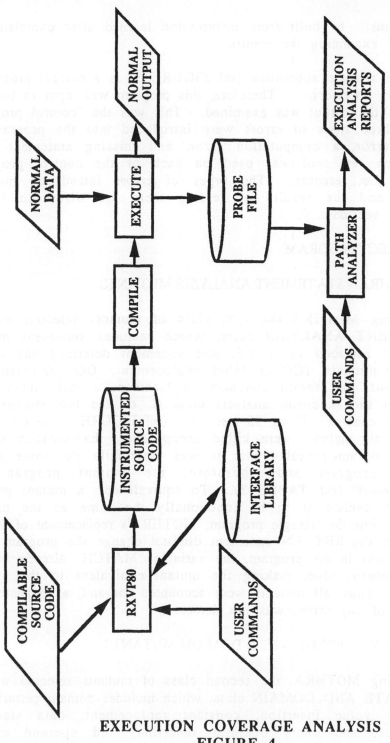

EXECUTION COVERAGE ANALYSIS
FIGURE 4

cases must be built from information learned after exercising the tools and examining the results.

The triangle subroutine (ref FIGURE 5) is a correct program -- it contains no errors. Therefore, this program was input to both test tools and the output was examined. This was the "control program." Next, three types of errors were introduced into the program: a domain error, a computation error, and missing statement error. Then each test tool was used on each of the control program's variants (i.e., errors). The types of errors introduced into the variants and the results of testing them are discussed in the following sections.

6.0 CORRECT PROGRAM

6.1 MOTHRA - STATEMENT ANALYSIS MUTANTS

Using MOTHRA the first class of mutants selected was the STATEMENT ANALYSIS class, which includes statement mutants (statement replaced by TRAP, and statement deletion) and control structure mutants (GOTO label replacement, DO statement end replacement, and return statement replacement). All mutants that belong to the statement analysis class (i. e., the test strength was 100) were enabled. Using 35 test cases (ref FIGURE 6) on the correct program, all mutants were killed except one. Examination of this mutant program revealed that it was essentially the same as the original program and, therefore, the mutant program was "equivalenced" (ref TABLE 3). To equivalence a mutant program means to declare it to be functionally the same as the original program. For the triangle program, MOTHRA's replacement of "GOTO 110" with the RETURN statement did not change the program since, at that point in the program, the variable "MATCH" already had the correct return value, making the mutant equivalent to the original program. Thus, all mutants were accounted for and, as expected, the presence of any errors was not detected.

6.2 MOTHRA - PREDICATE & DOMAIN MUTANTS

Using MOTHRA, the second class of mutants selected was the PREDICATE AND DOMAIN class, which includes domain perturbations (absolute value insertion, constant replacement, data statement alterations, and unary operator insertion) and operand mutants (logical connector replacement, and relational operator replacement).

```
          SUBROUTINE TRIANGLE(I,J,K,MATCH)

          integer  i,j,k,match

C         MATCH is output from the subroutine:
C         MATCH = 1 IF THE TRIANGLE IS SCALENE
C         MATCH = 2 IF THE TRIANGLE IS ISOSCELES
C         MATCH = 3 IF THE TRIANGLE IS EQUILATERAL
C         MATCH = 4 IF NOT A TRIANGLE

C         After a quick confirmation that it's a legal
C         triangle, detect any sides of equal length
          IF (I .LE. 0 .OR. J .LE. 0 .OR. K .LE. 0) GOTO 500
          MATCH=0
          IF (I.NE.J) GOTO 10
          MATCH=MATCH+1
10        IF (I.NE.K) GOTO 20
          MATCH=MATCH+2
20        IF (J.NE.K) GOTO 30
          MATCH=MATCH+3
30        IF (MATCH.NE.0) GOTO 100

C         Confirm it's a legal triangle before declaring it to be scalene
          IF (I+J.LE.K)  GOTO 500
          IF (J+K.LE.I)  GOTO 500
          IF (I+K.LE.J)  GOTO 500
          MATCH=1
          Return

C         Confirm it's a legal triangle before declaring
C         it to be isosceles or equilateral
100       IF (MATCH.NE.1) GOTO 200
          IF (I+J.LE.K) GOTO 500
110       MATCH=2
          RETURN
200       IF (MATCH.NE.2) GOTO 300
          IF (I+K.LE.J)  GOTO 500
          GOTO 110
300       IF (MATCH.NE.3) GOTO 400
          IF (J+K.LE.I)  GOTO 500
          GOTO 110
400       MATCH=3
          RETURN

C         Can't fool this program, that's not a triangle
500       MATCH=4
          RETURN
          END
```

CORRECT TRIANGLE PROGRAM

FIGURE 5

Test Cases for triangle.tc.

Values for case 1.   Values for case 2.
I 3   I 2
J 4   J 2
K 5   K 2

Values for case 3.   Values for case 4.
I 2   I 5
J 2   J 4
K 1   K 3

Values for case 5.   Values for case 6.
I 0   I -1
J 0   J 0
K 0   K 3

Values for case 7.   Values for case 8.
I 4   I 2
J 3   J 3
K 2   K 4

Values for case 9.   Values for case 10.
I 2   I 6
J 4   J 8
K 2   K 10

Values for case 11.   Values for case 12.
I -1   I -1
J -1   J 2
K -1   K -1

Values for case 13.   Values for case 14.
I 2   I 2
J 1   J 0
K 2   K 2

INITIAL SET OF TEST CASES

FIGURE 6

Values for case 15.
I 2
J 2
K -1

Values for case 16.
I 1
J 2
K 2

Values for case 17.
I 1
J 1
K 1

Values for case 18.
I 0
J 1
K 2

Values for case 19.
I 1
J 2
K 0

Values for case 20.
I 1
J -2
K 5

Values for case 21.
I 3
J 3
K 2

Values for case 22.
I 1
J 5
K 5

Values for case 23.
I 7
J 5
K 5

Values for case 24.
I 10
J 5
K 5

Values for case 25.
I 5
J 5
K 10

Values for case 26.
I 5
J 10
K 5

Values for case 27.
I 0
J 0
K 2

Values for case 28.
I 2
J 0
K 0

INITIAL SET OF TEST CASES

FIGURE 6 (continued)

Values for case 29.
I 1
J 1
K 2

Values for case 30.
I 3
J 3
K 3

Values for case 31.
I 0
J 3
K 7

Values for case 32.
I 1
J 5
K 9

Values for case 33.
I -1
J 5
K 1

Values for case 34.
I 1
J 0
K 5

Values for case 35.
I -20
J -20
K -20

INITIAL SET OF TEST CASES

FIGURE 6 (continued)

TYPE	GENERATED	LIVE	%LIVE	EQUIV	DEAD
glr	126	0	0.0	0	128
rsr	38	0	0.0	1	37
san	36	0	0.0	0	36
sdl	41	0	0.0	0	41
TOTALS	243	0	0.0	1	242

CLASS	GENERATED	LIVE	%LIVE	EQUIV	DEAD
ary	0	0	0.0	0	0
con	0	0	0.0	0	0
ctl	166	0	0.0	1	165
dmn	0	0	0.0	0	0
opm	0	0	0.0	0	0
prd	0	0	0.0	0	0
scl	0	0	0.0	0	0
stm	77	0	0.0	0	77

SUPERCL	GENERATED	LIVE	%LIVE	EQUIV	DEAD
all	243	0	0.0	1	242
cca	0	0	0.0	0	0
pda	0	0	0.0	0	0
sal	243	0	0.0	1	242

MOTHRA - STATEMENT ANALYSIS MUTANTS
(CORRECT PROGRAM)

TABLE 3

Using the same 35 test cases as in the statement analysis mutants test run described in section 6.1 above, 108 mutants remained alive. The mutants were then examined and it was found that many of them could be equivalenced. For example, the absolute value insertion mutant type (abs) was equivalenced at several points in the program since at those points, negative values were impossible due to the structure of the code. Thirty-one mutants were then left remaining. With these few remaining mutants, it was much easier to see which statements were not being executed. Additional test cases were then added and the remaining mutants were killed (ref TABLE 4). This confirmed the expected output, since it was known that the program was correct.

TYPE	GENERATED	LIVE	%LIVE	EQUIV	DEAD
abs	126	0	0.0	77	49
crp	29	0	0.0	0	29
lsr	13	0	0.0	1	12
ror	99	0	0.0	4	95
uoi	83	0	0.0	2	81
TOTALS	350	0	0.0	84	266

CLASS	GENERATED	LIVE	%LIVE	EQUIV	DEAD
ary	0	0	0.0	0	0
con	0	0	0.0	0	0
ctl	0	0	0.0	0	0
dmn	238	0	0.0	79	159
opm	0	0	0.0	0	0
prd	112	0	0.0	5	107
scl	0	0	0.0	0	0
stm	0	0	0.0	0	0

SUPERCL	GENERATED	LIVE	%LIVE	EQUIV	DEAD
all	350	0	0.0	84	266
cca	0	0	0.0	0	0
pda	350	0	0.0	84	266
sal	0	0	0.0	0	0

**MOTHRA - DOMAIN & PREDICATE MUTANTS
(CORRECT PROGRAM)**

TABLE 4

6.3 RXVP80

Using RXVP80, an output report was created which identified all the DD-PATHs in the triangle program (ref FIGURE 7). A DD-PATH tree (ref FIGURE 8) was manually created to aid understanding of the triangle program and determine exactly how RXVP80 created the DD-PATHs.   On entry to a function or subroutine, the entry point is always DD-PATH 1. For IF statements, the TRUE branch is assigned an even number DD-PATH and the FALSE branch an odd number DD-PATH.

By using RXVP80 on the triangle program, it was found that the original 35 test cases exercised 100% of the program DD-PATHs, and that the output from each test case was correct (as it should be, since this is a correct program).   Thus, as was expected, no errors were found.

7.0 DOMAIN ERROR

An error was introduced into the correct program, and both the MOTHRA and RXVP80 were used to see if they would detect the error.   The triangle program was modified such that a domain error was created.   A domain error occurs when a specific input follows the wrong path due to an error in the control flow of the program.[1] The error was created by modifying the predicate on line 18 of the triangle subroutine (ref FIGURE 9).   Line 18, IF (I .NE. J) GOTO 10, was changed to: IF (-I .NE. J) GOTO 10.

7.1 MOTHRA - STATEMENT ANALYSIS MUTANTS

The domain error was created via the VAX/ULTRIX editor.   The program was then entered into the MOTHRA system.   The statement analysis class was selected, and all mutants belonging to that class were enabled (i. e., the test strength was 100).

When the test cases were entered, test case 3, test input (2,2,1) gave an incorrect output.   The triangle program output identified the triangle as scalene when it should have been isosceles. This incorrect

---

[1]   White, Cohen, and Zeil, "A Domain Strategy for Computer Program Testing," Computer Program Testing, September 1981, 103-113.

```
DD-PATH DEFINITIONS
STMT NEST LINE  SOURCE...      SUBROUTINE TRIANGLE ( I , J , K , MATCH )

              1
              2                                                        ** DDPATH 1 IS PROCEDURE ENTRY
  1           3               SUBROUTINE TRIANGLE(I,J,K,MATCH)

              5
  2           6      C        INTEGER I,J,K,MATCH

              7      C  MATCH is output from the subroutine:
              8      C  MATCH = 1 IF THE TRIANGLE IS SCALENE
              9      C  MATCH = 2 IF THE TRIANGLE IS ISOSCELES
             10      C  MATCH = 3 IF THE TRIANGLE IS EQUILATERAL
             11      C  MATCH = 4 IF NOT A TRIANGLE
             12
             13      C  After a quick confirmation that it's a legal
             14      C  triangle, detect any sides of equal length
  3          16      C        IF (I .LE. 0 .OR. J .LE. 0 .OR. K .LE. 0) GOTO 500
                                                                       ** DDPATH 2 IS TRUE BRANCH
                                                                       ** DDPATH 3 IS FALSE BRANCH

  5          17               MATCH=0
  6          18               IF (-I.NE.J) GOTO 10
                                                                       ** DDPATH 4 IS TRUE BRANCH
                                                                       ** DDPATH 5 IS FALSE BRANCH

  8          19               MATCH=MATCH+1
  9          20            10 IF (I.NE.K) GOTO 20
                                                                       ** DDPATH 6 IS TRUE BRANCH
                                                                       ** DDPATH 7 IS FALSE BRANCH

 11          21               MATCH=MATCH+2
 12          22            20 IF (J.NE.K) GOTO 30
                                                                       ** DDPATH 8 IS TRUE BRANCH
                                                                       ** DDPATH 9 IS FALSE BRANCH

 14          23               MATCH=MATCH+3
 15          24            30 IF (MATCH.NE.0) GOTO 100
                                                                       ** DDPATH 10 IS TRUE BRANCH
                                                                       ** DDPATH 11 IS FALSE BRANCH

             25
             26      C  Confirm it's a legal triangle before declaring
             27      C  it to be scalene

 17          29               IF (I+J.LE.K) GOTO 500
                                                                       ** DDPATH 12 IS TRUE BRANCH
                                                                       ** DDPATH 13 IS FALSE BRANCH

 19          30               IF (J+K.LE.I) GOTO 500
                                                                       ** DDPATH 14 IS TRUE BRANCH
                                                                       ** DDPATH 15 IS FALSE BRANCH

 21          31               IF (I+K.LE.J) GOTO 500
                                                                       ** DDPATH 16 IS TRUE BRANCH
                                                                       ** DDPATH 17 IS FALSE BRANCH

 23          32               MATCH=1
 24          33               RETURN
             34
```

TRIANGLE PROGRAM DD-PATHS

FIGURE 7

```
DD-PATH DEFINITIONS          SUBROUTINE TRIANGLE ( I , J , K , MATCH )
STMT NEST LINE  SOURCE....

          35   C    Confirm is't a legal triangle before declaring
          36   C    it to be isosceles or equilateral
   25     38  100   IF (MATCH.NE.1) GOTO 200                    ** DDPATH 18 IS TRUE BRANCH
                                                                ** DDPATH 19 IS FALSE BRANCH

   27     39        IF (I+J.LE.K) GOTO 500                      ** DDPATH 20 IS TRUE BRANCH
                                                                ** DDPATH 21 IS FALSE BRANCH

   29     40  110   MATCH=2
   30     41        RETURN
   31     42  200   IF (MATCH.NE.2) GOTO 300                    ** DDPATH 22 IS TRUE BRANCH
                                                                ** DDPATH 23 IS FALSE BRANCH

   33     43        IF (I+K.LE.J)  GOTO 500                     ** DDPATH 24 IS TRUE BRANCH
                                                                ** DDPATH 25 IS FALSE BRANCH

   35     44        GOTO 110
   36     45  300   IF (MATCH.NE.3) GOTO 400                    ** DDPATH 26 IS TRUE BRANCH
                                                                ** DDPATH 27 IS FALSE BRANCH

   38     46        IF (J+K.LE.I)  GOTO 500                     ** DDPATH 28 IS TRUE BRANCH
                                                                ** DDPATH 29 IS FALSE BRANCH

   40     47        GOTO 110
   41     48  400   MATCH=3
   42     49        RETURN
          50   C    Can't fool this program, thats not a triangle
   43     51  500   MATCH=4
   44     54        RETURN
   45     55        END
```

TRIANGLE PROGRAM DD-PATHS

FIGURE 7 (continued)

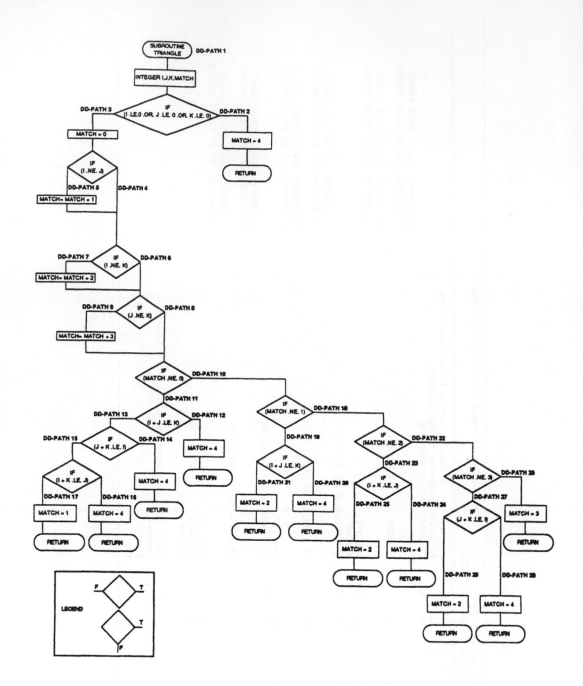

DD-PATH TREE

FIGURE 8

```
      SUBROUTINE TRIANGLE(I,J,K,MATCH)

      integer   i,j,k,match

C     MATCH is output from the subroutine:
C     MATCH = 1 IF THE TRIANGLE IS SCALENE
C     MATCH = 2 IF THE TRIANGLE IS ISOSCELES
C     MATCH = 3 IF THE TRIANGLE IS EQUILATERAL
C     MATCH = 4 IF NOT A TRIANGLE

C     After a quick confirmation that it's a legal
C     triangle, detect any sides of equal length
      IF (I .LE. 0 .OR. J .LE. 0 .OR. K .LE. 0) GOTO 500
      MATCH=0
      IF (-I.NE.J) GOTO 10 -- DOMAIN ERROR
      MATCH=MATCH+1
10    IF (I.NE.K) GOTO 20
      MATCH=MATCH+2
20    IF (J.NE.K) GOTO 30
      MATCH=MATCH+3
30    IF (MATCH.NE.0) GOTO 100

C     Confirm it's a legal triangle before declaring it to be scalene
      IF (I+J.LE.K)  GOTO 500
      IF (J+K.LE.I)  GOTO 500
      IF (I+K.LE.J)  GOTO 500
      MATCH=1
      Return

C     Confirm it's a legal triangle before declaring it to be isosceles or
C     equilateral
100   IF (MATCH.NE.1) GOTO 200
      IF (I+J.LE.K) GOTO 500
110   MATCH=2
      RETURN
200   IF (MATCH.NE.2) GOTO 300
      IF (I+K.LE.J)  GOTO 500
      GOTO 110
300   IF (MATCH.NE.3) GOTO 400
      IF (J+K.LE.I)  GOTO 500
      GOTO 110
400   MATCH=3
      RETURN

C     Can't fool this program, that's not a triangle
500   MATCH=4
      RETURN
      END
```

TRIANGLE PROGRAM (DOMAIN ERROR)

FIGURE 9

output immediately indicates there is an error. MOTHRA was then used to help pinpoint the error.

After inputting the original 35 test cases plus several additional test cases, 18 mutants were still alive (ref TABLE 5). The same mutant described in section 6.1 was equivalenced. Next, possible reasons for the remaining mutants were examined. Examination of Figure 10 shows that there are two groups of remaining live mutants (mutants are identified in the program via the "#" symbol). One group represents the mutants that are created to replace the statement: IF (I+J .LE. K) GOTO 500. As shown in Figure 10, the mutant statements for each original statement are displayed beneath the statement they replace. When MOTHRA executes, it replaces the original statement with one mutant statement. Thus, as many new programs are created as mutant statements. None of these were killed. Further examination shows that this statement was never executed because of the statement directly above it: IF (MATCH .NE. 1) GOTO 200. MATCH was never being set to 1 so the program execution was always jumping to statement 200. To find the reason for this, the other group of mutants, those that were created to replace the statement: MATCH = MATCH + 1, were checked. It was clear that this statement was not being executed. The statement directly above it was examined: IF (-I .NE. J) GOTO 10. What was happening was that the program was always going to statement 10 because there was an error in the IF statement. The error was found!

7.2 MOTHRA - PREDICATE & DOMAIN MUTANTS

Using MOTHRA, the predicate and domain class of mutants was selected. Using the same test cases as those input to the correct program previously mutated using the predicate and domain class, three inputs gave incorrect outputs. Obviously the program was in error and MOTHRA was used to try to find the error. After numerous test case inputs, fifty-three mutants were remaining (ref TABLE 6). The live mutants were examined (ref FIGURE 11). The first set of mutants replaced the statement: MATCH = MATCH + 1. It was clear that this statement was not being executed. To find a reason for this, the code was examined. The previous statement: IF (-I .NE. J) GOTO 10 indicated that the program execution was going to statement 10 and not executing the MATCH = MATCH + 1 statement.

TYPE	GENERATED	LIVE	%LIVE	EQUIV	DEAD
glr	128	8	6.3	0	120
rsr	38	4	10.5	0	34
san	36	3	8.3	0	34
sdl	41	3	7.3	0	38
TOTALS	243	18	7.4	0	225

CLASS	GENERATED	LIVE	%LIVE	EQUIV	DEAD
ary	0	0	0.0	0	0
con	0	0	0.0	0	0
ctl	166	12	7.2	0	154
dmn	0	0	0.0	0	0
opm	0	0	0.0	0	0
prd	0	0	0.0	0	0
scl	0	0	0.0	0	0
stm	77	6	7.8	0	71

SUPERCL	GENERATED	LIVE	%LIVE	EQUIV	DEAD
all	243	18	7.4	0	225
cca	0	0	0.0	0	0
pda	0	0	0.0	0	0
sal	243	18	7.4	0	225

MOTHRA - STATEMENT ANALYSIS MUTANTS
DOMAIN ERROR

TABLE 5

```
        SUBROUTINE TRIANGLE(I,J,K,MATCH)

        integer  i,j,k,match

C       MATCH is output from the subroutine:
C       MATCH = 1 IF THE TRIANGLE IS SCALENE
C       MATCH = 2 IF THE TRIANGLE IS ISOSCELES
C       MATCH = 3 IF THE TRIANGLE IS EQUILATERAL
C       MATCH = 4 IF NOT A TRIANGLE

C       After a quick confirmation that it's a legal
C       triangle, detect any sides of equal length
        IF (I .LE. 0 .OR. J .LE. 0 .OR. K .LE. 0) GOTO 500
        MATCH=0
        IF (-I.NE.J) GOTO 10 -- DOMAIN ERROR
        MATCH=MATCH+1
#   rsr      134   #       RETURN
#   san      170   #   *** TRAP  ***
#   sdl      208   #       CONTINUE
10      IF (I.NE.K) GOTO 20
        MATCH=MATCH+2
20      IF (J.NE.K) GOTO 30
        MATCH=MATCH+3
30      IF (MATCH.NE.0) GOTO 100

C       Confirm it's a legal triangle before declaring it to be scalene
        IF (I+J.LE.K)  GOTO 500
        IF (J+K.LE.I)  GOTO 500
        IF (I+K.LE.J)  GOTO 500
        MATCH=1
        Return

C       Confirm it's a legal triangle before declaring it to be isosceles
C       or  equilateral
100     IF (MATCH.NE.1) GOTO 200
        IF (I+J.LE.K) GOTO 500
#   rsr      152   #       RETURN
#   san      188   #   *** TRAP  ***
#   sdl      227   #       CONTINUE
#   rsr      153   #       IF ((I + J) .LE. K) RETURN
#   san      189   #       IF ((I + J) .LE. K) *** TRAP ***
#   sdl      228   #       IF ((I + J) .LE. K) CONTINUE
#   glr       73   #       IF ((I + J) .LE. K) GO TO 400
#   glr       74   #       IF ((I + J) .LE. K) GO TO 300
#   glr       75   #       IF ((I + J) .LE. K) GO TO 200
#   glr       76   #       IF ((I + J) .LE. K) GO TO 110
```

MOTHRA - "LIVE" STATEMENT ANALYSIS MUTANTS
DOMAIN ERROR

FIGURE 10

```
#    glr      77     #      IF ((I + J) .LE. K) GO TO 100
#    glr      78     #      IF ((I + J) .LE. K) GO TO 30
#    glr      79     #      IF ((I + J) .LE. K) GO TO 20
#    glr      80     #      IF ((I + J) .LE. K) GO TO 10
110       MATCH=2
          RETURN
200       IF (MATCH.NE.2) GOTO 300
          IF (I+K.LE.J)  GOTO 500
          GOTO 110
#    rsr     159     #      RETURN
300       IF (MATCH.NE.3) GOTO 400
          IF (J+K.LE.I)  GOTO 500
          GOTO 110
400       MATCH=3
          RETURN

C         Can't fool this program, that's not a triangle
500       MATCH=4
          RETURN
          END
```

MOTHRA - "LIVE" STATEMENT ANALYSIS MUTANTS
DOMAIN ERROR

FIGURE 10 (continued)

TYPE	GENERATED	LIVE	%LIVE	EQUIV	DEAD
abs	126	27	21.4	21	78
crp	29	2	6.9	0	27
lsr	13	0	0.0	0	13
ror	99	11	11.1	0	88
uoi	83	13	15.7	0	70
TOTALS	350	53	15.1	21	276

CLASS	GENERATED	LIVE	%LIVE	EQUIV	DEAD
ary	0	0	0.0	0	0
con	0	0	0.0	0	0
ctl	0	0	0.0	0	0
dmn	238	42	17.6	21	175
opm	0	0	0.0	0	0
prd	112	11	9.8	0	101
scl	0	0	0.0	0	0
stm	0	0	0.0	0	0

SUPERCL	GENERATED	LIVE	%LIVE	EQUIV	DEAD
all	350	53	15.1	21	276
cca	0	0	0.0	0	0
pda	350	53	15.1	21	276
sal	0	0	0.0	0	0

MOTHRA - PREDICATE & DOMAIN MUTANTS
DOMAIN ERROR

TABLE 6

```
       SUBROUTINE TRIANGLE(I,J,K,MATCH)

       integer  i,j,k,match
C      MATCH is output from the subroutine:
C      MATCH = 1 IF THE TRIANGLE IS SCALENE
C      MATCH = 2 IF THE TRIANGLE IS ISOSCELES
C      MATCH = 3 IF THE TRIANGLE IS EQUILATERAL
C      MATCH = 4 IF NOT A TRIANGLE
C      After a quick confirmation that it's a legal
C      triangle, detect any sides of equal length
       IF (I .LE. 0 .OR. J .LE. 0 .OR. K .LE. 0) GOTO 500
       MATCH=0
```

IF (-I.NE.J) GOTO 10 -- DOMAIN ERROR

```
       MATCH=MATCH+1
#  abs 17    #        MATCH = NEGABS (MATCH) + 1
#  abs 18    #        MATCH = ZPUSH (MATCH) + 1
#  uoi 283   #        MATCH = ( - MATCH) + 1
#  crp 135   #        MATCH = ZPUSH (MATCH) + 1
#  abs 20    #        MATCH = NEGABS (MATCH + 1)
#  abs 21    #        MATCH = ZPUSH (MATCH + 1)
#  uoi 284   #        MATCH = - (MATCH + 1)
#  uoi 285   #        MATCH = ++ (MATCH + 1)
#  uoi 286   #        MATCH = - - (MATCH + 1)
10     IF (I.NE.K) GOTO 20
       MATCH=MATCH+2
#  abs 29    #        MATCH = NEGABS (MATCH) + 2
#  uoi 291   #        MATCH = ( - MATCH) + 2
#  abs 33    #        MATCH = ZPUSH (MATCH + 2)
20     IF (J.NE.K) GOTO 30
       MATCH=MATCH+3
#  abs 45    #        MATCH = ZPUSH (MATCH + 3)
30     IF (MATCH.NE.0) GOTO 100
C      Confirm it's a legal triangle before declaring it to be scalene
       IF (I+J.LE.K)  GOTO 500
       IF (J+K.LE.I)  GOTO 500
       IF (I+K.LE.J)  GOTO 500
       MATCH=1
       Return
C      Confirm it's a legal triangle before declaring it to be isosceles
C      or equilateral
100    IF (MATCH.NE.1) GOTO 200
#  abs   83   #    100   IF (NEGABS (MATCH) .NE. 1) GO TO 200
#  abs   84   #    100   IF (ZPUSH (MATCH) .NE. 1) GO TO 200
#  uoi   321  #    100   IF (( - MATCH) .NE. 1) GO TO 200
#  uoi   322  #    100   IF (( ++ MATCH) .NE. 1) GO TO 200
#  crp   144  #    100   IF (MATCH .NE. 0) GO TO 200
#  uoi   324  #    100   IF (MATCH .NE. (- 1)) GO TO 200
#  ror   235  #    100   IF (MATCH .GT. 1) GO TO 200
```

MOTHRA - "LIVE" PREDICATE & DOMAIN MUTANTS
DOMAIN ERROR

FIGURE 11

```
#      ror 236   #        100    IF (MATCH .GE. 1) GO TO 200
#      ror 237   #        100    IF (.TRUE.) GO TO 200
             IF (I+J.LE.K) GOTO 500
#      abs 86    #          IF ((NEGABS (I) + J) .LE. K) GO TO 500
#      abs 87    #          IF ((ZPUSH (I) + J) .LE. K) GO TO 500
#      uoi 325   #        IF (((- I) + J) .LE. K) GO TO 500
#      abs 88    #          IF ((I + NEGABS (J)) .LE. K) GO TO 500
#      abs 90    #          IF ((I + ZPUSH(J)) .LE. K) GO TO 500
#      abs 92    #          IF (NEGABS (I - J) .LE. K) GO TO 500
#      abs 93    #          IF (ZPUSH(I + J) .LE. K) GO TO 500
#      uoi 326   #        IF ((- (I + J)) .LE. K) GO TO 500
#      uoi 327   #        IF ((++ (I + J)) .LE. K) GO TO 500
#      uoi 328   #        IF ((- - (I + J)) .LE. K) GO TO 500
#      abs 95    #          IF ( (I + J) .LE. NEGABS (K)) GO TO 500
#      abs 96    #          IF ((I + J) .LE. ZPUSH (K)) GO TO 500
#      uoi 329   #        IF ((I + J) .LE. (- K)) GO TO 500
#      ror 238   #        IF ((I + J) .LT. K) GO TO 500
#      ror 239   #        IF ((I + J) .EQ. K) GO TO 500
#      ror 240   #        IF ((I + J) .NE. K) GO TO 500
#      ror 241   #        IF ((I + J) .GT. K) GO TO 500
#      ror 242   #        IF ((I + J) .GE. K) GO TO 500
#      ror 243   #        IF (.TRUE.) GO TO 500
110        MATCH=2
           RETURN
200        IF (MATCH.NE.2) GOTO 300
#      abs 99    # 200    IF (ZPUSH (MATCH) .NE. 2) GO TO 300
#      ror 247 # 200      IF (MATCH .GT. 2) GO TO 300
             IF (I+K.LE.J)  GOTO 500
#      abs 102   #          IF ((ZPUSH (I) + K) .LE. J) GO TO 500
#      abs 105   #          IF ((I + ZPUSH(K)) .LE. J) GO TO 500
#      abs 108   #          IF (ZPUSH(I + K) .LE. J) GO TO 500
#      abs 111   #          IF ((I + K) .LE. ZPUSH (J)) GO TO 500
             GOTO 110
300        IF (MATCH.NE.3) GOTO 400
#      abs 114   # 300    IF (ZPUSH (MATCH) .NE. 3) GO TO 400
#      ror 259   # 300    IF (MATCH .GT. 3) GO TO 400
             IF (J+K.LE.I) GOTO 500
#      abs 117   #          IF ((ZPUSH (J) + K) .LE. I) GO TO 500
#      abs 120   #          IF ((J + ZPUSH(K)) .LE. I) GO TO 500
#      abs 123   #          IF (ZPUSH(J + K) .LE. I) GO TO 500
#      abs 126   #          IF ((J + K) .LE. ZPUSH (I)) GO TO 500
             GOTO 110
400        MATCH=3
           RETURN
C          Can't fool this program, that's not a triangle
500        MATCH=4
           RETURN
           END
```

MOTHRA - "LIVE" PREDICATE & DOMAIN MUTANTS
DOMAIN ERROR

FIGURE 11 (continued)

The next large group of mutants which were not killed were examined. These replaced the statement: IF (I+J .LE. K) GOTO 500. Again, by the large number of mutants remaining in this group, it was clear that this statement was not being executed. Looking at the previous statement: IF (MATCH .NE. 1) GOTO 200 indicated that MATCH was not being set to 1. MATCH was not set to 1 because, as indicated by the first group of mutants, the statement MATCH = MATCH + 1 was not executed. For each group of mutants, the flow of execution returned to the same point and it was finally noticed that the IF statement: IF (-I .NE. J) GOTO 10 was in error. It should have been: IF (I .NE. J) GOTO 10!

Overall, it was found that mutating for predicate and domain mutants provided too much information for this small non-critical testing experiment.   It was easier to locate an error (domain error) when statement analysis mutants were created.   However, the same conclusions were drawn as to what caused the error in the program - it just took the test personnel much longer.

7.3 RXVP80

The same domain error was created by modifying the subroutine triangle via the VAX/VMS editor. The program was then input to RXVP80, instrumented (insertion of software probes) for DD-PATH coverage and run against the previous set of test cases. After additional test cases were added, only 86% of the paths had been executed. RXVP80 identified DD-PATHs 5, 19, 20 and 21 as paths that were not executed (ref FIGURE 12).

This led to investigation of the DD-PATH report which identifies each DD-PATH, ref FIGURE 7. DD-PATH 5 is the FALSE branch of: IF (-I .NE. J) GOTO 10, which meant that for none of the test cases was -I = J. On first examination of the program, it appears that inputting (2,-2,2) for the sides of the triangle would cause this DD-PATH to be traversed.   However, closer examination revealed that a previous statement checked for negative input values. If negative input was encountered, then the program control flow jumps to a statement at the end of the program. The result is that this DD-PATH could never be exercised, and that the assignment statement on this DD-PATH which sets MATCH to 1 would not occur. DD-PATHs 19, 20, and 21 were also not exercised.   DD-PATH 19, 20, and 21 emerge from the false branch of: IF (MATCH .NE. 1) GOTO 200. This means that   for

PATH ANALYZER CUMULATIVE CUMULATIVE DETAILED REPORT

FOR MODULE TRIANGLE

CUMULATIVE RESULTS OF   39 TEST CASES

DD-PATH NUMBER	NUMBER NOT EXECUTED	NUMBER OF EXECUTIONS (NORMALIZED TO MAXIMUM) .----20.----40.----60.----80.----100	DD-PATH NUMBER	NUMBER OF TRAVERSALS
1		XXXXXXXXXXXXXXXXXXXXXXXXXXXXXXXXXXXXXXXXXXXXXXXXXXX	1	39
2		XXXXXXXXXXXXXXXXXXXXXXX	2	17
3		XXXXXXXXXXXXXXXXXXXXXXXXXXXXX	3	22
4		XXXXXXXXXXXXXXXXXXXXXXXXXXXXX	4	22
5	(5)			
6		XXXXXXXXXXXXXXXXXXXXXXX	6	17
7		XXXXXX	7	5
8		XXXXXXXXXXXXXXXXXXXX	8	15
9		XXXXXXXXX	9	7
10		XXXXXXXXXXXXX	10	10
11		XXXXXXXXXXXXXXXX	11	12
12		XXXXX	12	4
13		XXXXXXXXXX	13	8
14		X	14	1
15		XXXXXXXXX	15	7
16		X	16	1
17		XXXXXXXX	17	6
18		XXXXXXXXXX	18	10
19	(19)		...	
21	(21)			
22		XXXXXXXXX	22	7
23		XXX	23	3
24		XX	24	2
25		X	25	1
26		XX	26	2
27		XXXXXX	27	5
28		X	28	1
29		XXXXX	29	4

TOTAL NUMBER OF DD-PATH TRAVERSALS = 228

TOTAL NUMBER OF DD-PATHS NOT EXECUTED = 4
TOTAL NUMBER OF DD-PATHS EXECUTED   = 25
** PERCENT EXECUTED 86.21 **

**DD-PATH EXECUTION
(DOMAIN ERROR)**

FIGURE 12

these DD-PATHs never to be executed, MATCH must not equal 1 at any point in the program. Looking back again at FIGURE 8, MATCH never equals 1 because DD-PATH 5 was never exercised by the test data. Thus DD-PATHS 19, 20, and 21 these can never be exercised because DD-PATH 5 was never taken. Upon close examination of the predicate of DD-PATH 5: IF (-I .NE. J) the error was realized. It should be: IF (I .NE. J)!

8.0 MISSING STATEMENT ERROR

The triangle program was modified, such that statement 17, MATCH = 0 was removed from the program (ref FIGURE 13).

8.1 MOTHRA

Using MOTHRA the statement analysis class of mutants was selected. There were 242 mutants created for the triangle subroutine. Using the original set of test cases, test case 1, test input (3,4,5) gave an incorrect output on the changed program. The output showed that the triangle was "isosceles", however the correct output for these values is a "scalene" triangle. Twelve other test cases gave incorrect outputs. At the end of 23 test cases, 71 mutants remained alive (ref TABLE 7).

In checking the live mutants, it was evident that certain statements were not being executed and thus the mutants could not be killed (ref FIGURE 14). These statements followed the false branch of the predicate: IF (MATCH .NE. 0) GOTO 100, which means that if MATCH = 0 the control flow goes to the statement IF (I+J .LE. K) GOTO 500. However, his statement was never being executed. Thus, it was clear that there was a problem in the program such that MATCH was never set to zero and the missing statement (i. e., MATCH = 0) was found.

8.2 RXVP80

The modified triangle program was input to RXVP80 along with the same test cases as previously entered. The DD-PATH execution report showed that 100% execution coverage was obtained (ref FIGURE 15)! The reason was that VMS was automatically initializing memory (and therefore MATCH), to zero, and the missing statement error was not found. The static analysis capability of RXVP80 was then used to identify SET/USE errors. SET/USE errors occur when

```
        SUBROUTINE TRIANGLE(I,J,K,MATCH)

        integer  i,j,k,match

C       MATCH is output from the subroutine:
C       MATCH = 1 IF THE TRIANGLE IS SCALENE
C       MATCH = 2 IF THE TRIANGLE IS ISOSCELES
C       MATCH = 3 IF THE TRIANGLE IS EQUILATERAL
C       MATCH = 4 IF NOT A TRIANGLE

C       After a quick confirmation that it's a legal
C       triangle, detect any sides of equal length
        IF (I .LE. 0 .OR. J .LE. 0 .OR. K .LE. 0) GOTO 500
        MATCH = 0      --   MISSING STATEMENT
        IF (I.NE.J) GOTO 10
        MATCH=MATCH+1
10      IF (I.NE.K) GOTO 20
        MATCH=MATCH+2
20      IF (J.NE.K) GOTO 30
        MATCH=MATCH+3
30      IF (MATCH.NE.0) GOTO 100

C       Confirm it's a legal triangle before declaring it to be scalene
        IF (I+J.LE.K)  GOTO 500
        IF (J+K.LE.I)  GOTO 500
        IF (I+K.LE.J)  GOTO 500
        MATCH=1
        Return

C       Confirm it's a legal triangle before declaring
C       it to be isosceles or equilateral
100     IF (MATCH.NE.1) GOTO 200
        IF (I+J.LE.K) GOTO 500
110     MATCH=2
        RETURN
200     IF (MATCH.NE.2) GOTO 300
        IF (I+K.LE.J)  GOTO 500
        GOTO 110
300     IF (MATCH.NE.3) GOTO 400
        IF (J+K.LE.I)  GOTO 500
        GOTO 110
400     MATCH=3
        RETURN

C       Can't fool this program, that's not a triangle
500     MATCH=4
        RETURN
        END
```

TRIANGLE PROGRAM (MISSING STATEMENT)

FIGURE 13

TYPE	GENERATED	LIVE	%LIVE	EQUIV	DEAD
glr	128	40	31.3	0	88
rsr	37	10	27.0	0	27
san	37	10	27.0	0	27
sdl	40	11	27.5	0	29
TOTALS	242	71	29.3	0	171

CLASS	GENERATED	LIVE	%LIVE	EQUIV	DEAD
ary	0	0	0.0	0	0
con	0	0	0.0	0	0
ctl	165	50	30.3	0	115
dmn	0	0	0.0	0	0
opm	0	0	0.0	0	0
prd	0	0	0.0	0	0
scl	0	0	0.0	0	0
stm	77	21	27.3	0	56

SUPERCL	GENERATED	LIVE	%LIVE	EQUIV	DEAD
all	242	71	29.3	0	171
cca	0	0	0.0	0	0
pda	0	0	0.0	0	0
sal	242	71	29.3	0	171

MOTHRA - STATEMENT ANALYSIS MUTANTS
MISSING STATEMENT ERROR

TABLE 7

```
            SUBROUTINE TRIANGLE(I,J,K,MATCH)

            integer  i,j,k,match

C           MATCH is output from the subroutine:
C           MATCH = 1 IF THE TRIANGLE IS SCALENE
C           MATCH = 2 IF THE TRIANGLE IS ISOSCELES
C           MATCH = 3 IF THE TRIANGLE IS EQUILATERAL
C           MATCH = 4 IF NOT A TRIANGLE
C           After a quick confirmation that it's a legal
C           triangle, detect any sides of equal length
            IF (I .LE. 0 .OR. J .LE. 0 .OR. K .LE. 0) GOTO 500
```

MATCH = 0 --   MISSING STATEMENT

```
            IF (I.NE.J) GOTO 10
            MATCH=MATCH+1
10          IF (I.NE.K) GOTO 20
            MATCH=MATCH+2
20          IF (J.NE.K) GOTO 30
            MATCH=MATCH+3
30          IF (MATCH.NE.0) GOTO 100

C           Confirm it's a legal triangle before declaring it to be scalene
            IF (I+J.LE.K)  GOTO 500
    #   rsr  142    #       RETURN
    #   san  179    #    ***   TRAP   ***
    #   sdl  216    #       CONTINUE
    #   rsr  143    #       IF ((I + J) .LE. K) RETURN
    #   san  180    #       IF ((I + J) .LE. K) *** TRAP ***
    #   sdl  217    #       IF ((I + J) .LE. K) CONTINUE
    #   glr  41     #       IF ((I + J) .LE. K) GO TO 400
    #   glr  42     #       IF ((I + J) .LE. K) GO TO 300
    #   glr  43     #       IF ((I + J) .LE. K) GO TO 200
    #   glr  44     #       IF ((I + J) .LE. K) GO TO 110
    #   glr  45     #       IF ((I + J) .LE. K) GO TO 100
    #   glr  46     #       IF ((I + J) .LE. K) GO TO 30
    #   glr  47     #       IF ((I + J) .LE. K) GO TO 20
    #   glr  48     #       IF ((I + J) .LE. K) GO TO 10
            IF (J+K.LE.I)  GOTO 500
    #   rsr  144    #       RETURN
    #   san  181    #    ***   TRAP   ***
    #   sdl  218    #       CONTINUE
    #   rsr  145    #       IF ((J + K) .LE. I) RETURN
    #   san  182    #       IF ((J + K) .LE. I) *** TRAP ***
    #   sdl  219    #       IF ((J + K) .LE. I) CONTINUE
    #   glr  49     #       IF ((J + K) .LE. I) GO TO 400
    #   glr  50     #       IF ((J + K) .LE. I) GO TO 300
    #   glr  51     #       IF ((J + K) .LE. I) GO TO 200
    #   glr  52     #       IF ((J + K) .LE. I) GO TO 110
```

MOTHRA - "LIVE" STATEMENT ANALYSIS MUTANTS
MISSING STATEMENT ERROR

FIGURE 14

```
#    glr   53    #       IF ((J + K) .LE. I) GO TO 100
#    glr   54    #       IF ((J + K) .LE. I) GO TO 30
#    glr   55    #       IF ((J + K) .LE. I) GO TO 20
#    glr   56    #       IF ((J + K) .LE. I) GO TO 10
       IF (I+K.LE.J)  GOTO 500
#    rsr   146   #          RETURN
#    san   183   #       ***  TRAP  ***
#    sdl   220   #        CONTINUE
#    rsr   147   #       IF ((I + K) .LE. J) RETURN
#    san   184   #        IF ((I + K) .LE. J) *** TRAP ***
#    sdl   221   #       IF ((I + K) .LE. J) CONTINUE
#    glr   57    #       IF ((I + K) .LE. J) GO TO 400
#    glr   58    #       IF ((I + K) .LE. J) GO TO 300
#    glr   59    #       IF ((I + K) .LE. J) GO TO 200
#    glr   60    #       IF ((I + K) .LE. J) GO TO 110
#    glr   61    #       IF ((I + K) .LE. J) GO TO 100
#    glr   62    #       IF ((I + K) .LE. J) GO TO 30
#    glr   63    #       IF ((I + K) .LE. J) GO TO 20
#    glr   64    #       IF ((I + K) .LE. J) GO TO 10
       MATCH=1
#    rsr   148   #          RETURN
#    san   185   #       ***  TRAP  ***
#    sdl   222   #        CONTINUE
       Return
#    sdl   223   #        CONTINUE
C       Confirm it's a legal triangle before declaring it to be isosceles
C       or equilateral
100     IF (MATCH.NE.1) GOTO 200
        IF (I+J.LE.K) GOTO 500
110     MATCH=2
        RETURN
200     IF (MATCH.NE.2) GOTO 300
        IF (I+K.LE.J)  GOTO 500
#    rsr   156   #          RETURN
#    san   193   #       ***  TRAP  ***
#    sdl   232   #        CONTINUE
#    rsr   157   #       IF ((I + K) .LE. J) RETURN
#    san   194   #        IF ((I + K) .LE. J) *** TRAP ***
#    sdl   233   #       IF ((I + K) .LE. J) CONTINUE
#    glr   89    #       IF ((I + K) .LE. J) GO TO 400
#    glr   90    #       IF ((I + K) .LE. J) GO TO 300
#    glr   91    #       IF ((I + K) .LE. J) GO TO 200
#    glr   92    #       IF ((I + K) .LE. J) GO TO 110
#    glr   93    #       IF ((I + K) .LE. J) GO TO 100
#    glr   94    #       IF ((I + K) .LE. J) GO TO 30
#    glr   95    #       IF ((I + K) .LE. J) GO TO 20
#    glr   96    #       IF ((I + K) .LE. J) GO TO 10
```

MOTHRA - "LIVE" STATEMENT ANALYSIS MUTANTS
MISSING STATEMENT ERROR

FIGURE   14   (continued)

```
            GOTO 110
    #    glr   97   #      GO TO 500
    #    glr   98   #      GO TO 400
    #    glr   99   #      GO TO 300
    #    glr  100   #      GO TO 200
    #    glr  101   #      GO TO 100
    #    glr  102   #      GO TO 30
    #    glr  103   #      GO TO 20
    #    glr  104   #      GO TO 10
    #    rsr  158   #      RETURN
    #    san  195   #   *** TRAP ***
    #    sdl  234   #      CONTINUE
300          IF (MATCH.NE.3) GOTO 400
             IF (J+K.LE.I)  GOTO 500
             GOTO 110
400          MATCH=3
             RETURN
C            Can't fool this program, that's not a triangle
500          MATCH=4
             RETURN
             END
```

MOTHRA - "LIVE" STATEMENT ANALYSIS MUTANTS
MISSING STATEMENT ERROR

FIGURE 14 (continued)

PATH ANALYZER CUMULATIVE DETAILED REPORT

FOR MODULE TRIANGLE

CUMULATIVE RESULTS OF   37 TEST CASES

DD-PATH NUMBER	NUMBER NOT EXECUTED	NUMBER OF EXECUTIONS (NORMALIZED TO MAXIMUM) . ----20.----40.----60.----80.----100	DD-PATH NUMBER	NUMBER OF TRAVERSALS
1		XXXXXXXXXXXXXXXXXXXXXXXXXXXXXXXXXXXXX	1	37
2		XXXXXXXXXXXXXXX	2	15
3		XXXXXXXXXXXXXXXXXXXXXX	3	22
4		XXXXXXXXXXXXXXXXX	4	17
5		XXXXX	5	5
6		XXXXXXXXXXXXXXXXX	6	17
7		XXXXX	7	5
8		XXXXXXXXXXXXXXX	8	15
9		XXXXXXX	9	7
10		XXXXXXXXXXXXX	10	13
11		XXXXXXXXX	11	9
12		XX	12	2
13		XXXXXXX	13	7
14		X	14	1
15		XXXXXX	15	6
16		X	16	1
17		XXXXX	17	5
18		XXXXXXXXXX	18	10
19		XXX	19	3
20		XX	20	2
21		X	21	1
22		XXXXXXX	22	7
23		XXX	23	3
24		XX	24	2
25		X	25	1
26		XX	26	2
27		XXXXXX	27	5
28		X	28	1
29		XXXXX	29	4

TOTAL NUMBER OF DD-PATH TRAVERSALS =   225

TOTAL NUMBER OF DD-PATHS NOT EXECUTED =   0
TOTAL NUMBER OF DD-PATHS EXECUTED   =   29
** PERCENT EXECUTED 100.00 **

DD-PATH EXECUTION
(MISSING STATEMENT ERROR)

FIGURE 15

variables are used before being assigned a value.   None were found. RXVP80 reports showed that MATCH was set to a value via the statements   MATCH = MATCH + 1,   MATCH = MATCH + 2,   and MATCH = MATCH + 3 and therefore, as far as RXVP80 was concerned, MATCH was set before being used.   This shows a limitation of the SET/USE capability of RXVP80!

9.0 COMPUTATION ERROR

The triangle program was modified such that statement 19, MATCH = MATCH + 1 was changed to MATCH = MATCH - 1 (ref FIGURE 16).

9.1 MOTHRA

Using MOTHRA, the class of mutants that belong to statement analysis was selected.   There were 243 mutants created for the triangle subroutine.   At the end of the set of test case inputs, 15 mutants   remained   alive.   Looking   at   each   mutant,   one   was equivalenced since MATCH was always equal to 2 at that point in the program.   There were then 14 live mutants remaining (ref TABLE 8). Examination of the location of the mutants in the program (ref FIGURE 17), showed that this was the result of the false branch of the predicate: IF (MATCH .NE. 1) never being executed (i.e., MATCH is never equal to 1).   Therefore, it was necessary to check statements where MATCH is assigned values.   Checking back in the program it was found that at:

line # 23, MATCH = MATCH + 3
line # 21, MATCH = MATCH + 2
line # 19, MATCH = MATCH - 1
line # 17, MATCH = 0

Since MATCH is originally set to zero, it never gets set to 1 on any of the subsequent branches.   It was determined that MATCH could be set to one if: the false branch of IF (I .NE. J) is taken and MATCH = MATCH - 1, resulting in MATCH = -1 and then the false branch of IF (I .NE. K) is taken and MATCH = MATCH + 2 resulting in MATCH = 1.   However, for these two conditions to be false, I would be equal to J and I would be equal to K, which means that J would be equal to K and the false branch of IF (J .NE. K) would be taken and MATCH = MATCH + 3 would be executed resulting in MATCH = 2.

```
            SUBROUTINE TRIANGLE(I,J,K,MATCH)

        integer i,j,k,match

C       MATCH is output from the subroutine:
C       MATCH = 1 IF THE TRIANGLE IS SCALENE
C       MATCH = 2 IF THE TRIANGLE IS ISOSCELES
C       MATCH = 3 IF THE TRIANGLE IS EQUILATERAL
C       MATCH = 4 IF NOT A TRIANGLE

C       After a quick confirmation that it's a legal
C       triangle, detect any sides of equal length
        IF (I .LE. 0 .OR. J .LE. 0 .OR. K .LE. 0) GOTO 500
        MATCH=0
        IF (I.NE.J) GOTO 10
```

MATCH=MATCH-1   -- COMPUTATION ERROR

```
10      IF (I.NE.K) GOTO 20
        MATCH=MATCH+2
20      IF (J.NE.K) GOTO 30
        MATCH=MATCH+3
30      IF (MATCH.NE.0) GOTO 100

C       Confirm it's a legal triangle before declaring it to be scalene
        IF (I+J.LE.K)  GOTO 500
        IF (J+K.LE.I)  GOTO 500
        IF (I+K.LE.J)  GOTO 500
        MATCH=1
        Return

C       Confirm it's a legal triangle before declaring
C       it to be isosceles or equilateral
100     IF (MATCH.NE.1) GOTO 200
        IF (I+J.LE.K) GOTO 500
110     MATCH=2
        RETURN
200     IF (MATCH.NE.2) GOTO 300
        IF (I+K.LE.J)  GOTO 500
        GOTO 110
300     IF (MATCH.NE.3) GOTO 400
        IF (J+K.LE.I)  GOTO 500
        GOTO 110
400     MATCH=3
        RETURN

C       Can't fool this program, that's not a triangle
500     MATCH=4
        RETURN
        END
```

TRIANGLE PROGRAM (COMPUTATION ERROR)

FIGURE 16

TYPE	GENERATED	LIVE	%LIVE	EQUIV	DEAD
glr	128	8	6.3	0	120
rsr	38	2	5.3	1	35
san	36	2	5.6	0	34
sdl	41	2	4.9	0	39
TOTALS	243	14	5.8	1	228

CLASS	GENERATED	LIVE	%LIVE	EQUIV	DEAD
ary	0	0	0.0	0	0
con	0	0	0.0	0	0
ctl	166	10	6.0	1	155
dmn	0	0	0.0	0	0
opm	0	0	0.0	0	0
prd	0	0	0.0	0	0
scl	0	0	0.0	0	0
stm	77	4	5.2	0	73

SUPERCL	GENERATED	LIVE	%LIVE	EQUIV	DEAD
all	243	14	5.8	1	228
cca	0	0	0.0	0	0
pda	0	0	0.0	0	0
sal	243	14	5.8	1	228

MOTHRA - STATEMENT ANALYSIS MUTANTS
COMPUTATION ERROR

TABLE 8

```
         SUBROUTINE TRIANGLE(I,J,K,MATCH)

         integer  i,j,k,match

C        MATCH is output from the subroutine:
C        MATCH = 1 IF THE TRIANGLE IS SCALENE
C        MATCH = 2 IF THE TRIANGLE IS ISOSCELES
C        MATCH = 3 IF THE TRIANGLE IS EQUILATERAL
C        MATCH = 4 IF NOT A TRIANGLE

C        After a quick confirmation that it's a legal
C        triangle, detect any sides of equal length
         IF (I .LE. 0 .OR. J .LE. 0 .OR. K .LE. 0) GOTO 500
         MATCH=0
         IF (I.NE.J) GOTO 10
         MATCH=MATCH-1 --    COMPUTATION ERROR
10       IF (I.NE.K) GOTO 20
         MATCH=MATCH+2
20       IF (J.NE.K) GOTO 30
         MATCH=MATCH+3
30       IF (MATCH.NE.0) GOTO 100

C        Confirm it's a legal triangle before declaring it to be scalene
         IF (I+J.LE.K)  GOTO 500
         IF (J+K.LE.I)  GOTO 500
         IF (I+K.LE.J)  GOTO 500
         MATCH=1
         Return

C        Confirm it's a legal triangle before declaring it to be isosceles
C        or  equilateral
100      IF (MATCH.NE.1) GOTO 200
         IF (I+J.LE.K) GOTO 500
    #  rsr  152  #       RETURN
    #  san  188  #   ***  TRAP  ***
    #  sdl  227  #       CONTINUE
    #  rsr  153  #      IF ((I + J) .LE. K) RETURN
    #  san  189  #      IF ((I + J) .LE. K) *** TRAP ***
    #  sdl  228  #      IF ((I + J) .LE. K) CONTINUE
    #  glr   73  #      IF ((I + J) .LE. K) GO TO 400
    #  glr   74  #      IF ((I + J) .LE. K) GO TO 300
    #  glr   75  #      IF ((I + J) .LE. K) GO TO 200
    #  glr   76  #      IF ((I + J) .LE. K) GO TO 110
    #  glr   77  #      IF ((I + J) .LE. K) GO TO 100
    #  glr   78  #      IF ((I + J) .LE. K) GO TO 30
    #  glr   79  #      IF ((I + J) .LE. K) GO TO 20
    #  glr   80  #      IF ((I + J) .LE. K) GO TO 10
110        MATCH=2
```

**MOTHRA - "LIVE" STATEMENT ANALYSIS MUTANTS
COMPUTATION ERROR**

FIGURE 17

```
          RETURN
200       IF (MATCH.NE.2) GOTO 300
          IF (I+K.LE.J)  GOTO 500
          GOTO 110
300       IF (MATCH.NE.3) GOTO 400
          IF (J+K.LE.I)  GOTO 500
          GOTO 110
400       MATCH=3
          RETURN

C         Can't fool this program, that's not a triangle
500       MATCH=4
          RETURN
          END
```

MOTHRA - "LIVE" STATEMENT ANALYSIS MUTANTS
COMPUTATION ERROR

FIGURE   17   (continued)

Therefore, it was clear that MATCH never stays equal to 1 for this program.   Upon closer examination, it was seen that this was a result of one of the assignment statements being in error and it was found that MATCH = MATCH - 1 on line 19.   It should be MATCH = MATCH + 1, therefore the error was found.

9.2 RXVP80

The modified triangle program was input to RXVP80, using the same set of test cases in addition to several new test cases.   The DD-PATH execution report showed that DD-PATHs 19, 20, and 21 were not executed (ref FIGURE 18).   Examination of the DD-PATHs not traversed showed that this was the result of DD-PATH 19 never being taken.   This meant that MATCH was never equal to one.   As in the MOTHRA system, the statements where MATCH is assigned a value were examined.   These statements were as follows:

> MATCH = MATCH + 3 on DD-PATH 9
> MATCH = MATCH + 2 on DD-PATH 7
> MATCH = MATCH - 1 on DD-PATH 5
> MATCH = 0   on DD-PATH 3

For the reasons stated in the previous MOTHRA section, it was clear that one of the assignment statements (i.e., MATCH = MATCH - 1) was in error.   Again, the error was found.

10.0 CONCLUSION

Both tools performed very well.   It was felt that RXVP80 was easier to learn and use, and easier to find the error types that were created.   The DD-PATH concept is very clear and the graphical chart that was manually created aided understanding of this test technique.   The DD-PATH concept has been used on many large-scale software development efforts and has proven its usefulness.

MOTHRA is a newer and much more complex system (but a more powerful testing system).   It was more difficult to learn and use and very time consuming to equivalence mutants.   With so many mutants being created, especially for the Predicate and Domain mutant class, using MOTHRA was difficult to detect the errors. Except for the Missing Statement Error, RXVP80 found the errors and displayed them to the tester in a more understandable manner. Overall, while mutation testing certainly has the potential to surpass

PATH ANALYZER CUMULATIVE DETAILED REPORT

FOR MODULE TRIANGLE

CUMULATIVE RESULTS OF   35 TEST CASES

DD-PATH NUMBER	NUMBER NOT EXECUTED	NUMBER OF EXECUTIONS (NORMALIZED TO MAXIMUM) .------20.------40.------60.------80.------100	DD-PATH NUMBER	NUMBER OF TRAVERSALS
1		XXXXXXXXXXXXXXXXXXXXXXXXXXXXXXXXXXXX	1	35
2		XXXXXXXXXXXXXX	2	13
3		XXXXXXXXXXXXXXXXXXXXXXX	3	22
4		XXXXXXXXXXXXXXXXXXX	4	18
5		XXXXX	5	4
6		XXXXXXXXXXXXXXXXXX	6	17
7		XXXXXX	7	5
8		XXXXXXXXXXXXXXX	8	14
9		XXXXXXXXX	9	8
10		XXXXXXXXXXXXXX	10	13
11		XXXXXXXXXX	11	9
12		XX	12	2
13		XXXXXXXX	13	7
14		X	14	1
15		XXXXXXX	15	6
16		X	16	1
17		XXXXXX	17	5
18		XXXXXXXXXXXXXX	18	13
(19)			...	
...				
(21)				
22		XXXXXXXXXXX	22	10
23		XXX	23	3
24		XX	24	2
25		X	25	1
26		XXXXX	26	4
27		XXXXXXX	27	6
28		XX	28	2
29		XXXXX	29	4

TOTAL NUMBER OF DD-PATH TRAVERSALS = 225

TOTAL NUMBER OF DD-PATHS NOT EXECUTED =   3
TOTAL NUMBER OF DD-PATHS EXECUTED = 26
** PERCENT EXECUTED 89.66 **

**DD-PATH EXECUTION
(COMPUTATION ERROR)**

FIGURE 18

all other forms of testing, for certain classes of errors (i.e., missing statement errors), the much easier to use static and dynamic style of testing provides comparable results.

Mutation Testing's different mutant operators, however, allow an extremely thorough testing strategy and is especially important for testing mission critical applications. It allows testers to match the degree of testing to the criticality of the application and the amount of resources available for testing.   Its statement mutants allow it to provide statement level coverage, which overlaps RXVP80's capabilities.

Future work is planned to enhance the MOTHRA system and ensure a more usable testing system.   As a result of this testing project, recommendations for enhancements include:

Automated support to determine equivalent mutants. If all classes of mutants are enabled, there are on the order of N^2 mutants created for an N line computer program!   A significant number of these, as shown in the test sample, may be equivalent to the original program.   Determining equivalent mutants is a time consuming process and requires detailed knowledge of the computer program. It could be very difficult for an independent tester to determine if a program is equivalent as intimate knowledge of the details of the program are necessary.   This limits the variety of personnel that can easily use the tool.   Automated support for determining equivalent programs would significantly increase the usability of the tool.

State-of-the-art user interface.   MOTHRA's current menu driven user interface,   while adequate, should be more helpful in guiding users through the proper sequence of steps necessary to execute the tool.   Determining the proper sequence to create the mutants, execute the program with/without mutants, compare the expected output with the mutant program's output, equivalence programs, etc. should be part of the tool's user interface.   It should display the menus with those options applicable only at that point in time in the testing process.   This would ensure that a user would not be allowed to, for example, perform equivalence functions without first creating mutants, and/or execute the mutant program without saving the correct output results.   In addition, on-line help at each menu option should also be available to explain each menu option.

Test case generation. Automated support to provide additional test cases to kill the remaining mutants would also enhance the tool's usability. Currently, test case generation, is a manual process which is assisted by the results of various MOTHRA reports which display the type of live mutants, number of equivalenced mutants and dead mutants. From this information, the user must deduce which test case(s) may kill those particular mutants. Automating the generation of test cases would relieve some of the burden from the user. While 100% automation may not be possible, some support would increase overall productivity of the tester and allow the testing process to be completed in a shorter time frame. This enhancement is applicable not only to MOTHRA but to most all testing tools (including RXVP80) and research is currently being performed in this area by academia, industry, and government.

Printed and bound by CPI Group (UK) Ltd, Croydon, CR0 4YY

03/10/2024

01040335-0008